# MOBILISING INTERNATIONAL LAW FOR 'GLOBAL JUSTICE'

*Mobilising International Law for 'Global Justice'* provides new insights into the dynamics between politics and international law and the roles played by state and civic actors in pursuing human rights, development, security, and justice through mobilisation of international law at local and international levels. This includes attempts to hold states, corporations, and individuals accountable for violations of international law. Second, this book examines how enforcing international law creates particular challenges for intergovernmental regulators seeking to manage tensions between incompatible legal systems and bring an end to harmful practices, such as foreign corruption and child abduction. Finally, it explores how international law has local resonance, whereby, for example, cities have taken it upon themselves to give effect to the spirit of international treaties that national governments fail to implement, or may even have refused to ratify.

JEFF HANDMAKER is a senior lecturer at the International Institute of Social Studies in The Hague, which forms part of Erasmus University Rotterdam. In 2017 he was a visiting research fellow in the Department of Sociology at Princeton University. He is also a senior research fellow of the Faculty of Law at the University of the Witwatersrand in Johannesburg and editor-in-chief of the South African Journal on Human Rights. Handmaker formerly worked as a practitioner in over fifteen countries, particularly in southern Africa, Europe, and the Middle East. He has also worked with the United Nations and the African Commission on Human and Peoples' Rights. As a socio-legal scholar, his research on legal mobilisation explores the social and political dimensions of instrumentalising international law in a variety of contexts.

KARIN ARTS holds a professorial chair in international law and development at the International Institute of Social Studies in The Hague, which forms part of Erasmus University Rotterdam. She studies international law as a major factor in processes of development and transition, either as an instrument of change or as a vehicle for guarding the status quo. Human rights–based approaches to development, and in particular child rights–based approaches, are central in her recent work. In addition to ample teaching and research experience, Arts has professional experience in nearly twenty countries. Through the Advisory Council on International Affairs, she advises the Dutch government and parliament on human rights matters. She is also a member of the supervisory board of the National UNICEF Committee of the Ne

T0382057

# MOBILISING INTERNATIONAL LAW FOR 'GLOBAL JUSTICE'

Edited by

## JEFF HANDMAKER
*Erasmus Universiteit Rotterdam*

## KARIN ARTS
*Erasmus Universiteit Rotterdam*

## CAMBRIDGE
### UNIVERSITY PRESS

University Printing House, Cambridge CB2 8BS, United Kingdom

One Liberty Plaza, 20th Floor, New York, NY 10006, USA

477 Williamstown Road, Port Melbourne, VIC 3207, Australia

314-321, 3rd Floor, Plot 3, Splendor Forum, Jasola District Centre, New Delhi - 110025, India

79 Anson Road, #06-04/06, Singapore 079906

Cambridge University Press is part of the University of Cambridge.

It furthers the University's mission by disseminating knowledge in the pursuit of education, learning and research at the highest international levels of excellence.

www.cambridge.org
Information on this title: www.cambridge.org/9781108466080
DOI: 10.1017/9781108586665

First published 2019
Reprinted 2019
First paperback edition 2020

*A catalogue record for this publication is available from the British Library*

*Library of Congress Cataloging in Publication data*
Names: Handmaker, Jeff, editor. | Arts, Karin, editor.
Title: Mobilising international law for 'global justice' / edited by Jeff Handmaker, Erasmus Universiteit Rotterdam; Karin Arts, Erasmus Universiteit Rotterdam.
Description: Cambridge, United Kingdom; New York, NY, USA : Cambridge University Press, 2018.
Identifiers: LCCN 2018026135 | ISBN 9781108497947
Subjects: LCSH: International law and human rights. | International law – Political aspects. | Humanitarian law – Political aspects.
Classification: LCC KZ1266 .M63 2018 | DDC 341–dc23
LC record available at https://lccn.loc.gov/2018026135

ISBN 978-1-108-49794-7 Hardback
ISBN 978-1-108-46608-0 Paperback

# CONTENTS

# CONTRIBUTORS

KARIN ARTS is Professor of International Law and Development at the International Institute of Social Studies (ISS) in The Hague, the Netherlands. She is a member of the editorial board of the *Netherlands Quarterly on Human Rights*, a member of the Human Rights Committee of the Dutch Advisory Council on International Affairs (AIV) and a member of the Supervisory Board of UNICEF (Netherlands).

MAJA GROFF is a Senior Legal Officer at the Permanent Bureau of the Hague Conference on Private International Law. She holds degrees from McGill University (LL.B. and B.C.L.), Harvard University (A.B.) and from Oxford University (M.Sc.). The views expressed in her chapter are her own and do not reflect the views of the Permanent Bureau or the Hague Conference on Private International Law.

JEFF HANDMAKER is Senior Lecturer in Law, Human Rights, and Development at the International Institute of Social Studies (ISS) in The Hague, the Netherlands, Senior Visiting Research Fellow in Law at the University of the Witwatersrand, South Africa, and editor-in-chief of the *South African Journal on Human Rights*. In 2017 he was a research fellow in the Sociology Department at Princeton University.

WARNER TEN KATE was United Nations adviser to the Juba peace process in Northern Uganda and currently is head of the United Nations Organization Stabilization Mission in the Democratic Republic of the Congo (MONUSCO). He previously served as a civil adviser for the United Nations Mission in Mali and as a senior policy adviser for the Dutch Ministry of Foreign Affairs. The views he expresses are his own.

MARK KERSTEN is a fellow at the Munk School of Global Affairs of the University of Toronto, Canada, and the deputy director of the Wayamo Foundation, where he was previously research director. He was previously a postdoctoral researcher and lecturer at the University of Toronto and has also taught at the London School of Economics and Political Science as well as the School of Oriental and African Studies.

MARTTI KOSKENNIEMI is Professor of International Law at the University of Helsinki, Finland, Hauser Global Visiting Professor of Law at New York University School of Law, and a professorial fellow at the Melbourne Law School, University of Melbourne (2014–2019). He has also held visiting positions at various other universities and worked in several capacities for the Ministry for Foreign Affairs of Finland between 1978 and 1994.

JASPER KROMMENDIJK is Assistant Professor of European Law at Radboud University Nijmegen, the Netherlands. He was previously a visiting researcher at the Erik Castrén Institute of International Law and Human Rights and at the Victoria University of Wellington. He has also served as a policy officer in the International and European Affairs Department of the Dutch Ministry of Justice.

ABIOLA MAKINWA is a senior lecturer in International and European Law at The Hague University of Applied Sciences, The Hague, the Netherlands. Previously, she was a senior lecturer at Lagos State University in Nigeria. She is a professional member of the International Compliance Association and chair of the Structured Criminal Settlements Sub-Committee of the International Bar Association Anti-Corruption Committee.

SARAH NOUWEN is Senior Lecturer in Law and co-deputy director of the Lauterpacht Centre for International Law and a fellow of Pembroke College at the University of Cambridge. In 2018, she was a visiting professor at the Graduate Institute of International and Development Studies in Geneva. She previously served as a legal adviser for the African Union High-Level Implementation Panel for Sudan and as a rule of law and governance adviser for the Netherlands Embassy in Sudan.

BARBARA OOMEN is Professor of Law and the Sociology of Human Rights at Utrecht University, the Netherlands. She works at University College Roosevelt, where she was previously dean. In 2016–2017 she was a senior Fernand Braudel fellow at the European University Institute in Florence. She was also Professor in Legal Pluralism at the

University of Amsterdam and a member of the Dutch Advisory Council on International Affairs (AIV).

AISLING O'SULLIVAN is a Lecturer in Law at Sussex Law School and researcher at the Sussex Centre for Human Rights Research at the University of Sussex, United Kingdom. She was previously an Irish Research Council project researcher at the Irish Centre for Human Rights, NUI Galway, and an Endeavour Research fellow at the Sydney Centre for International Law, University of Sydney.

CLAUDIA SABA is Lecturer in International Relations at the Blanquerna School of Communication and International Relations at Ramon Llull University in Barcelona, Spain. She is also a member of the teaching faculty at the Geneva Business School. She was previously a researcher and teaching assistant at University College Dublin and a parliamentary research assistant at the Irish National Parliament.

# ACKNOWLEDGEMENTS

The contributions to this book have emerged from a conference we organised in October 2012 at the International Institute of Social Studies (ISS) in The Hague entitled 'The Politics of Justice: From a Human Rights Revolution to Global Justice?'. The conference took place under the auspices of the Hague Academic Coalition (HAC) as part of its From Peace to Justice conference series. We were greatly helped by the very able support of the HAC coordinator at the time, Sofia Gerards. We also note the contributions of Nathanael Ali, Femke van der Vliet, and others in the organisation of the conference.

Nearly six years have passed since the conference took place and we value the patience and commitment of all contributors to this volume, and in particular Marti Koskenniemi, whose many contributions to the field of critical international legal studies have been a strong source of inspiration to us and feature so strongly in this volume. We further value the detailed feedback of the three anonymous reviewers of this volume; their comments improved the quality of the book. And thanks also to the fine staff of Cambridge University Press and Integra who eased our manuscript through the final stages of publication.

Institutionally, this book falls within the framework of the five-year Research Project, Integrating Normative and Functional Approaches of the Rule of Law and Human Rights (INFAR), a Research Excellence Initiative funded by Erasmus University Rotterdam. We appreciate our interactions with our colleagues in the INFAR project, led by Sanne Taekema, Professor of Jurisprudence at the Erasmus School of Law. INFAR is furthermore embedded in the Research Group on Governance, Law and Social Justice (GLSJ) that is part of the overall ISS research programme on global development and social justice. We cherish the academic freedom we enjoy at the ISS, which continues to be a highly motivating place to teach and research law and development and socio-legal issues.

Family remains the most important and sustaining force in our lives and we are ever grateful for the patience and support of our respective partners, Friederycke and Aart. Since starting this project, Jeff embarked on the uncertain but wonderfully fulfilling world of fatherhood thanks to Helena and Oliver, while Karin saw her two sons Fabian and Ramon grow into fine and tall young men.

As the contributions in this book attest, international law can be a force for positive change, but we need to more seriously engage with the politics of it all. In our modest roles as academics, we hope that our work can make a contribution to a world based on dignity, rights, and justice.

*Jeff Handmaker and Karin Arts, The Hague, the Netherlands, July 2018*

# Mobilising International Law as an Instrument of Global Justice: Introduction

JEFF HANDMAKER AND KARIN ARTS

## Globalisation and the Emergence of Global Justice

Globalisation is a hotly debated topic. There is a plethora of literature on the subject. Much of the debate is oriented around the economic and social dimensions of globalisation, leading to a situation in which, despite massive increases in global capital and foreign direct investment, previously existing inequalities have been exacerbated.[1] According to this literature, inequalities at global and national levels have led, correspondingly, to low wages, poverty, pressures to migrate, human insecurity, and ultimately global insecurity.

A prominent commentator on the topic, Saskia Sassen, has observed that the processes of globalisation cut across traditional institutions, including legal institutions. This, she has argued, 'does not mean that the old hierarchies [have] disappear[ed], but rather that rescalings [have] emerge[d] alongside the old ones'.[2] Economic globalisation in particular, she argued, has produced a process to 'negotiate the intersection of national law and the activities of foreign economic actors', a process that has been 'shaped and driven by often thick and complex

---

[1] Bernhard Gunter and Rolph van der Hoeven, 'The Social Dimension of Globalisation: A Review of the Literature', *International Labour Review*, 143 (2004), 7–43. And more recently: Alan Alexandroff and Andrew Cooper, eds, *Rising States, Rising Institutions: Challenges for Global Governance* (Washington: Brookings Institution, 2010); Andrew Gamble, *The Spectre at the Feast: Capitalist Crisis and the Politics of Recession* (Basingstoke: Palgrave, 2009); Gilford John Ikenberry, 'The Future of Liberal World Order', *Japanese Journal of Political Science*, 16 (2015), 450–5; Charles Kupchan, 'The Normative Foundations of Hegemony and the Coming Challenge to Pax Americana', *Security Studies*, 23 (2014), 219–57; Sijbren de Jong, Rem Korteweg, and Artur Usanov, eds, *New Players, New Game? The Impact of Emerging Economies on Global Governance* (Amsterdam: Amsterdam University Press, 2013); Thomas Weiss, *Global Governance: What? Why? Whither?* (Cambridge: Polity, 2013); Des Gasper and Thanh Dam Truong, eds, *Transnational Migration and Human Security* (Heidelberg: Springer, 2011).
[2] Saskia Sassen, 'Globalization or Denationalization?' *Review of International Political Economy*, 12 (2003), 1–22 at 6.

agendas . . . and an elaborate body of law'.[3] Furthermore, the content of this body of law, which has emerged over a relatively short period of just a few decades, has changed the traditionally 'exclusive territorial authority' of the nation state, 'to an extent not seen in earlier centuries'.[4] In practice, corporate protection has increased as a result of this legalisation[5] and entrenched corporate legal personality. Meanwhile, social protection has been reduced through legal measures that are produced through a liberal, democratic rule of law system, or what we refer to in this chapter as liberal lawmaking. For example, liberal lawmaking tends to prioritise property rights over social and economic rights, de-emphasises government regulation of the market, and is reluctant to interfere in matters that a judge determines to be primarily falling under another state's jurisdiction. This system of liberal democracy and lawmaking has furthermore been reproduced in other countries, and is indeed perfectly functional in authoritarian regimes.[6] Hence, civic actors across the globe have been left with few other avenues for social and economic redress than, often very confrontational, claims directed against both states and corporations. All in all, the developments sketched above have had a number of legal, social, and economic consequences that are the subject of critical attention in this book.

First, liberal lawmaking has led to what Koskenniemi has termed a 'fragmentation' of international law whereby lawyers must continually refine their understandings of the ever-changing nature and purpose of law.[7] This includes the ways in which international legal rules have been given expression at the domestic level. By extension, increased legalisation has spawned a plethora of what Koskenniemi in Chapter 2 of this book refers to as 'legal vocabularies'. In particular, human rights, as a legal normative project, comprise one of the vocabularies in international law that are often at odds with some aspects of liberal legal regimes. As discussed by nearly all contributors to this book, these tensions are especially apparent when human rights are instrumentalised, either by state or civic actors, and acquire a more explicitly political character. A positive illustration of this is the way in which human rights vocabulary has been 'socialised' or 'translated' into locally relevant contexts through mobilisation by civic

---

[3] Ibid. 7.
[4] Ibid. 8.
[5] Subhabrata Banerjee, 'Corporate Social Responsibility: The Good, the Bad and the Ugly', *Critical Sociology*, 34 (2008), 51–79 at 54.
[6] Ibid. 70.
[7] Martti Koskenniemi, *The Politics of International Law* (Oxford: Hart, 2011).

actors.[8] For example, as discussed in Chapter 10 by Oomen, municipal governments aware of social challenges – such as hate speech by right-wing political groups – are uniquely positioned to realise human rights protection in a culturally relevant manner, such as by preventing municipal funding to these groups. But international vocabularies also have the negative potential to obscure local cultural notions of justice and replace them with 'Western'-oriented notions of justice. A good example of the latter is the way in which the much-lauded *Gacaca* courts in Rwanda, billed as 'local' or 'customary' justice mechanisms, were essentially framed by Western donors and consultants.[9] Furthermore, some legal vocabularies have at best been rather impotent, and at worst played a role in subordinating people in developing countries to conquest and domination. The latter has led to a fundamental questioning of international law and its liberal underpinnings by scholars associated with Third World Approaches to International Law, or 'TWAIL'.[10]

The dysfunction of international law in addressing human rights concerns by way of concrete enforcement measures is one of the most challenging aspects of mobilising international law for global justice that the chapters in this book explore, at multiple levels of enforcement and in relation to different themes. Human rights treaties are often not self-executing. States may ratify human rights treaties as a symbolic gesture in order to avoid international criticism. Lax monitoring and weak enforcement mechanisms for non-compliance permit states to 'get away with continued human rights violations'.[11] Moreover, while formal institutions at national and international levels have largely fallen short in operationalising human rights – including the pursuit of international

---

[8] Thomas Risse, Steve Ropp, and Kathryn Sikkink, eds, *The Power of Human Rights: International Norms and Domestic Change* (New York: Cambridge University Press, 1999); Sally Merry, 'Translating Human Rights and Local Activism: Mapping the Middle', *American Anthropologist*, 108 (2006), 38–51.

[9] Barbara Oomen, 'Donor Driven Justice and Its Discontents: The Case of Rwanda', *Development and Change*, 36 (2005), 887–910.

[10] See e.g. Makau Mutua, 'What Is Twail?' American Society of International Law, Proceedings of the 94th Annual Meeting (2000), 31–9; Antony Anghie, 'TWAIL: Past and Future', *International Community Law Review*, 10 (2008), 470–81; James Gathii, 'TWAIL: A Brief History of Its Origins, Its Decentralized Network, and a Tentative Bibliography', *Trade, Law and Development*, 3/1 (2011), 26–64; M. Sornarajah, 'On Fighting Global Justice: The Role of a Third World International Lawyer', *Third World Quarterly* 37/11 2016), 1972–89. But see also S.G. Sreejith, 'An Auto-Critique of TWAIL's Historical Fallacy: Sketching an Alternative Manifesto', *Third World Quarterly*, 37/11 (2016), 1511–30.

[11] Oomen (2005), 927.

criminal justice, one of the specific themes explored in this book – the possibilities for creative responses by civic actors using the law to support broader forms of legal mobilisation have correspondingly increased. Examples include the capacity of non-governmental organisations (NGOs) to interact with the International Criminal Court, either by bringing evidence of crimes to the attention of the prosecutor, by supporting individuals in witness protection programmes, or by offering legal and logistical support to victims who wish to participate in hearings. In that space, law is wielded in a strategic way to promote progressive structural change.[12]

Second, liberal lawmaking has created particular challenges for intergovernmental regulators seeking to end problematic practices taking place on a global scale, such as the financing of international terrorism[13] or international child abduction. The latter receives detailed attention in this book in Chapter 5 by Maja Groff. International regulators seeking to end such practices have found themselves managing tensions between diverse national legal systems. They have also had to recognise the need for more proactive human rights approaches to guide the direction of global regulation and resist bureaucratic solutions to complex social problems that lie at the core of such problematic practices. Furthermore, the highly contested relationship between national and international legal orders is a key challenge in enforcing international law. While indeed this observation as such is not particularly new, these contestations have become especially visible in the efforts of national regulators to address other global issues, such as transboundary corruption. As discussed by Abiola Makinwa in Chapter 6 of this book, the enforcement of transboundary corruption has revealed not only the challenges of selective national enforcement of anti-corruption laws, but also a very patchy record of corporate self-regulation that has singularly failed to address the social and economic factors driving corruption.

Third, liberal lawmaking has generated a number of vague but rhetorically significant and globally enforceable doctrines and principles. Paralleling the retreat of the state to directly regulating individual or corporate misbehaviour, civic actors who have been forced to make claims themselves have instrumentalised these doctrines and principles at multiple jurisdictional levels. This has created possibilities for

---

[12] Jeff Handmaker, 'Peering through the Legal Mobilisation Lens to Analyse the Potential of Legal Advocacy', presentation in Leiden Socio-Legal Series, Leiden University, 2017.

[13] Nathanael Ali, 'Dynamism and the Erosion of Procedural Safeguards in International Governance of Terrorism', PhD thesis, Erasmus University, Rotterdam, 2015.

individuals, for example, military commanders and even corporate managers, such as board members, to be held directly responsible for serious international crimes. Such crimes are prosecutable not only through international criminal courts, but also by national authorities, and even through civil claims on the basis of the principle of universal jurisdiction.[14] In such instances, the focus of international law has dramatically shifted away from the state (although not entirely of course) and has more explicitly engaged individuals who had hitherto been regarded as passive 'objects' of international law. While civic participation in international (criminal) law has expanded, the retreat of the state has been matched by a general reluctance of, and a high degree of selectivity by, states in exercising jurisdiction over international crimes.[15] Accordingly, this tendency towards cosmopolitanism or global constitutionalism has been at odds with the tendency of some, often quite powerful, states to pursue an exceptionalist agenda that negates these universal principles and is premised on a claim of hegemonic legitimacy by these states. For example, Richard Falk has criticised the United States of America for exercising forceful military intervention without sanction of the UN Security Council, arguing that this is in contravention of international law, and has led to double standards being applied.[16] Similarly, Saba in Chapter 5 of this book explains how Israel's extreme use of force against civilians, negating principles of protection enshrined in the Geneva Conventions, reveals its profound disregard for international legal rules.

Finally, as the line between international and national becomes increasingly difficult to distinguish, it is becoming clear that the consequences of liberal lawmaking are more acutely felt 'at home', including at the level of the city. The conventional functioning of multiple vocabularies in international law through national (state-level) institutions and international organisations have led to normative contestations, bureaucratic solutions, and inconsistent enforcement. By contrast, the forces of globalisation have had a more positive influence from a municipal standpoint, where in some cases there is greater respect for international law norms than at the national level. Challenging Koskenniemi's

---

[14] Jeff Handmaker and Liesbeth Zegveld, 'Universal Jurisdiction: State of Affairs and Ways Ahead. A Policy Paper', Working Paper 532 (2012), International Institute of Social Studies, Erasmus University, Rotterdam. https://repub.eur.nl/pub/31137

[15] Robert Cryer *Prosecuting International Crimes: Selectivity and the International Criminal Law Regime* (Cambridge: Cambridge University Press, 2005).

[16] Richard Falk, 'Legality and Legitimacy: The Quest for Principled Flexibility and Restraint', *Review of International Studies*, 31 (2005), 33–50.

observations that the power of human rights tends to be lost when they are instrumentalised by public authorities, Chapter 10 by Oomen reveals that, in contrast to national government authorities that tend to 'rank' rights in accordance with what is all too often a security agenda, human rights-based approaches are being incorporated directly into some municipal policies and programmes, including the symbolic ratification of international human rights treaties that national governments may refuse to ratify.

The liberal lawmaking project has had a number of consequences for those engaged in mobilising international law for global justice. Fragmentation in international law has been matched by a proliferation of legal vocabularies. International regulators have struggled to counter specific practices (such as child abduction and foreign corruption) that cause great harm on a global scale. Vague but rhetorically significant and globally enforceable concepts, such as the Responsibility to Protect and obligations to prosecute international crimes, are rarely enforced by states. So what is the potential for mobilising global justice in a world of liberal states? How indeed can the concept be understood?

## The Elusive Concept of (Global) Justice

Just as is the case with the term globalisation, notions of justice, and even more so global justice, have been elusive and difficult to define. Thomas Pogge and others have attempted to do so, emphasising a pro-poor orientation that promotes rights-based approaches and takes issue with the influence of multinational corporations and other powerful interests in international policymaking and governance.[17] However, Pogge framed his definition of global justice in Rawlsian terms, falling short of fundamentally critiquing the liberal underpinnings of lawmaking that trigger the need for global justice, such as the liberal legal characterisation of corporations as legal persons.

Hence, Pogge's notion of global justice is associated with liberal articulations of social justice, drawing broadly on the work of Rawls that stresses social and economic inequalities.[18] Liberal endorsers of social justice often pay attention to promoting the interests of the poor through realising access

---

[17] Thomas Pogge, *Global Justice* (Oxford: Blackwell, 2001); Florian Wettstein, *Multinational Corporations and Global Justice* (Stanford: Stanford University Press, 2009).

[18] Ibid.

to justice and are inspired by iconic figures such as Nelson Mandela, who also endorsed a liberal vision of social justice.[19]

The United Nations approach to social justice was recently rearticulated in the Sustainable Development Goals. They focus on the need to narrow yawning gaps in wealth between rich and poor countries and between citizens within countries; eliminate poverty; protect the environment; and ensure health, shelter, education, and non-violence for all.[20] The Sustainable Development Goals uphold the liberal position that states are expected to live up to their human rights obligations. This formalistic position that is exclusively oriented around the rule of law fails to fully acknowledge the structural circumstances in which individuals are often forced to make claims against the state regarding their rights. This liberal premise is reinforced by Golub, Khan, Banik, and others who, during the mid- to late-2000s, emphasised the need for legal empowerment of those living in poverty. They grounded their social justice perspective in the everyday realities of the poor and recognised that there were multiple ways in which the poor could be supported through intermediary, legal, and other mechanisms.[21] The legal empowerment concept has also become a basis for substantive rule of law interventions, for example by the International Development Law Organisation (IDLO).[22]

Similarly, Pogge identified access to medicines coupled with measures to track outreach efforts and cost-effectiveness in health system delivery and challenging the interests of pharmaceutical companies as primary features of global health justice.[23] While Nagel critiqued Rawls's notions of egalitarianism, and in particular his tolerance for non-liberal states, his

---

[19] Nelson Mandela, 'The Continuing Struggle for Social Justice', in International Labour Office, *Visions of the Future of Social Justice: Essays on the Occasion of the ILO's 75th Anniversary* (Geneva: ILO Publications, 1994), 183–5.

[20] Addressing inequality, so as to 'leave no one behind', is a central notion in the Sustainable Development Goals, which are the core of the development agenda pursued by the United Nations in the period 2016–2030. See *UN Doc.* A/RES/70/1, 21 October 2015. See also Karin Arts, 'Inclusive Sustainable Development: A Human Rights Perspective', *Current Opinion in Environmental Sustainability*, 24 (2017), 58–62.

[21] Stephen Golub, *Beyond Rule of Law Orthodoxy: The Legal Empowerment Alternative* (Washington, DC: Carnegie Endowment for International Peace, 2003); Irene Khan, *The Unheard Truth: Poverty and Human Rights* (New York: Norton, 2009); Dan Banik, 'Legal Empowerment as a Conceptual and Operational Tool in Poverty Eradication' Hague *Journal on the Rule of Law*, 1 (2009), 117–31.

[22] Stephen Golub, ed., *Legal Empowerment: Practitioners Perspectives* (Rome: IDLO, 2010).

[23] Thomas Pogge, 'The Health Impact Fund: Enhancing Justice and Efficiency in Global Health', *Journal of Human Development and Capabilities*, 13 (2012), 537–59.

position was still fundamentally a liberal one. Underlining the challenges of defining global justice from a human rights or humanitarian perspective, a principal emphasis of this book, Thomas Nagel has argued that: 'The normative force of the most basic human rights against violence, enslavement, and coercion, and of the most basic humanitarian duties of rescue from immediate danger, depends only on our capacity to put ourselves in other people's shoes.'[24] But does either of these conceptualisations of global justice go far enough? Even if notions of global justice place an emphasis on either the social or socio-economic characteristics of justice, failing to critique the shortcomings of liberal lawmaking and institutions may be an oversight.

By contrast, Adrian Bedner's reconceptualisation of what is meant by the rule of law concept has highlighted the function of the rule of law, rather than its normative content. He has emphasised that the rule of law concept is highly contested, particularly in pluralistic legal systems.[25] More specifically, he has questioned the capacity of liberal lawmaking and institutions to address state power:

> one may establish legal rules and procedures to be followed to call the state to order on this matter, but if such behaviour is widespread even the most 'liberal' procedures applied by the most independent of judiciaries cannot control it. In the end it is the behaviour of state bodies themselves which is decisive. In most, if not all rule of law conceptions this is a major litmus test to establish whether a state can be labelled as obeying the rule of law.[26]

To drive home this point, Bedner has further reflected on the practice of rule of law interventions, observing that 'those developing rule of law indicators may lose sight of the legal issues and only focus on state practices'.[27] He has also stressed the importance of relating what one knows about the legal system to explaining people's experience with 'formal legality'.[28] In making the case for a socio-legal approach to studying the rule of law, which takes into account legal practice as well as normative legal questions, Bedner joins other socio-legal scholars who have made a strong

---

[24] Thomas Nagel, 'The Problem of Global Justice', *Philosophy and Public Affairs*, 33 (2005), 113–47 at 131.
[25] Adrian Bedner, 'An Elementary Approach to the Rule of Law', *Hague Journal on the Rule of Law*, 2 (2010), 48–74.
[26] Ibid. 59.
[27] Ibid. 60.
[28] Ibid. 62.

case for addressing the function of law, rather than simply its normative content.

By a similar token, driven by the practices of international transitional and criminal justice mechanisms, scholarly literature relating to global justice has increasingly focused on criminal justice, and primarily on ending impunity. Particular attention has been devoted to the role of the International Criminal Court and other criminal justice mechanisms.[29] This institutional form of global justice has primarily involved punishing individuals for particular human rights violations qualified as international crimes (such as torture, war crimes, and crimes against humanity). Attempts to apply this have extended to former world leaders such as Augusto Pinochet from Chile, Hissène Habré from Chad, and Charles Taylor from Liberia. These developments have furthermore been underpinned by the post-World War Two utopian ideal 'never again', which refers to the response of world powers to some of the horrors of war by establishing the UN; codifying human rights; and creating international criminal tribunals to prosecute individual violators, for example in Nuremberg, Tokyo, and later in The Hague and Arusha, as well as hybrid-international criminal tribunals in Freetown and Phnom Penh.

While doctrinal accounts of international criminal justice mechanisms, and a still liberal orientation concerning rule of law questions have tended to dominate the scholarly debate on global justice, broader questions have also come up, which question the function of law as an instrument of global justice. Such questions have explored, among other issues, the politics of state (non-)compliance with international human rights and the strategic challenges involved in accomplishing global justice.[30] Nouwen and Werner have critiqued the institutionalisation of formal criminal justice mechanisms, particularly when labelled as global justice interventions, to monopolise justice discourses. They argue that this preference for global solutions has resulted in the sidelining of what

---

[29] Frédéric Mégret 'What Sort of Global Justice Is International Criminal Justice?' *International Journal of Criminal Justice*, 13 (2015), 77–96; Geoffrey Robertson, *Crimes against Humanity: The Struggle for Global Justice* (New York: New Press, 2006); Luis Moreno Ocampo, 'The International Criminal Court: Seeking Global Justice', *Case Western Reserve Journal of International Law*, 40 (2009), 216–26; Marlies Glasius, 'What Is Global Justice and Who Decides? Civil Society and Victim Responses to the International Criminal Court's First Investigations' *Human Rights Quarterly*, 31 (2009), 496–520.

[30] David Barnhizer, *Effective Strategies for Protecting Human Rights* (Aldershot: Ashgate, 2001); Christopher Lamont, *International Criminal Justice and the Politics of Non-Compliance* (Aldershot: Ashgate, 2010).

they term 'alternative' conceptualisations of justice, thereby transcending 'the values, institutions and interests of directly affected communities'.[31] Accordingly, we now turn to the function of law as an instrument for pursuing global justice.

## The Function of Law as an Instrument for Pursuing Global Justice

Similar to conceptualisations of justice, the function of law as an instrument for global justice has an ambiguous character. Law and legal institutions articulate bold promises yet contain very definite limits to what they can deliver, let alone explain in relation to complex social phenomena.

Legal perspectives have a very different starting point than other scholarly perspectives, particularly within the social sciences. While there are numerous perspectives among legal scholars about the content of law, its origins and interpretations, and the institutions created to enforce it, legal scholarship has generally resisted multidisciplinary or interdisciplinary study. Many lawyers and legal scholars continue to regard law either as a given product (*lex lata*, law as it is) or as something of the future (*lex ferenda*, law as it should be). Positivist or doctrinal legal scholars continue to make claims to objectivity.[32]

Legal scholars such as Rosalyn Higgins have departed from a purely doctrinal understanding of law, and in particular of international law, recognising the value of seeing law as process. For instance, Higgins has characterised the primary function of international law as a 'co-ordination of clashing wills', or, alternatively, to reflect certain realities and aspirations of peoples in relation to what they hope international law may achieve, for example in realising self-determination.[33] Higgins's characterisation of law as process recognises the pluralistic nature of international law, beyond its normative content. Such an approach allows for a critique of international law's function by interacting with other disciplines such as sociology, politics, and anthropology. Such approaches furthermore recognise the complexity of participants involved in legal process and their interactions

---

[31] Sarah Nouwen and Wouter Werner, 'Monopolizing Global Justice: International Criminal Law as Challenge to Human Diversity', *Journal of International Criminal Justice*, 13 (2015), 157–76 at 158.

[32] Veronica Rodriguez-Blanco, 'Objectivity in Law', *Philosophy Compass*, 5 (2010), 240–9.

[33] Rosalyn Higgins, *International Law and How We Use It* (Oxford: Oxford University Press, 1994) 11–12.

with liberal lawmaking processes, with legal institutions, and indeed with each other.

On the other side of the scholarly plain, social scientists often misunderstand law. Law has been regarded as irrelevant, particularly by scholars studying culture in relation to identity, race, lifestyle, ritual, and other factors, who may conceptualise law and culture as 'distinct realms of action and only marginally related to one another'.[34] Countering this perspective, Mezey has argued: 'Law, at first glance, appears easier to grasp if considered in opposition to culture as the articulated rules and rights set forth in constitutions, statutes, judicial opinions, the formality of dispute resolution, and the foundation of social order. In most conceptions of culture, law is occasionally a component, but it is most often peripheral or irrelevant.'[35] Such an assumption, according to Mezey, is 'profoundly wrong', just as wrong as legal scholars dismissing the cultural implications of law.[36]

Indeed, law is a cultural system in itself. As Cotterell deftly put it: 'legal ideas are a means of structuring the social world'.[37] Society structures law, and law structures relationships within society. Law is also highly political, whether in the manner in which it is made, the circumstances and ways in which it is understood and interpreted, or the extent to which it is respected (or not). Social justice advocates invoke law in order to underpin claims for self-determination or to try and hold states or corporations accountable by way of campaigns and sometimes audacious acts of civil disobedience. Examples include: a Greenpeace action to interrupt a Formula One racing event by drawing attention to its primary sponsor, a multinational oil corporation implicated in violations of environmental law, including damage to the environment in the Arctic;[38] large-scale demonstrations at meetings of the World Economic Forum in Davos from 2005 until 2015 to emphasise alleged failures of the Forum's organisers to adequately address human rights violations by corporations, particularly in the extractive industries (although as of 2016 the protests were largely abandoned following a 'lifetime achievement

---

[34] Naomi Mezey, 'Law as Culture', *Yale Law Journal*, 13 (2001), 35–67 at 35.
[35] Ibid.
[36] Ibid. See also e.g. Lan Cao, *Culture in Law and Development: Nurturing Positive Change* (Oxford: Oxford University Press, 2016); Kate Nash, *The Cultural Politics of Human Rights: Comparing the US and the UK* (Cambridge: Cambridge University Press, 2009).
[37] Roger Cotterrell, 'Why Must Legal Ideas Be Interpreted Sociologically', *Journal of Law and Society*, 25 (1998), 171–92 at 192.
[38] Greenpeace, 'Shell's priceless Grand Prix Moment', 2013. www.greenpeace.org/australia/en/news/climate/Shells-priceless-Grand-Prix-moment

award' to Chevron Corporation);[39] and, as explained in Chapter 4, repeated efforts by civil society activists to 'break the blockade' in Gaza by sailing boats to the Israeli-occupied territory.[40]

Law also functions as the framework for administering international organisations in order to prevent a proliferation of conflicts or to intervene by way of forceful measures in order to try and resolve a conflict, although it often fails to do so and is argued to be hopelessly outdated in this regard.[41] The work done in and by international organisations is embedded within high-level negotiations that are featured by massive power differentials (for example in the United Nations Security Council). Law should also function to regulate the behaviour of states, of individuals, and of corporations but is often limited by nationalist and hegemonic acts of protectionism, reinforced by complex webs of interests involving powerful governments and politicians, and above all the market.

International development interventions too have an explicit legal basis, whether in functioning to eradicate poverty and improving the quality of healthcare in developing countries or introducing preferential trade measures in order to enable developing countries to participate in international markets on a more equitable basis. As elaborated earlier in this introduction, both international and national law are also a basis for efforts to end impunity for international crimes.

In these and so many other respects, law fulfils a central function in society, in political discourse, and in social relations. But its resistance to other scholarly perspectives and the way in which some legal scholars fail to critically address the normative, liberal bias embedded in law have served as impediments to understanding the complex interactions between politics and law, not to mention its structural potential as a vehicle for delivering global justice.

## The Structural Bias in International Law: What Have We Learned?

Koskenniemi has argued that there is a 'structural bias' embedded within global governance institutions, itself a consequence of the fragmentation

---

[39] Samuel Oakford, 'This Year in Davos, Opponents Aren't Even Bothering to Protest', *ViceNews* (20 January 2016). https://news.vice.com/article/this-year-in-davos-oppo nents-of-the-world-economic-forum-arent-even-bothering-to-protest

[40] This particular example is discussed in Chapter 4 of this book by Claudia Saba.

[41] Christine Chinkin and Mary Kaldor, *International Law and New Wars* (Cambridge: Cambridge University Press, 2017).

of international law.[42] According to this concept, international law is not the homogenous system it once was but has evolved into 'a wide variety of specialist vocabularies and institutions'.[43] As discussed earlier, these include the international legal vocabularies of human rights and criminal law. However, according to Koskenniemi, the rhetoric of rights has lost its 'transformative effect' through over-legalistic explanations and is 'not as powerful as it claims to be'.[44]

Related to the structural bias, Koskenniemi has also raised concerns about the extent to which international legal institutions are characterised by an excessive managerialism, 'that envisages law beyond the state as an instrument for particular values, interests, preferences'.[45] While acknowledging that it is highly difficult to manage anything on a global scale, Koskenniemi has argued that the 'unforeseeability of future events, including the effect that any determining rules might have in practice suggests that such rules ought not to be laid out at the outset'.[46]

Similar to Higgins, who stressed the processual nature of law, Koskenniemi's declaration of the malleability of law has represented a serious shift away from the preoccupation of legal scholars with what has been regarded as legal doctrinal argumentation. Regarding law as inherently political thus represented a fundamental challenge to widely held assumptions within legal scholarship about the nature of law and also helped to explain why legal instruments and administrative institutions have so inadequately served as a vehicle for delivering social justice.

Koskenniemi's reflections on the structural bias contained in international law and the dangers of managerialism build on nearly three decades of critical scholarship. This first gained wide attention through his seminal article on the politics of international law in 1990 in the first issue of the European Journal of International Law.[47] Directed primarily to international lawyers, both scholars and practitioners, he argued that one should look beyond the normative liberal tendency that underpins the world view of many lawyers, that is, to look beyond the content of law. On the one hand, Koskenniemi argued that international law has been

---

[42] Martti Koskenniemi 'The politics of international law: 20 years later', *European Journal of International Law*, 20/1 (2009), 7–19 at 9.

[43] Ibid. 12.

[44] Koskenniemi (2011), 133.

[45] Martti Koskenniemi 'Constitutionalism, Managerialism and the Ethos of Legal Education', *European Journal of Legal Studies*, 1 (2007), 1–18 at 2.

[46] Ibid. 8.

[47] Martti Koskenniemi, 'The Politics of International Law', *European Journal of International Law*, 1 (1990), 4–32.

criticised as 'too apologetic to be taken seriously' because of its depen-
dence on the political power, and thus the power politics, of states.[48] On
the other hand, international law has been considered to be too far
removed from power politics and thus 'too utopian' (or speculative) to
meet the challenges of a complex globalised world.[49] Rather than forming
an objective system of 'concrete and normative' and therefore 'valid' and
'binding' rules, as many lawyers claim them to be, Koskenniemi observed
that international legal rules were, in fact, highly malleable. Thus, he
asserted that:

> it is impossible to prove that a rule, principle or doctrine (in short, an
> argument) is both concrete and normative simultaneously. The two
> requirements *cancel each other out*. An argument about concreteness is
> an argument about the closeness of a particular rule, principle or doctrine
> to state practice. But the closer to state practice an argument is, the less
> normative and the more political it seems. ... An argument about nor-
> mativity, on the other hand, is an argument which intends to demonstrate
> the rule's distance from state will and practice. The more normative a rule,
> the more political [the rule] seems because the less it is possible to argue
> [the rule] by reference to social context. It seems utopian and – like
> theories of natural justice – manipulable at will.[50]

So what has been the response to Koskenniemi's critique in the intervening years, if any? The picture is mixed. While conventional legal
scholars maintain a largely doctrinal discussion, debating 'simply' the
content of international law, other legal scholars have ventured into the
social, cultural, political, and economic underpinnings of international
law and governance institutions.[51] For example, Balakrishnan Rajagopal
has studied the role of transnational and so-called third world social
movements both in resisting and using international law 'from below'
and in seeking to redefine its content in the course of social justice
struggles, at both national and global levels.[52] John Hagan, Sarah
Nouwen, Wouter Werner, and others have critically studied the

[48] Ibid. 9.
[49] Ibid.
[50] Ibid. 8 (emphasis in original text).
[51] Edwin Egede and Peter Sutch, *The Politics of International Law and International Justice* (Edinburgh: Edinburgh University Press, 2013); Mezey (2001); Dana Gold, ed., *Law and Economics: Towards Social Justice* (Bingley: JAI Press, 2009).
[52] Balakrishnan Rajagopal, *International Law From Below: Development, Social Movements and Third World Resistance* (Cambridge: Cambridge University Press, 2003). See also Jeff Handmaker, *Advocating for Accountability: Civic-State Interactions to Protect Refugees in South Africa* (Antwerpen, Intersentia, 2009).

administration of international criminal justice.[53] Makau Mutua has made a political and cultural critique of the human rights corpus, the NGOs and institutions involved in the articulation of social problems, and the construction of justice mechanisms intended to address those problems.[54] Doris Buss has studied how international criminal law and its enforcement institutions draw on various forms of expert knowledge (sociology, anthropology, history, and other disciplines) in the course of delivering criminal justice.[55]

Similarly, Barbara Oomen has been studying the disconnect between national and global justice. Taking on the human rights corpus, which others such as Mutua have criticised, Oomen has sought to explain why there is a lack of national enforcement of international human rights norms by analysing the example of the Dutch government 'exporting' human rights norms and values while it simultaneously ignored critical human rights issues at home.[56]

From a growing critical literature on the politics of international law, and the justice mechanisms that accompany these normative frameworks, new discussions have emerged. This has been especially evident in the vocabulary of human rights, including Barnhizer and colleagues' extensive evaluation of human rights as an important 'strategic system' in global governance.[57] While most studies focus on the nature of legal concepts, and several of these concepts feature in the contributions to this book as well – for example in relation to the Responsibility to Protect,[58]

[53] John Hagan, *Justice in the Balkans: Prosecuting War Crimes in the Hague Tribunal* (Chicago: University of Chicago Press, 2003); Sarah Nouwen, *Complementarity in the Line of Fire* (Cambridge: Cambridge University Press, 2013); Sarah Nouwen and Wouter Werner, 'Doing Justice to the Political: The International Criminal Court in Uganda and Sudan', *European Journal of International Law*, 21 (2010), 941–65.

[54] Makau Mutua, 'Savages, Victims and Saviors: The Metaphor of Human Rights', *Harvard Human Rights Journal*, 42 (2001), 201–45.

[55] Doris Buss, 'Expert Witnesses and International War Crimes Trials: Making Sense of Large-Scale Violence in Rwanda', in Dubravka Zarkov and Marlies Glasius, eds, *Narratives of Justice in and Out of the Courtroom* (Heidelberg: Springer, 2014).

[56] Barbara Oomen, *Rights for Others: The Slow Home-Coming of Human Rights in the Netherlands* (Cambridge: Cambridge University Press, 2013). See also Karin Arts, 'Reflections on Human Rights in the Netherlands', *Netherlands Quarterly of Human Rights*, 33/4 (2015), 374–81 and Jasper Krommendijk's chapter in this book.

[57] Barnhizer (2001).

[58] Anne Orford, *International Authority and the Responsibility to Protect* (Cambridge: Cambridge University Press, 2011); Karin Wester, 'Promise and Pitfalls of the Responsibility to Protect and Lessons to Be Learned from the Case of Libya', PhD thesis, University of Amsterdam, 2016.

obligations *erga omnes*,[59] and universal jurisdiction[60] – some address the challenges of enforcement.[61]

This book as a whole shows in various ways how the invoking of legal vocabularies have framed the possibilities for mobilising international law for global justice. In addition to showing how this legal mobilisation can potentially hold states, corporations, or individuals accountable for violations of international law, numerous inconsistencies within the global liberal legal order are revealed.

## Structure of the Book and Chapter Summaries

The potential for realising justice through invoking the law by way of different kinds of engagements is the core theme of this book. Accordingly, this book is organised in three parts that each address the realisation of justice from a different vantage point. The first part of the book explores how realising justice requires a conscious and critical engagement with the nature and role of international law and the multiple 'vocabularies' that international law produces. The second part of the book explores three empirical examples of how instrumentalising specific legal vocabularies to realise justice can solve political problems in some cases, and in other cases creates new problems altogether. The third and last part of the book explores the particular challenges of realising justice by embedding international legal principles in a national or local setting.

The first part of the book presents three critical perspectives on the nature and role of international law and justice in addressing social problems. The chapter by Martti Koskenniemi, which substantially sets the tone of the book and to which all authors make reference, addresses what he refers to as the 'competing vocabularies' of international justice, international politics, and international law and their relationship with each other, highlighting justice as the most important and difficult to define of the three. Koskenniemi draws on the theories of Morgenthau and Lauterpacht to illustrate the tensions between these competing vocabularies. He argues that both scholars had valid perspectives on how to realise justice. Koskenniemi then proceeds to highlight how

---

[59] Jochen A. Frohwein, 'Obligations *Erga Omnes*', *Max Planck Encyclopedia of Public International Law* (Oxford University Press, 2015).

[60] Cedric Ryngaert, *Jurisdiction in International Law* (Oxford, Oxford University Press, 2008).

[61] Christian Tams, *Enforcing Obligations Erga Omnes in International Law* (Cambridge: Cambridge University Press, 2005).

lawyers and political observers view these concepts differently through the use of these different frames. He observes that there is no correct response to the question: who is right, 'the jurist or the politician'[62] and often it is a matter of looking through frames simultaneously, while also explicitly recognising the differences and the implications of each other's positions. He concludes Chapter 2 by revisiting his often-stated critique on the fragmentation of international law, emphasising the importance of legal learning on the failure of international law to resolve social problems, which he characterises as the 'politics of re-description'. He further observes that lawyers need to engage with this rather than avoid it (which lawyers are inclined to do).

Chapter 3 by Warner Ten Kate and Sarah Nouwen develops this theme in the specific context of international criminal justice. The authors provide explanations for why the views of some individuals and groups are re-described or amplified in the discourse on international criminal justice while others are silenced. This, they argue 'is not the inevitable consequence of a technical development',[63] but is the culmination of what Koskenniemi in this book refers to as 'the politics of re-description'.[64]

Nouwen and Ten Kate argue that the spaces for civic participation, according to the 'language' of international law, are very limited, especially with regard to the prosecution of international crimes. Nouwen and Ten Kate then discuss in more detail the participation of various stakeholders in transitional justice processes. In an earlier work, Nouwen and Werner had argued that, in the course of legal and political processes, punishment tends to be much more emphasised than reconciliation and other forms of justice.[65]

Chapter 4 by Claudia Saba complements Nouwen and Ten Kate's analysis by revealing efforts on the part of civil society organisations to provide a justice solution when states and international authorities fail to do so. In particular, she focuses on the role of the so-called 'Freedom Flotilla', which sought to provide concrete humanitarian assistance, notably medical supplies, to Palestinians in the Israeli-occupied territory of Gaza and generate international attention for their situation. Saba's chapter vividly reveals the strategic importance of engaging with the political character of law, towards the realisation of justice.

---

[62] Chapter 2, 27.
[63] Chapter 3, 46.
[64] Chapter 2, 40–44.
[65] Nouwen and Werner (2015).

Accordingly, she addresses issues concerning: legal versus political discourse and efforts to make them 'talk' to each other; the mobilisation of international law, including deliberately misinterpreting it for one's own purposes; the powerlessness of law against the existing political order; and bringing Palestinian voices to the fore by mobilising international law arguments. In so doing, Saba illustrates how civil society organisations can contribute to attempts to re-describe international law and, by explicitly engaging in the political and legal implications of their actions, promote justice.

The second part of the book, on new vocabularies in international law, addresses various dimensions of how law has emerged to solve political problems, or in some cases has made matters worse. As the authors in this section reveal, the plethora of legal vocabularies has given rise to new challenges in the functioning of international legal norms relating to, respectively: harmonising public and private international law, as illustrated by the work of the Hague Conference on Private International Law; combating foreign-based corruption; implementing the 'Responsibility to Protect'; and addressing the challenges of universal jurisdiction for international crimes.

Maja Groff, in Chapter 5, seeks to counter some prominent critiques of international law (including Koskenniemi's ideas about an over-reliance on formalistic rules and lack of appropriate interdisciplinary engagement; excessive 'managerialism' in international institutions; the indeterminacy of international legal norms; and Eurocentrism), choosing rather to focus on potential avenues of further progress in international law. She does so on the basis of the work done by the Hague Conference on Private International Law, especially as regards child support, abduction, and protection orders. The relationship between private and public international law principles plays a significant role in her chapter.

Next, in Chapter 6, Abiola Makinwa discusses global efforts to end impunity for foreign-based corruption. She critically explores the formidable challenges faced by both lawyers and politicians in seeking to introduce concrete measures. She evaluates the global regime to address international corruption, including 'smart' measures and the complementary measures taken by states to address international corruption, including the US Foreign Corrupt Practices Act and the UK Bribery Act. She also shares some observations concerning the fragmentation of international law, building on Koskenniemi's characterisation of conceptual 'boxes', each of which comes with its own vocabulary. Abiola argues that, due to the lack of a coherent set of rules and regulations governing international efforts to tackle foreign-based corruption, 'multiple boxes are emerging'. The resulting fragmentation leads to different standards of compliance among countries that ought to be harmonising their efforts in order to tackle the extraterritorial nature of international corruption practices. Accordingly, she notes various general lessons that can be drawn from this global effort at norm-making to address international corruption, also based on her larger study of this area.[66]

In Chapter 7, Mark Kersten introduces the concept of the Responsibility to Protect (RtoP) and in particular addresses the relationship between the RtoP concept and the role of the International Criminal Court (ICC). Using the lenses of liberalism and cosmopolitanism, he argues that, although both the RtoP and the ICC have emerged from liberal cosmopolitan values, the role of the UN Security Council in determining their scope and function has eroded these values.

Kersten makes particular reference to Libya, drawing on numerous empirical examples that illustrate the extensive range of unilateral, regional (NATO), and multilateral efforts to try and resolve the crisis in that country. Accordingly, he highlights various military, humanitarian, and other justifications for intervening in Libya's affairs, measuring these interventions against the principles underpinning the RtoP. This allows him to make certain observations about the utility of both the concept of the RtoP and the functioning of the ICC, based on Koskenniemi's characterisation of international law serving as a form of political apology or utopian ideal.

The third section of the book refers to localised efforts to realise justice through 'bringing human rights home' by introducing national and even municipal measures to implement international human rights obligations. These last four chapters address the practical normative and functional challenges of realising global values at the national and local levels while confronting diverse socio-cultural and political contexts. From the national prosecution of international crimes and the associated recognition of humanitarian law to the realisation of children's rights and establishment of 'human rights cities', the authors in this section explore the hard issues of domesticating, and even translating, human rights in a locally relevant manner.[67]

---

[66] Abiola Makinwa, *Private Remedies for Corruption: Towards an International Framework* (The Hague: Eleven International, 2013).

[67] Merry (2006).

Aisling O'Sullivan in Chapter 8 discusses the many tensions of the national exercise of universal jurisdiction for international crimes, which lay bare the exceptional challenges of addressing the pluralistic and often politicised character of international criminal law that were alluded to by Nouwen and Ten Kate in Chapter 2. O'Sullivan's chapter explores various positions concerning the universal jurisdiction debate, and in particular the politically sensitive question of whether it is legally possible to prosecute someone for international crimes through a national court without the physical presence (i.e. *in absentia*) of the accused on the territory involved. The implications of deciding whether or not to prosecute in turn relate to more complicated matters as to whether prosecutions in these circumstances are desirable and raise multiple and competing questions of realising justice: for the accused, for the victims of international crimes, and/or for 'humanity' in general. In weighing these different and often competing considerations, O'Sullivan engages with a classic debate – which she acknowledges as irreconcilable – on whether law ought first and foremost to meet the justice needs of the so-called international community or of individuals.

This is followed by Jasper Krommendijk's chapter (Chapter 9), which provides insight into the extent to which states have been influenced by the Concluding Observations of the Committee on the Rights of the Child when introducing national measures aimed at the realisation of children's rights. Evaluating the extent to which the Netherlands has given effect to its obligations under the Convention on the Rights of the Child by domesticating these international human rights norms, and drawing on international law and international relations theory, Krommendijk reveals whether the Committee has exerted a 'compliance pull' or has affected the extent to which states act on the findings of the Committee by giving concrete effect to them in their policies and legislation.

Finally, in Chapter 10, Barbara Oomen analyses efforts to go beyond pure formal domestication of international legal norms and more deeply embed or translate global human rights obligations at a local level through the establishment of so-called human rights cities. Realising human rights at the municipal level, Oomen argues, holds tremendous potential for fostering a culture of constitutionalism. Accordingly, she questions whether the tensions between the various 'global' vocabularies referred to by Koskenniemi present fundamental problems when crafting human rights policies, particularly at the local level where municipal government responses often are more grounded in the local realities of rights violation and realisation. Oomen suggests that Koskenniemi's distinction between talking either 'Rabbit' or 'Duckalese', respectively the language of politics or that of the law, might not be that simple in local practice.

The book concludes with final reflections (Chapter 11) on the various chapters that re-engage with Koskenniemi's politics of re-description and how three key dilemmas faced by those mobilising the law in order to realise justice are revealed, namely: the cultural embeddedness of justice understandings, the non-enforcement of international legal obligations, and the existence of significant socio-economic gaps at the global level.

# 2

# Speaking the Language of International Law and Politics: Or, of Ducks, Rabbits, and Then Some

MARTTI KOSKENNIEMI*

## Introduction

Together with a number of colleagues, I have often reflected on the relations between international justice, international politics, and international law. These three notions have an ambivalent relationship to each other. I usually think of them as competing normative vocabularies, accompanied by academic specialisations, systems of expertise, and professional and ideological biases. In some contexts justice vocabularies seem persuasive. In other contexts we rather prefer the more sober languages of law or politics.

In this contribution I adopt the common sense assumption that, out of the three notions, justice is both the most abstract and obscure and also the most important. We see this in the way speakers in the realms of both law and politics usually suggest that it is the very point of those vocabularies to reach justice and frequently quarrel over their respective abilities to attain it. This chapter will first bracket the independent question of 'justice' and instead examine the relations between international law and international politics, as they have arisen in a number of familiar contexts where it has seemed imperative to make a choice between the two. We often query whether something is 'legal' or 'political'. However, I suggest that this question is pointless, as most important problems can be examined from both legal and political perspectives. The real problem lies in which perspective to choose, and that cannot be decided in abstraction from the types of outcome we prefer or, if you wish, from what we feel may be a 'just' solution.

This chapter continues with an examination of the uncomfortable relationship between international politics and international law by referring to two important twentieth century jurists, Hans Morgenthau

---

* This contribution is based on a spoken address and preserves the informality appropriate for the spoken word.

and Hersch Lauterpacht. Each had interesting things to say about that relationship, although the conclusions they drew were very different, even contradictory. In my view, both were right. In order to deal with a situation where two contrary positions are both right – and yet point in different directions – it is useful to turn to Wittgenstein. A substantial part of this chapter will then be used to illustrate what Wittgenstein might have said, had he been an international lawyer, by reference to three practical examples. One stems from recent developments in international criminal law, another from debates on international intervention and the Responsibility to Protect, and the third example centres on human rights law. I will conclude this chapter with a few words on the sociological meaning of the much-debated problem of the fragmentation of international law. This will enable me to introduce what I think of as the most important politics in the international world today: the politics of re-description.

## Morgenthau vs. Lauterpacht

Hans Morgenthau, widely regarded as the founder of international relations as an academic discipline, submitted his doctoral thesis to the University of Frankfurt in 1929. This thesis was entitled *Die Internationale Rechtspflege: Ihr Wesen und Ihre Grenzen* (*The International Administration of Justice: Its Nature and Limits*). Morgenthau discussed the question, much debated in his time, of the meaning of the reservation that many states had made to their international agreements according to which they would accept arbitration, except for cases dealing with 'vital interests, honour and sovereignty',[1] issues that were often summarised as political. Like many other jurists at the time, Morgenthau was anxious about the effect of this reservation. Was it not the case that the suggested 'political' nature of an issue could not be determined irrespectively of the state's own view of it? And, if the state's own view was decisive, did this not undermine the binding force of the arbitration clause, and with it perhaps the whole agreement? Or, to put the matter in another way, could issues of 'vital interest, honour or sovereignty' be somehow delimited by an (objective) rule independently of the state's own view? Morgenthau's view was a resounding 'no'. What belongs to the vital interests of a state or raises

---

[1] See Hans Morgenthau, *Die Internationale Rechtspflege: Ihr Wesen und Ihre Grenzen* (Leipzig: Notzke, 1929), or e.g. Hans-Jürgen Schlochauer, 'Arbitration', in R. Bernhardt et al., eds, Encyclopedia of Public International Law, *viii* (Amsterdam: North-Holland, 1981), 13–28 at 22.

issues of its honour or sovereignty cannot be independently determined.[2] They were, he suggested, purely political questions.

What is a political question? In Morgenthau's view it was a question that we feel especially intensely about. This did not necessarily mean that it needed to be large and important. It was often the case that a small issue, e.g. about a remote frontier territory, turned into a symbol of a deep-felt political antagonism and therefore became unavailable for legal settlement. Though the matter at hand may have appeared small, it was felt strongly about. For Morgenthau, politics was an 'intensity concept' that could attach itself to *any* substance, large or small.[3] Morgenthau's point was that there was no objective criterion for defining what questions touch upon the vital interests, honour, or sovereignty of a state. In his view it was always up to the state to determine this. This view left very little room for international law; it was reduced into a shadowy reflection of things that people did not care too much about. No surprise that, later in his career, Morgenthau's ambition shifted away from international law to international politics. In 1948 he published his famous classical realist manifesto, *Politics Among Nations*,[4] that would become the most widely used textbook in international relations at US universities in the latter half of the twentieth century.

Morgenthau's dissertation was favourably received but its conclusions dissented from those drawn by another central European lawyer, Hersch Lauterpacht. Lauterpacht's *The Function of Law in the International Community*[5] also enquired into the effect of reservations having to do with vital interest and honour, sovereignty, or the interests of peace. He agreed with Morgenthau that it did not seem possible to define the content of such notions by a general rule. But contrary to the latter, he thought that it was perfectly possible, and in fact common, that such questions were determined by the arbitration body or the court itself to which such claim was made. In his view, if the content of such reservations could only be determined by the state itself, this would mean an unlimited right to opt out from binding third-party settlement. This

---

[2] Morgenthau (1929), 62–72, *passim*.

[3] Martti Koskenniemi, *The Gentle Civilizer of Nations: The Rise and Fall of International Law 1870–1960* (Cambridge: Cambridge University Press, 2002), 436.

[4] Hans Morgenthau, *Politics among Nations: The Struggle for Power and Peace* (New York: Knopf, 1948).

[5] Hersch Lauterpacht, *The Function of Law in the International Community* (Oxford: Clarendon, 1933).

would be a *reductio ad absurdum* that would make the arbitration clause meaningless. The same concerned sovereignty. If a state was entitled to determine which questions dealt with its sovereignty and on that basis opt out from legal settlement, then no international obligation was really binding. But it could not be assumed that important treaties, including the Covenant of the League of Nations, were actually non-binding. This would defeat their point and purpose. Lauterpacht's conclusion was that, although reservations about vital interests, honour, or sovereignty could not be determined by an *ex ante* applicable rule, their content could still be fixed by an arbitral or judicial body for each case separately. Such reservation is like any other treaty clause: it is for the settlement organ to interpret it in a way that is binding on the parties. Lauterpacht remarked further that, if something was indeed of great interest to a state, then it is hard to conceive that it would not deal with a legal right and therefore be suitable for judicial assessment. He also dealt with the objection that law was sometimes contrary to the interest of peace, and in such cases should yield. This, Lauterpacht thought, was pure nonsense. Since peace was an eminently legal concept, if something were really necessary for peace, then it would be enshrined by law as well.[6]

From premises similar to Morgenthau's, Lauterpacht drew the exact opposite conclusion. The fact that sovereignty, peace, or vital interests and honour were hard to determine and had political aspects in no way prevented actors from dealing with their legal aspects. For example, in response to claims about a legal body's jurisdiction (or lack thereof), it would be up to the legal body itself to determine what these terms meant. As Lauterpacht demonstrated, in practice this had often been done. The contrast between Morgenthau and Lauterpacht opens into two completely different conceptual worlds. From one perspective, the world is above all political, and law appears only as a marginal phenomenon, preoccupied with issues of minor interest. From another, the world is above all legal and most things are determined by laws and courts that sometimes leave issues for politicians to decide.

These views are as present in today's international debates as they were in the 1920s and 1930s. We still discuss international law's strength or weakness in the way Morgenthau and Lauterpacht did, disagreeing about whether matters are 'political' or 'legal', thereby grappling towards a determination of whether they would be better dealt with by politicians or lawyers. Not far behind the substantive quarrel, there is a conflict of

---

[6] Ibid. 336–47.

**Figure 1:** Duck-Rabbit Illusion, 1892
Source: Jastrow, J. 'The mind's eye', *Popular Science Monthly*, 54 (1899), 299–312.
https://commons.wikimedia.org/wiki/File:Duck-Rabbit_illusion.jpg

ambitions. Nowadays I think that this debate is based on a mistaken view of the nature of politics and law.

## The Duck-Rabbit

How then should we think about the relationship between politics and law? I suggest that Wittgenstein already resolved the problem with his famous duck-rabbit image (Figure 1). The question about whether something is 'really' law or 'really' politics is as meaningful or meaningless as the question of whether the Wittgenstein image is *really* that of a duck or a rabbit. Now what can this possibly mean?

First of all, this draws attention to the fact that there is no objective reality to which the distinction would refer; it is just an image. Whether we see a rabbit or whether we see a duck is not something that is determined by the relationship of the image to the world but by its operation in our minds. The image is one, but the message(s) that it conveys are two. What we see depends on what we are inclined to see, or, technically, our cognitive bias. This also applies to our ability to 'see' law or politics in some issue. Whether we think of something – sovereignty, for example – as law or politics is not dependent on what there 'really' is in the world, i.e. the intrinsic nature of sovereignty, but on our perspective on it, the conceptual frame from which we observe it. Jurists are just as accustomed to dealing with sovereignty as politicians are. For the jurists, sovereignty is a basic legal principle, included in a huge number of legal instruments. For political observers, again, it is a quintessentially political notion, inextricable from power and ideology, the stuff of their expertise. To persist in asking the question 'but is the jurist or the politician right?' is like asking whether the image really *is* that of a rabbit or a duck. All depends on the background assumptions against which we examine the image, the vocabulary through which we try to grasp its meaning. In most cases, this is a deeply institutionalised vocabulary. In The Hague, at times referred to as the 'legal capital of the world', there are a lot of ducks (or jurists), for example within the International Court of Justice (ICJ) and the International Criminal Court (ICC). They all speak 'Duckalese' (or legal language) and are perfectly able to deal with sovereignty, peace, vital interests, and honour by their legal words and concepts. In fact, that is what we demand of them. If you went to the court and spoke like a rabbit (that is politics), you would not be understood, and you would certainly lose your case. When with ducks, speak like ducks. Likewise, in political institutions, such as a meeting between diplomats in a foreign ministry's political department, or the United Nations Security Council, what you will find are rabbits (political experts), quite unselfconsciously doing what rabbits do, namely speaking Rabbit. The question that everybody is obsessed with there is not 'what does the law say?' but 'what is the right political solution?' Again, if you go there as a Duck-lawyer, with your duck-legal texts and duck-arguments, your colleagues will look at you surprised and perhaps embarrassed. They know that you are out of order and they will show you the door. When with rabbits, speak Rabbit!

Through socialisation, we learn with whom we should speak, with the duck or with the rabbit, in Duckalese or in Rabbit. The relationship between politics and law is like that. The two are not out there, in the world, but in here with us, as part of our conceptual vocabularies, institutions and systems of expertise,[7] each equally capable of describing the whole world. Asking whether the international world is 'really' a world of law or a world of politics is like asking whether the Wittgenstein image is 'really' one of a duck or a rabbit. Of course it is both at the same time. The only interesting question concerns the choice between them. Which frame should we adopt, what language might be

---

[7] See e.g. Monika Ambrus et al., eds, *The Role of Experts in International Decision-Making* (Cambridge: Cambridge University Press, 2014); David Kennedy, A *World of Struggle: How Power, Law and Expertise Shape Global Political Economy* (Princeton, NJ: Princeton University Press, 2016).

more just, produce the better outcome, be more useful, and so on? This can be translated into a question of institutional authority as well (and is usually so understood by the legal/political experts themselves). Should we be ruled by lawyers or politicians, by institutions where legal or political arguments are appreciated? Notice again that the relevant question is not about what the world is like as a matter of *fact*: is it 'legal' or 'political'? Rather, it is about values and objectives: which language would be better, which experts more capable of dealing with the problem in an acceptable way?

Notice moreover that we never see half-a-duck or half-a-rabbit in the image. The animal appears as a whole and not as some kind of monster (that is why it is used as an example of the holistic nature of the human psyche). So it is also with law and politics. Things are never half-law and half-politics but always wholly either one or the other. When pleading in the ICC, everything you say *is* law, whereas when you are a foreign policy decision maker in government *grosso modo* all that you do is politics. This is not a matter of what you think but an institutional fact about you, a fact that everyone in the institution understands. Each vocabulary is always a whole, providing a coherent interpretation of the world. That is the very point of vocabulary. Institutional vocabularies such as law and politics smoothen the rough edges of the world, simplify its complexities and make things fit in larger conceptual wholes. They do this so as to explain the world to us in view of some larger system of ideas making it familiar to enable us to act in it in a meaningful way. Finally, it is also useful to notice the familiar fact that the longer we examine the duck-rabbit image, the easier it becomes to shift from one image to the other. This applies to law and politics too. In order to be effective operators in the world of global institutions, we should be able to shift quite smoothly from the language of politics to the language of law, depending on the audience we are speaking to or whom it is we wish to persuade. Failing to display the kind of authority that is expected results not just in a cultural embarrassment; it will also undermine the interest that we wish to advance.

The relationship between law and politics in the international (but also the domestic) world is that between two vocabularies and expert systems, two types of institutional practice and authority. These vocabularies and their corresponding institutions have effects in the world. Therefore, it is very important to decide whether some matter is best treated by law or by politics, that is to say, by applying to it those conceptual tools and institutional practices that go with such expert vocabularies.

I will now move on to three particular fields of international law and politics that are analysed more deeply in their own right further along in this book: international criminal law, humanitarian intervention, and human rights. In each field, the duck-rabbit quality of the professional approach may obscure our ability to view these fields of international law in a comprehensive light, and thus, perhaps, prevent us from dealing intelligently with them.

## International Criminal Justice

One area where the law-politics opposition regularly emerges is in the turn to criminal justice in international affairs. Are international criminal tribunals about legal punishment or show trials?; the enforcement of law or of Western/imperial bias?; legal or victor's justice? Much of this seems at stake in an assessment of the Yugoslavian or Rwandan war crimes proceedings, or the work of the International Criminal Court. Indeed, the very legitimacy of international trials seems to depend on whether we can regard them as law instead of politics. We lawyers have an interest, a legitimate interest, in trying to make them seem as legal as possible, by pointing to the objective fact-orientation of the process; the safeguards of impartiality constructed into criminal law; and the semiotics of blind justice (wigs, gowns, and the formalism of it all). Nevertheless, it seems always possible also to tell the trial as a political event, a story of rabbits instead of ducks. Why is that?[8]

Let's begin at the beginning. What is the point of bringing law to issues of massive violence, atrocities, and war? Some suggest that we do this in order to persuade people in general not to engage in such horrific actions, whereas others admit that even if such general prevention may not work at least the punishment will remove those individuals who have already been proven to be dangerous. Yet there are many plausible objections to the thesis about international criminal law's preventive capacity. The *mens rea* is lacking. For people who are convinced that they are fighting for a just cause, international criminal law has no effect. To the contrary, for such people the trial may appear as yet another vicious instrument of their adversary, a prolongation of earlier fighting. For centuries, just war rhetoric was used by one side as moral condemnation

---

[8] This section is largely based on Martti Koskenniemi, 'Between Impunity and Show Trials', in Armin von Bogdandy et al., eds, Max Planck Yearbook of United Nations Law, *vi* (Leiden: Brill-Nijhoff, 2002), 1–36, also published in Martti Koskenniemi, *The Politics of International Law* (Oxford: Hart, 2011), 171–97.

of the adversary, while seen on the other side as political manipulation of public opinion. For such (and other) reasons, most people nowadays claim that the point of criminal trials is not so much prevention but revolves around the need to have a historical record of what has happened, an 'archive' for the use of victims and future generations. The judgment produced at the end of the day will make people learn about what happened; victims will be vindicated and the way to reconstruction opened. Trials are about the truth and the law will bring it to us.

And yet, nothing is more difficult to attain, more contestable (and contested) than the truth brought about by a criminal law process.[9] At the outset of the Milosevic trial, the then prosecutor Carla Del Ponte of the International Criminal Tribunal for the Former Yugoslavia (ICTY) suggested that the Serbian nation was not on trial, only one individual was. There was no collective punishment, no political judgement over the whole Serbian nation. We are all just lawyers, she was hoping to assure her audience, and the only question we need to answer is: Did the accused do it? Was he there at the time of the crime? Did he have a weapon and a motive, did he give the order?

But what kind of a history would suggest that the Balkan tragedy is the result of the doings of one man? Individuals operate as part of structures : command structures, but also larger social and economic wholes pushed and pulled by complex historical causalities. After the Second World War, many Germans blamed the Nazi atrocities on Adolf Hitler, thus exculpating German society and the German economy, forgetting about the willing participation of large masses in the Nazi surge. If the point of criminal trials is to attain the truth, then pinning the guilt on individuals is the surest way to fail. No self-respecting historian would attribute the Balkan wars to a few individuals who happened to be in office at the time. Large historical and institutional causalities were at issue. But these are contested causalities: socialism and Cold War: how to assess them? So is the role of colonialism or neocolonialism in Rwanda in 1994. What about economic deprivation, greed, and imperial interests? These 'truths' are not accessible through law, they are matters of political assessment, and preference. This does not undermine law, of course, but merely makes (or should make) lawyers reflect on law's political role in particular situations.

---

[9] A message many a time impressed on the reader in Telford Taylor's classic, *The Anatomy of the Nuremberg Trials* (Boston: Little & Brown, 1992).

Something is a crime, and someone is a criminal, only against some interpretative background, some narrative about what is 'normal' and acceptable, and what not. We think nothing of soldiers killing each other because we think (perversely) that this is the way wars are fought. But when a civilian dies, we are scandalised. The boundary between what we accept and what we righteously reject may be legally clear but morally blurry and contested. As lawyers we need to know that boundary, but also be aware of its arbitrariness. Think of the East German *Stasi* (State Security Service) officials or informers who were tried as criminals after the fall of the Berlin wall. Where was their crime? What if they were merely trying to have a decent life for themselves and their children by complying to the standards of a society that happened to be profoundly unjust. Would you have acted otherwise?

The point is not to say that there should be no criminal trials, or that they should be conducted in some other way, only that, in order to pin down 'criminality' in contexts such as the Yugoslavian succession wars or postcolonial Africa, large assumptions are involved about the context against which behaviour is being adjudicated: what about nationalism, racism, imperialism? Of course law – ducks – cannot stand in judgement of those larger structures. Law does its own work, useful but limited as it is. A little pond in the forest. But this does not prevent us from thinking about those trials as rabbits would do: as political from beginning to end. For them, the meaning of the pond and the role of the pond-dwellers lies in how they are seen from the perspective of the forest. A trial appears 'political' as soon as such issues as the role of imperialism, nationalism, economic interests, institutional ambitions, etc. are included in the conceptual frame, and it is good to remember that refraining from engaging with these issues is just as political as engaging with them.

There has always been both a legal and a political story about the Yugoslavian succession wars and about Rwanda in 1994, just like there has been on the fight against terrorism and Responsibility to Protect. Each story focuses on some aspect of the events, ignoring others. Each plays to its own audience, ducks or rabbits, and will never be quite persuaded by the alternative. But both have their places. The criminal law story is about an orderly world where legal rules and institutions provide security, communicate values, and enable adversaries to live in peace. The political story situates law and courts as parts of the landscape of struggle and compromise, adversity and reconciliation, power and ideology. Both stories are well known and true in their own (limited) way. Apart from what they tell us about the world, they also communicate about the character and preferences of the people who tell the stories. International criminal law is also about the role that criminal lawyers should play in the international institutional world. Large groups of professionals – lawyers and political scientists – have much at stake in the appeal of their respective stories. On both sides their stories are not only about 'truth' but also about professional ambition and bias.

To believe that the point of criminal law is to find the truth so as to bring about reconciliation is to close one's eyes to the deeply unhistorical nature of the formalism of criminal trial. The individualisation of the past is not a plausible way to think about history. The adversarial nature of the trial, its formal methods of evidence gathering and measurement as well as the closeness of the trial to the events being adjudged all contribute to widening the gap between a proper historical understanding and the truth of a criminal trial, brought to light by legal forms and rules of evidence. Moreover, the criminal trial always produces an account that is convenient to the powers on the shoulders of which the court itself sits.

It is a criminological commonplace that criminal law is one of the repressive mechanisms whereby elites of a society keep the masses in check, an instrument of hegemony through and through. This is even more obviously true of international criminal trials that need the backing of an overwhelming power that is able to set such trials in motion, pay the costs, and determine who among the parties to a conflict will be branded as a criminal. Nuremberg and Tokyo may have set legal precedents but they were also victors' justice. Acquittals of high-ranking Croatian and Serbian military officials by the ICTY Appeals Chamber was widely seen as deference to a power responsible for the existence of that Tribunal, itself beyond its jurisdiction.[10] These are aspects of the criminal process in which journalists, political historians, and international relations scholars revel. For them, criminal trials are always (also) show trials. They aim to solidify the structures of power in the (international) society and brand as criminals those who are, among other things, the political adversaries of the victorious powers. Such facts, however undeniable, are hardly reconcilable with the commitment of many legal professionals to the virtues of trials.[11] And yet this is hardly

---

[10] For a discussion, see e.g. Janine Natalya Clark, 'Courting Controversy: The ICTY's Acquittal of Croatian Generals Gotovina and Markac', *Journal of International Criminal Law*, 11 (2013), 399–423.

[11] This faith is beautifully discussed in Sarah Nouwen, 'Justifying Justice', in James Crawford and Martti Koskenniemi, *The Cambridge Companion to International Law* (Cambridge: Cambridge University Press, 2012), 338–45.

a scandal: the journalist and the jurist – the rabbit and the duck – each carrying out a distinct job, each speaking to a distinct audience, with different expectations. The fact that atrocities *were* committed is, after all, no less a truth than the political character of the trial. And just lawyers will continue to debate the appropriateness of judging atrocity in the first place and the legal correctness of the verdict, political experts will continue to disagree about its political appropriateness.

The lesson from the duck-rabbit image in regard to international criminal law is not that trials are wrong (though it does not exclude that possibility). Rather, it is to remind us that trials are perceived differently by different audiences. If one then asks about the relative merits of audience perspectives, and in particular those of the lawyer and the political analyst, it is important to bear in mind that there is no superior 'third dimension' that could produce that assessment with authority. We are always either lawyers or political analysts, ducks or rabbits, delivering a specific kind of knowledge that language (one is tempted to use the Wittgensteinian phrase, 'forms of life') reflects: a professionally competent reading of criminal law or a politically competent analysis of the meaning of that reading. Both depend on each other, neither can be reduced to the other. The presence in the world of ducks and rabbits is not a problem to be resolved but an existential situation which we had better make good use of.

## Humanitarian Intervention

Another set of questions about the relation between law and politics arises in the context of forcible intervention for ostensibly humanitarian causes. Ever since the NATO bombing of Serbia during the Kosovo crisis in 1999 and well into the debates on the Responsibility to Protect (RtoP) and the controversies over Western action in Libya in 2011 and inaction in Syria thereafter, lawyers and political scientists have anxiously tried to figure out whether such intervention is really about the enforcement of humanitarian principles or paternalistic discipline over misbehaving minors. Many international lawyers, myself included, have found themselves answering journalists, when questioned about intervention without Security Council authorisation in the Kosovo situation, that it was 'illegal, but legitimate'. What did this mean?[12] There is an aspect of trying to be

---

[12] See further Martti Koskenniemi,'The Lady Doth Protest too Much: Kosovo and the Turn to Ethics in International Law', *The Modern Law Review*, 65 (2002), 159–75, also

both a duck and a rabbit simultaneously: to convey a message that would appear both professionally competent and politically acceptable. 'Illegal but legitimate' was a way to admit that the two did not always go hand in hand, that a legal-technical and a moral-political way to observe the situation did not always generate the same description or an identical program of action, but also that neither was sufficient without the existence of the other.

But then, how informative or useful was such a response? Surely lawyers are not expected to act as Delphic oracles, producing ambiguous and contradicting messages to a concerned public. The dissatisfaction led to a number of research projects and reports in the early 2000s by domestic think tanks and international institutions about the present and future of humanitarian intervention. The most famous of these, discussed in Chapter 7 of this book, was titled 'Responsibility to Protect' and was referred to in several UN contexts, including the 2005 report of the High-Level Meeting of the General Assembly.[13] However, in the aftermath of the widespread dissatisfaction with the Western action in the Libyan civil conflict in the spring of 2011, and the occupation of Crimea three years later, the future of the Responsibility to Protect seems very uncertain. Common to the anxious reports produced in the early 2000s was the hope that the legal situation would be clarified by laying out once and for all the legal parameters of international violence so as to be able to distinguish acceptable humanitarian action from the advancement of imperial interest. The effort has met with little success. The law and the politics of intervention are still completely entangled with each other. But this cannot be avoided. There is always both a legal and a political perspective to any humanitarian situation and responsible (in contrast to dogmatic) action must somehow involve a deliberate consideration in both. Any intervention will invoke rules and principles, practices and precedent to which lawyers cannot be indifferent, but it will also sustain some constellation of power and some set of values over others that inform how those legal materials appear.

Many believe that a legal rule on humanitarian intervention is required to prevent the destruction of innocent lives. What content should such

published in Martti Koskenniemi, *The Politics of International Law* (Oxford: Hart, 2011), 112–30.

[13] For the relevant part of the World Summit document, see UNGA Res A/60/L.1, 15 September 2005, paras. 138–40. The best discussion of the intellectual contexts of humanitarian intervention is Anne Orford, *International Authority and the Responsibility to Protect* (Cambridge: Cambridge University Press, 2011).

rule have? The most obvious suggestion would be to simply repeat the following policy-objective: *Intervention shall take place when innocent lives are being destroyed.* That would be an excellent rule to the extent that it gives precise expression to the overriding objective. But it would also be a stupid rule. It would be too open for discretion – who is 'innocent' anyway, and what does 'destruction' mean? Its open-endedness would only support interests that have the capacity of action and a propaganda machinery to support it. A rule is needed not because there is a lack of agreement that the innocent should not be destroyed – everyone agrees to that – but because the open-endedness of the expression leaves too much room for misuse: imperialism in the guise of humanitarian action.

So, we need a tougher rule, one that leaves no room for discretion. What might be such a rule? Perhaps the following would do: military intervention is allowed (or perhaps called for) when 500 people are killed. This would be an excellent rule in that it would leave no room for discretion and misuse. Compliance could be measured by a body count. Of course this would also be a bad rule. Like every hard-and-fast rule, it is also a permission to do precisely what is not prohibited in it. And lawyers are trained not only to tell their clients what rules prohibit but, in fact much more commonly, what they allow. Now, imagine a dictator wanting to relocate a minority from its traditional home. Her intuition is just to destroy the population. Before doing that, however, she asks the legal advisor how she can get rid of these people. The legal advisor would answer that, according to international law, if 500 die, you will face an intervention force. 'But', the dictator would respond 'you are the legal advisor. It is your task to tell me how I can get rid of them without breaking the law.' To which the advisor would now respond: 'Tell your soldiers to go, kill one member of every family, while informing others that the killing will stop immediately as they leave. You can be sure that people will have abandoned their homes before the 500th person is killed. And if they do not, then the soldiers would stop at 499 (and start the killing somewhere else).'

Here, the rule does not prohibit what the dictator wants to do, it just tells her how to go about it. This is how legal rules work. They never just tell you what you should *not* do, but always also *how you should* do what you want without breaking the law. The case of humanitarian intervention is a perfect example of the kind of limits that are intrinsic to law in the pursuit of desirable political objectives. Law comes to us as rules and principles, linguistic formulations that are either too open-ended or not open-ended enough. They leave too much room for discretion that can then be used to advance interests other than those the rules were designed to protect. Or, if they leave no room for discretion at all, they fail to include either cases that would have been desirable to include (the very commencement of the killing) or cases that had not been thought of but that could be read into the narrow limits of the rule by the adversary. An example might be the thousands of cases of abortion practiced daily in the secular West. In other words, whether the law is broad or narrow, allows discretion or does not allow discretion, it will fail without more. And that 'more' can only be found by an assessment of what small injustice we are able to tolerate as the inevitable cost that the rule will produce in relation to the advantages that we can gain by having it.[14]

What this perhaps crude example shows is that, whatever the content of the law, it is insufficient as a full description and program of action. It is too approximate either too wide or too narrow. Which is why the law itself may sometimes become a (political) problem. A rule that encourages powerful states to use their military force to discipline others as well as one that shields ruthless dictators would be a bad rule. *Fiat justitia, pereat mundus*, or let there be justice even if the world would perish, is a useful reminder that law is not 'all', and that we need often to assess its political wisdom. There are more animals than ducks in the forest and more ways to understand the world than suggested to us by the vision from the pond. Ducks and rabbits both have their own kind of wisdom, but it is a limited wisdom. In a complex international world, one needs both kinds.

Like international criminal trials, the laws of humanitarian intervention are profoundly legal and profoundly political at the same time. They are operated by lawyers and legal institutions through legal mechanisms, but their operation relies on a constellation of political power. Finland will never intervene in the Crimea and Uganda will never intervene in race riots in Baltimore. It will always be states with large military and economic resources and worldwide interests to protect that are liberated by a rule on humanitarian intervention. This is not an accident but the result of many years of international history: a history of (some) progress but also of much violence and injustice. A hegemon, political analysts tell us, is often needed for a system of international governance to emerge and, perhaps, to

---

[14] A very useful discussion of the ways in which rules operate is found in Frederick Schauer, *Playing by the Rules: A Philosophical Examination of Rule-Based Decision-Making in Law and in Life* (Oxford: Clarendon Press, 1991).

operate efficiently.[15] But hegemons agree to be enlisted only on conditions laid out by them. It is *their* soldiers and *their* prestige that are involved. The fate of the League of Nations' security system during the interwar period provides a reminder that when the great powers are *not* entitled to control the course of action (the League's Council operated with majority voting and no right of veto), then they will leave the system as soon as it turns against them (as happened in the cases of Germany, Japan, and Italy). A rule that treats everyone as equals in matters of military force does not cease to be a political rule, it is a *stupid* political rule. That is why the five great powers have the right of veto in the UN Security Council. And that is why every suggestion about humanitarian force must pass through the Security Council. This is the law. And the law tries hard not to be an ass. That the Council's decisions are based on political considerations does not mean that applying the UN Charter would not be a legal matter. The provisions of the UN Charter and the way they are applied are *both* politics and law, about the wisdom of ducks as well as rabbits.

## Human Rights

Let me finally touch upon a few things about law and politics in human rights. We often think that the introduction of rights vocabulary in domestic or international government is about bringing the rule of law to those institutions. The rule of law, again, we think, is precisely the contrary to discretion, favouritism, and political bias. And perhaps it is sometimes like that. But it certainly is not like that always or necessarily. Rights, like other governmental vocabularies, are techniques for justifying one type of rule and one type of behaviour over others. I often wonder why there is not more awareness of the fact that, historically speaking, the most significant subjective right has been, and continues to be, the right of private property. When subjective rights emerged inside the Catholic Church in the fourteenth century, they did so in the context of the Franciscan poverty controversy that was precisely about the validity of the right of exclusion that is involved in property claims.[16] The natural lawyers Hugo Grotius and John Locke, writing in the seventeenth century, linked their very influential subjective rights theories to property

---

[15] Robert Keohane, *After Hegemony. Cooperation and Discord in the World Political Economy* (Princeton, NJ: Princeton University Press, 1984).

[16] See e.g. Annabel Brett, *Liberty, Right and Nature: Individual Rights in Later Scholastic Thought* (Cambridge: Cambridge University Press, 1997), pp. 12–20.

claims within Dutch and English colonisation.[17] Still today, by far the most national jurisprudence has to do with rights involving claims of recognition of property. And yet, of course, claims of property rights are at the root of many significant injustices in global modernity.

There is a new interest in writing the history of human rights. The question of when exactly human rights emerged has been answered differently, with references being made to canon law, to the Spanish scholastics, to the French Revolution, and to the American Revolution.[18] Much More recent work suggests that, as a cultural and political phenomenon, human rights emerged only in the 1970s.[19] There is much to be said for the latter view. When I took my exam in Finnish constitutional law forty years ago not a word was said about human rights. It was all about the powers of the highest state organs. Meanwhile, the jurisprudence class had just started to read a hugely popular book *Taking Rights Seriously,*[20] and by the early 1980s Finnish jurists were rehearsing their skills in speaking about the rights of factions of Finnish citizenry. As a result, the new Finnish Constitution of the year 2000 came to include a substantial Bill of Rights.[21] And yet, when I look around at home in Finland and ask myself how much we have changed – I must admit, not that much. The re-description of Finland in rights terms may have signified a fundamental jurisprudential change. But its effect on the lives of Finns has still been negligible.

The history of the rise of rights-talk is broadly similar in most Western societies. Rights are everywhere. It is hard to find a social conflict today in which both sides are not able to translate their grievances into rights terms. And because rights are all over the place, it has become routine in administrations and legal institutions, including human rights courts and tribunals, to 'balance' rights, to limit rights by countervailing rights and, in the process, to put the values represented by rights in a hierarchical order. Here is a skeletal history of how this came about. Early in the

---

[17] Eric Wilson, *Savage Republic: De Indis of Hugo Grotius, Republicanism and Dutch Hegemony within the Early Modern World-System (c. 1600–1619)* (Leiden: Nijhoff, 2008); Barbara Arneil, *John Locke and America: The Defence of English* Colonization (Oxford: Oxford University Press 2007).

[18] See Martti Koskenniemi 'Rights, History, Critique', in Adam Etinson, ed., *Human Rights: Moral or Political?* (Oxford: Oxford University Press, 2018), 41–61.

[19] See Samuel Moyn, *The Last Utopia: Human Rights in History* (Cambridge MA: Harvard University Press, 2010).

[20] Ronald Dworkin, *Taking Rights Seriously* (Cambridge MA: Harvard University Press, 1977).

[21] The Constitution of Finland, 731/1999, Chapter 2.<INTEGRA: no link>

twentieth century, Max Weber, another famous lawyer, put forward the view of law of late modern society as deformalised law. Modernity, Weber once explained, involved increased social complexity. This was reflected in the legal system by a move from clear-cut, universal and generally applicable rules to soft and flexible standards that allowed taking into account the factual differences between situations, including good faith, reasonableness, proportionality, and balancing.[22] With open-ended legislation, social power was shifted from legislators to law-appliers, governments, and administrative bodies. In the late 1960s and early 1970s, the increase of public authorities' discretion began to seem worrying, however. It was felt that strict rules were again needed that would put an end to discretion and that would allow expressing things such as: 'you cannot do that even if, all things considered, it would be socially useful or economically optimal. You cannot because I have a right.' This was a powerful strategy to limit decision-making by public authorities and to shift power in favour of those that legislators decided to inaugurate as rights-holders.

Soon however, everyone learned to translate their interests into rights-claims, with the result that the original power of 'having a right' was lost. It was now again up to public authorities to determine how we should be treated by limiting rights vis-à-vis other rights, ranking them, and providing them with meanings that made them compatible with governmental agendas, including security agendas. This would not have been the case had there existed some public authority-independent way of identifying 'real' rights in contrast to merely spurious or political rights. But where would such criteria come from? Lawyers once found a theory of natural rights, assumed as unchanging, invariable, and universal. But natural rights theories soon showed themselves as deeply political, subjective, and arbitrary – good instruments for revolutionary agitation, but unsuitable for administering societies. They were theologies in disguise (which is how the first natural lawyers, Grotius, Locke, and Pufendorf actually thought of them). However, the alternative – thinking of them in purely positive, legislative terms – made their content and rank dependent on governmental coalitions and the interests of their constituencies.

---

[22] See e.g. Max Rheinstein, ed., *Max Weber: On Law in Economy and Society* (New York: Simon and Schuster, 1954), 305–321 and comments in Roberto Mangabeira Unger, *Law in Modern Society* (New York: Free Press, 1976).

As was the case with criminal justice and the lawful use of force, human rights too oscillated between law and politics, between technical vocabularies and institutions on the one side and the heterogeneity of the interests of social groups (as well as the power on which the latter can be settled) on the other side.[23] It is ducks and rabbits once again. To think that human rights speak truth to politics (and politicians) is a dogmatic, even ideological aspect of duck-speech, the effort by lawyers (ducks) to dictate social preferences to others (rabbits). But ducks have no monopoly on rights language that is, while legal, also thoroughly political. What rights there are and how they can be limited and balanced against countervailing rights both takes place in legal process by distinctly legal ways of argument and depends on political priorities. This does not mean that rights are completely malleable. For lawyers, they are fixed in legal institutions and practices with a hardness and verifiability that enables jurists to operate them. For politicians, they appear in party programs and governmental projects that constitute, however abstractly, the focal points that enable likeminded individuals to recognise each other as allies. For both groups, rights language offers a platform on which abstract ideals are fitted with institutional realities. Both worlds, the abstract and the concrete, delimit and inform each other in the constant struggle over the distribution of social values.

### Fragmentation and the Politics of Re-Description

International law is a messy world of ideas and institutions where it is often hard to understand the ubiquitous tensions between politics and law. The proliferation of rights has a parallel phenomenon elsewhere in international institutions, in the proliferation of legal vocabularies, such as trade law, humanitarian law, sports law, investment law, environmental law, and so on. Every vocabulary comes with its own specialist institutions and experts whose training and professional experiences and expectations make them share reasonably coherent political preferences. In practice, this has meant that political conflict in the international space has come to focus on jurisdiction: how should authority between expert groups be distributed so as to deal with particular problems? 'Trade and environment' describes one such set of problems of distribution: should an issue be dealt with by trade experts in trade

---

[23] See further Martti Koskenniemi, 'Human Rights, Politics and Love', in *The Politics of International Law* (Oxford: Hart, 2011), 153–68.

institutions and under trade law, or should it rather be debated among environmental experts in environmental bodies under environmental standards?[24] Everything about how the problem will be dealt with is involved in that choice. Or think of the ubiquitous theme of 'security and human rights'. Under which vocabulary (read: expert system) should issues of political deviance, immigration, or life in the suburbs be administered?[25] Once we know who will deal with the issue we also know how it will be dealt with. All of us are able to distinguish such expert groups by some sociological criteria, somewhat like we are able to distinguish ducks from rabbits. How does the person speak? Does he or she wear a lounge suit or a Norwegian sweater? Well, then that person is either a member of the WTO appellate body or an activist of Greenpeace. The way an expert speaks, what he or she reads, and whom he or she associates with (including for whom he or she votes) are all on a par with the way experts analyse a problem and suggest solutions to it. The choice of the relevant law (human rights or trade law?) is in this sense always already political. This makes the totality of international institutions look a bit like the familiar painting by Kandinsky displayed in full colour on the cover of this book (Figure 2). Researching a theme such as the fragmentation of international law is somewhat like analysing an early non-figurative art work. Both express a sense that a tradition is breaking down, that the world is one of plurality and not singularity, and that there are innumerable ways of describing and re-describing the world in order to give expression to the countless experiences of it.

When Kandinsky first came up with artistic complexity as expressed in 'Composition 8', audiences had a hard time figuring out what to think of it. Is this really art? And if it is, what does it mean? Today many people are comfortable with an image like this. Popular culture and college art history classes have turned it into a perfectly banal specimen of one type of early twentieth century artistic experimentation. We are no longer puzzled by the complexity of the work in the way early audiences were. One lesson to be learned from the cultural moments that we have learned to associate with Kandinsky is that there is nothing to worry about concerning the plurality of the experiences we have of the world. It is all right, and even welcome as a reminder of life's manifoldness and mystery. One can see many things in an image like this. Ducks might be

---

[24] See e.g. Monika Ambrus et al. ( 2014), for various chapters on experts, environment, and trade. See also David Kennedy, 'Challenging Expert Rule: The Politics of Global Governance', *Sydney Law Review*, 25 (2005), 5–28.

[25] Ambrus et al. (2014), chapter on migration.

Figure 2: Vassily Kandinsky, *Composition 8*, 1923, Guggenheim Museum, New York
Source: https://commons.wikimedia.org/wiki/File:Vassily_Kandinsky,_1923_-
Composition_8,_huile_sur_toile,_140_cm_x_201_cm,_Mus%C3%A9e_Guggenheim,
_New_York.jpg

inclined to view crumbs of bread while rabbits might imagine it to deal
with carrots (perhaps displaying then a tragic absence of carrots). This is
how experts operate. They see in the world what they have been trained to
see there. A human rights expert sees human rights problems everywhere, while for the trade lawyer the world appears as a mass of
incentives and hindrances to commerce. I do not think there is any
super-image that would offer a description of the world as it 'really' is,
and to which we should then adjust the images that our professional
training has taught us to believe in. Instead, especially for academics,
what seems worth aspiring to is the ability to see the world through
different eyes, and to learn about how others experience the world.
No doubt, even as professionals, seeing the world through different
eyes might seem important for our ability to understand and to govern
the world in a beneficial way.

So what are the relations between international law and international
politics? They are relations between specialist vocabularies, each with
their own priorities. Each may be good for something and not so good for
something else. Lawyers, political scientists, diplomats, and academics

are all experts in specialised languages through which we try to persuade our audiences. To succeed we must be sensitive to whom we are in conversation with, whom we try to persuade. What language has power in what context? With ducks, one should speak Duckalese, with rabbits, one should speak Rabbit. Otherwise, one will not be understood. But which language is 'good' or 'right' to speak in relation to a particular matter? This is the question of 'justice' to which I promised to come at the end. That question, I am afraid, cannot be answered in an abstract or all-encompassing way. To do that would require a meta-language or super-expertise. It is true that, in their quest for influence, expert vocabularies have often tried to present themselves as a kind of Esperanto. Theology once imagined itself as the queen of the sciences: law then, politics not so long ago, economics more recently. There is no reason to accept such claims at face value. English is now spoken everywhere, but the world it conveys is no truer than, say, the world described in Finnish.

As many of us learned at school, it is good to know many languages, because they also give access to the lives, cultures, and thinking of native speakers. And it is good to know the world from many sides. This seems as true to me now as it seemed when I went to school. But there is an additional catch to this truism. No language is completely homogenous and closed. Each has its mainstream but also its heterodoxy. Law, politics, and other expert systems are also live fields of internal contestation. It is not possible to participate in the effort to create a just society without doing this from some expert position, without recourse to some data (and preferences), collected by experts (of trade, environment, human rights, foreign policy, whatever). There is no area of pure justice in which the question of the right way to act could be decided outside of what we know of the world. But precisely because the languages are open, the forms of expertise have themselves become fields of conflict and contestation. Economic experts quarrel over the effects of foreign investment on development just like environmental experts disagree on the respective dangers of coal and nuclear power. In fact, it often seems that the most important questions of social justice today have become internal to systems of knowledge. They highlight the fragility of the presumptions under which disagreements between experts, and scientific uncertainties are resolved.[26]

---

[26] See further, Martti Koskenniemi, 'Hegemonic Regimes', in Margaret Young, ed., *Regime Interaction in International Law: Facing Fragmentation* (Cambridge: Cambridge University Press, 2011), 305–24.

To lawyers frustrated about the injustices of the world, I often say that we should learn to be better at the politics of re-description. We should examine problems, whether these be international problems, domestic problems, problems of distribution or violence, by seeking to re-describe them in alternative languages, so as to understand them from many sides: our own expertise of course, but also that of other disciplines. For sometimes law's narrow view of the world lies at the root of some injustice. Sometimes, again, injustice emerges from action produced by politicians, economists, soldiers or engineers – though sometimes any one of them might possess insights that we ignore at out peril. This is why I cannot think of a better, or more relevant way to advance *justice* than by engaging in constant re-descriptions; that is to say, in a persistent effort to rid ourselves as experts of the prison-house of the inherited biases of our disciplines, our standard ways of explaining the world. Re-description sensitises us to those biases and ways in which we ourselves (our kind of expertise, our biases) might have become 'the problem'.

## Conclusion

Most of us agree that the world is a terribly unjust place, even as we disagree on precisely where the injustice lies, what has caused it, and how to change things. One way to commence this work is by describing the world anew, focusing on what was previously unseen, telling a new story, or recovering an old one that simply has not been heard from the surrounding noise. In the conditions of today's backlash it often seems that liberal and cosmopolitan projects, including the projects of international criminal law, humanitarian intervention, and human rights, have become stale and autistic, unable to speak to those not already committed. No doubt, they are in desperate need of new, more engaging background narratives, instead of just endless calls for institutional reform. It is time to enquire into what our inherited legal and political vocabularies actually do: how they are related to the will formation of large communities and in what ways they participate in the distribution of material and spiritual values. Who do they lift into decision-making positions and who do they sideline or silence? Like other expert systems, international law and politics are forms of literature, types of narrating the world. They are not just about making the world a better place, they are also complicit in the world's injustices. But – and this is crucial – we cannot wish them away. There are no *a priori* truer or more authentic ways of seeing and experiencing the world. Ignorance is still not a virtue.

But what we can do is to engage in the internal debates within the worlds of expertise that are ours: how solid are our presuppositions, how confident our conclusions? Could our inherited institutions be imagined in other ways as well? What are the distributive consequences of the knowledge in which we excel? Trying to take such questions seriously requires thinking of legal and political expertise not as separate worlds, but as alternative descriptions of a single world, each in possession of its own kind of wisdom. They are complex and often contradictory and contested descriptions, which is why a certain dialectic is required in working with them. We need the technical wisdom of law and politics, but also sharp insight into the consequences of how their respective outcomes enter the lives of human communities. Whether internal and external, or professional and experiential: without embracing both viewpoints, it is hard to see how the specialised languages of law and politics can retrieve the promise of helping in the construction of just societies, which we once believed was their very point.

3

# The Globalisation of Justice: Amplifying and Silencing Voices at the ICC

WARNER TEN KATE AND SARAH M.H. NOUWEN*

## The Globalisation of Justice

As a process of both dominance and resistance, globalisation often ends up amplifying some voices and silencing others. Some people manage to use globalisation to get their voice heard internationally. Others are out-voiced by stronger, yet more globalised, voices. This applies to globalisation in the sense of economics (local companies losing the competition with multinationals), politics (domestic lobby groups reaching international audiences by rallying with international counterparts), culture (local customs and traditions marginalised by globalised manifestations of culture) and, as this chapter will argue, justice. The globalisation of justice, which in fact is often shorthand for the globalisation of international criminal justice, amplifies some voices and diminishes or silences others.

This process of amplification and silencing of voices is not the inevi-table consequence of a technical development. It stems at least in part from what Martti Koskenniemi calls 'the politics of re-description'.[1] Whereas Koskenniemi uses this term particularly to refer to the struggle among various legal vocabularies to describe the same fact pattern, the term is also appropriate for the more preliminary struggle over whether to describe that fact pattern in a legal or other type of language, for instance, that of diplomacy, reconciliation, or economics. Each of these languages comes with its own preferences in values, institutions, and solutions. In the language of international criminal law, for instance, the focus is on individuals. The structures within which these individuals operate are less relevant. The language of international criminal law

* Nouwen finished this chapter while funded by the Economic and Social Research Council (Grant Number ES/L010976/1), the Leverhulme Trust (PLP-2014–067), and the Isaac Newton Trust (RG79578).
[1] See M. Koskenniemi, Chapter 2 of this book.

comes with courts and prisons, not with peace negotiations or Marshall plans. And the language of international criminal law offers solutions in terms of individual criminal accountability and punishment; not in terms of forgiveness, amnesties, or distributive justice.

The choice of language can make all the difference. While the fact pattern of the situation at hand may have barely changed, a different description might highlight different elements of the situation and thus a different type of solution. Processes of globalisation may thus trigger a struggle over the language in which to describe a particular situation with a view to identifying which elements and institutions are relevant, and which solutions should be considered. The globalisation of international criminal justice implies the emergence and dominance of the language of international criminal law, the amplification of the voices of those who master the language of international criminal law, and the silencing of those who adopt different, non-legal, languages.

The very first situation before the International Criminal Court (ICC), that concerning northern Uganda, is illustrative of these politics of re-description, of the globalisation of international criminal justice and of the ensuing amplification of some voices (those within the Ugandan executive advocating for military solutions to the conflict with the Lord's Resistance Army, those of human rights and transitional justice activists, and those of internationally oriented Ugandan technocrats) and the silencing of others (the voices of the Ugandan Parliament, judiciary, advocates for comprehensive solutions, and last but not least the population most directly affected by the conflict). This chapter will illustrate this process by showing four instances of re-description attempts of the conflict in northern Uganda: (1) the struggle between a military approach and reconciliation efforts in the period prior to ICC intervention; (2) the ICC referral as a way to re-describe the conflict and to continue a military approach; (3) the Juba peace process as a negotiation between legal and other approaches; and (4) the post-Juba period, in which a political agreement is approached legalistically.

Four preliminary clarifications are in place. First, when we speak of amplifying or silencing, we do not necessarily imply intention, in other words, that certain actors actively try to strengthen some voices or diminish others: sometimes they may have that intent, sometimes they may not. What we are interested in is the process of amplifying and silencing of voices and the outcome. Secondly, although the developments that we describe are related to the ICC, we do not argue that the ICC is the only actor involved in these processes. Nonetheless, the ICC is a key actor that sets in motion developments, inspires other actors, or intensifies existing processes. Thirdly, there are as many voices as there are people. This chapter does not argue that those of specific groups, for instance, so-called local, national, or international actors, are always in unison. Rather, we are interested in illustrating how some voices get amplified to the detriment of others. Finally, in this chapter we are primarily interested in the processes, in the 'what happens?' Whether what happens is good or bad depends on one's normative and political framework.

## The Conflict in Northern Uganda: A Military Approach versus Reconciliation Efforts

When the ICC opened an investigation into northern Uganda in 2004, it entered into a long-standing conflict.[2] While the military conflict between the Government of Uganda and the Lord's Resistance Army (LRA) and its predecessors existed since 1986, tensions between northern and southern Uganda had endured since before Uganda's independence. The problems between the regions were never properly resolved and led in 1981 to a civil war. This war was won in 1986 by the southerner Yoweri Museveni, who forcefully dislodged a junta of Acholi, one of the main ethnic groups in northern Uganda. After 1986, the situation in northern Uganda remained fluid, with many rebel groups emerging and vanishing.

The most persistent rebel movement has been the LRA. After a short period in which it may have enjoyed some popular support for its fight against Museveni, the LRA lost most of this when it turned its arms against the local population, blaming them for supporting the national government. A cult-based organisation, the LRA looted from local people, maimed and killed them, and abducted children to fill its ranks. In

---

[2] For more elaborate information on the conflict in northern Uganda, on which this section is based, see A. Seftel, ed., *Uganda: The Bloodstained Pearl of Africa and Its Struggle for Peace: From the Pages of Drum* (Kampala: Fountain Publishers, 1994); R. R. Atkinson, *The Roots of Ethnicity: Origins of the Acholi of Uganda* (2nd edn, Kampala: Fountain Publishers, 2010); H. Behrend, *Alice Lakwena & the Holy Spirits: War in Northern Uganda, 1985–97* (Oxford: James Currey, 1999); S. Finnström, *Living with Bad Surroundings: War, History, and Everyday Moments in Northern Uganda* (Durham/London: Duke University Press, 2008); C. Dolan, *Social Torture: The Case of Northern Uganda 1986–2006* (Oxford: Berghahn Books, 2011); T. Allen and K. Vlassenroot, eds, *The Lord's Resistance Army: Myth and Reality* (London/New York: Zed Books, 2010); C. R. Soto, *Tall Grass, Stories of Suffering and Peace in Northern Uganda* (Kampala: Fountain Publishers, 2009).

sum, the LRA is notorious for the atrocious crimes it committed against the very population its leaders originated from.

At the same time, the northern Ugandans received little protection from the Ugandan government. President Museveni's government usually prioritised an offensive military approach, which proved disastrous for the local population. Certainly in the early years, the Ugandan army (the UPDF) committed grave human rights violations during its military operations.[3] In later years, it forced people to move to camps for internally displaced people with a view to facilitating the military operation against the LRA. However, the conditions in these camps proved to be at times more hazardous for the people than the LRA itself.[4] The government did not have the conflict high on its political agenda. As a result, the UPDF engaged in corrupt practices (e.g. officers would pocket salaries for deceased soldiers – 'ghost soldiers' – by manipulating the army payroll; as a result there were far fewer soldiers in northern Uganda than on the records) and was not always active in its fight against the LRA.[5] The camps for internally displaced persons (IDPs) were poorly protected and became a target for LRA raids.

Northern Ugandans, in particular the Acholi, were therefore in a dire situation. They found themselves between, on the one hand, a rebel group that they did not support but that consisted mainly of their missing children and, on the other hand, a government that had put them into camps and did not sufficiently try to resolve the conflict.

Acholi civil society, informally led by religious and traditional leaders of the region, took a stance against the government's attempts militarily to defeat the LRA. Instead, it argued for reconciliation, with a view to both addressing the strained relations between northern and southern Uganda and re-integrating children abducted by the LRA into the local population.[6] Throughout the years of the conflict they made several

---

[3] Human Rights Watch, 'Uprooted and Forgotten: Impunity and Human Rights Abuses in Northern Uganda', 17/12A (September 2005). http://hrw.org/reports/2005/uganda0905/ uganda0905.pdf accessed 8 January 2018.

[4] See, for instance, 'Uganda: 1,000 Displaced Die Every Week in War-Torn North: Report', IRIN (29 August 2005). www.irinnews.org/news/2005/08/29/1000-displaced-die-every-week-war-torn-north-report accessed 8 January 2018.

[5] A. Mwenda, 'Uganda's Politics of Foreign Aid and Violent Conflict: The Political Uses of the LRA Rebellion', in Allen and Vlassenroot, *Lord's Resistance Army*, 45–58 at 52.

[6] See e.g. G. M. Khadiagala, 'The Role of the Acholi Religious Leaders Peace Initiative (ARLPI) in Peace Building in Northern Uganda', *Greater Horn of Africa Peace Building Project* [Case Study Two] (March 2001). pdf.usaid.gov/pdf_docs/PNACY566.pdf accessed 8 January 2018; K. P. Apuuli, 'Peace over Justice: The Acholi Religious Peace Initiative

attempts at promoting dialogue with the LRA. Eventually, all of these proved unsuccessful due to obstruction by both the government and the LRA.

In order to enable the LRA to abandon rebellion, the Acholi community leaders also lobbied the Ugandan parliament, which until then had not concerned itself with the situation in northern Uganda, to adopt an Amnesty Act. They did so successfully: an Amnesty Bill was introduced. When the executive tried to exclude certain crimes from the scope of the Act,[7] parliament insisted on a general amnesty, in a rather unique moment of parliamentary independence from the executive. In 2000, the Amnesty Act was adopted.[8]

By comparison to amnesty acts across the world, the Ugandan Amnesty Act 2000 stands out in that it was advocated for not by the direct beneficiaries of the promise of non-prosecution, but by the community directly affected by the conflict and the many crimes committed. The voice of those most directly affected, calling for a peaceful resolution, was taken into account by the government, which usually favoured a military approach to the LRA problem.[9]

## Involving the ICC: A Legal Re-Description of a Continuing Military Approach

### Proponents of a Military Solution Bypass Parliament and the Acholi

Whereas in the Lauterpachtian world view recourse to an international court is perceived as a peaceful means of conflict resolution,[10] in Uganda the referral was more in line with a military than a peaceful approach.[11] It

---

(ARLPI) vs. the International Criminal Court (ICC) in Northern Uganda', *Studies in Ethnicity and Nationalism*, 11 (2011) 116–29.

[7] See B. Afako, 'Reconciliation and Justice: *"Mato Oput"* and the Amnesty Act', in O. Lucima, ed., *Protracted Conflict, Elusive Peace*, Accord series (London: Conciliation Resources, 2002). www.c-r.org/downloads/Accord%2011_13Reconciliation%20and%20justice_2002_ENG.pdf accessed 8 January 2018.

[8] Amnesty Act 2000, *Laws of Uganda*, chapter 294.

[9] See, for instance, 'Interview with President Yoweri Museveni', IRIN (9 June 2005). www.irinnews.org/report/54853/uganda-interview-president-yoweri-museveni accessed 8 January 2018.

[10] See M. Koskenniemi, Chapter 2 of this book.

[11] See S. M. H. Nouwen, *Complementarity in the Line of Fire: The Catalysing Effect of the International Criminal Court in Uganda and Sudan* (Cambridge: Cambridge University Press, 2013), 111–243; K. A. Rodman and P. Booth, 'Manipulated Commitments: The International Criminal Court in Uganda', *Human Rights Quarterly*, 35 (2013), 271–303.

was the Minister of Defence who convinced President Museveni of the utility of a referral. Faced with increasing criticism on human rights violations in northern Uganda and Western calls for a peaceful solution, the government legitimised its military approach by involving the ICC. ICC-supporting Western states would not criticise the military's counter-insurgency campaign when fought against internationally wanted 'war criminals'. The conflict in northern Uganda was thus re-described in the language of international criminal law, but this served as a new cloak to sustain the preferred option of the military, while silencing Western allies by taking recourse to their preferred instrument: the ICC.[12]

It is thus that in December 2003 the Ugandan government referred 'the situation concerning the LRA' to the ICC. In a twenty-seven-page letter, the government argued that it, '[h]aving exhausted every other means of bringing an end to this terrible suffering ... now turn[ed] to the newly established ICC and its promise of global justice'.[13] The referral happened without consultation of the Acholi and even without consultation of parliament. It could be argued that a referral is an act of the executive that constitutionally does not require parliamentary consultation, let alone approval. However, in Uganda, the entire ratification of the Rome Statute had happened without parliamentary involvement, even though national law seemed to require such involvement given that ratification could necessitate constitutional amendments.[14] Whether constitutionally required or not, politically such consultation would have seemed essential. The effect of the referral was to reduce substantially the value of parliament's Amnesty Act by triggering the jurisdiction of a court not bound by Ugandan law. The referral went against the spirit of an act of parliament and against the wish of the Acholi who had lobbied for the Act. In a weak democratic system and against the background of strained north-south relations, the referral to the ICC thus amplified the voice of the executive vis-à-vis the legislative, and of the southerners who preferred a military solution vis-à-vis the northerners who preferred a peaceful solution.

---

[12] See, more elaborately, S. M. H. Nouwen and W. G. Werner, 'Doing Justice to the Political: The International Criminal Court in Uganda and Sudan', *European Journal of International Law*, 21 (2010), 941–65 at 948–9.

[13] Government of Uganda, Referral of the Situation Concerning the Lord's Resistance Army Submitted by the Republic of Uganda, 16 December 2003, para. 6, on file with authors.

[14] See the aborted case before the Constitutional Court of Uganda in Kampala, *John Magezi, Judy Obitre-Gama, Henry Onoria v. Attorney General*, Constitutional Court, Constitutional Petition No. 10, 27 July 2005.

## Local Resistance to ICC Involvement

While Michael Ignatieff has argued that human rights have 'real power in the international political arena',[15] for people in northern Uganda it was astonishing that, for the purposes of arresting the LRA, the ICC relied on the very army that had failed to do so over the previous two decades. They feared that without its own enforcement powers, the ICC would make an end to the conflict only more difficult. First, ICC involvement went against the idea of the general amnesty that the Acholi had demanded and of which thousands of people had made use to return to civil life. ICC involvement also threatened the implementation of the Act by undermining legal certainty. Finally, ICC involvement jeopardised local initiatives preparing for dialogue with the LRA.[16]

Lobbying against ICC involvement, the Acholi began to emphasise the merits of their own traditional justice and reconciliation mechanisms as an alternative.[17] They did so with some success: the *mato oput* ceremony ('drinking the bitter root') became not only part of the national vocabulary, but also gained international attention.[18] Scholars, international lawyers, and transitional justice activists also came to northern Uganda to study the mechanisms.

However, because the ICC was accepted as the point of reference for 'justice', Acholi justice and reconciliation mechanisms were evaluated from the perspective and within the framework of ICC-style justice. More specifically, the question was whether the traditional mechanisms fulfilled the standards of the ICC's complementarity principle, according to which domestic investigations and prosecutions enjoy primacy to the ICC.[19] According to many human rights activists, the Acholi

---

[15] M. Ignatieff, *Whose Universal Values? The Crisis in Human Rights* (Amsterdam: Stichting Praemium Erasmianum, 1999), 11.

[16] See Z. Lomo and L. Hovil, 'Whose Justice? Perceptions of Uganda's Amnesty Act 2000: The Potential for Conflict Resolution and Long-Term Reconciliation' (15 February 2005). http://allafrica.com/download/resource/main/main/idatcs/00010394:ad20eceb262e2 b1268108ea5971c2783.pdf accessed 8 January 2018; Nouwen, *Complementarity in the Line of Fire*, 111–243.

[17] See Ibid.; T. Allen, *Trial Justice: The International Criminal Court and the Lord's Resistance Army* (African Arguments, London/New York: Zed Books, 2006).

[18] See, for instance, M. Lacey, 'Atrocity Victims in Uganda Choose to Forgive', *New York Times* (18 April 2005). www.nytimes.com/2005/04/18/world/africa/atrocity-victims-in-uganda-choose-to-forgive.html accessed 8 January 2018; B. Afako, 'Traditional Drink Unites Ugandans', *BBC Focus On Africa Magazine* (29 September 2006). http://news.bbc .co.uk/2/hi/africa/5382816.stm accessed 8 January 2018.

[19] Rome Statute of the International Criminal Court, Rome, 17 July 1998, in force 1 July 2002, 2187 UNTS 90, tenth preambular recital and arts. 1 and 17.

mechanisms did not meet the standards of complementarity. An ICC judge, indeed the Ugandan judge, publicly stated:

> Crimes against humanity, genocide, aggression against other states and war crimes are internationally condemned and cannot be tried by traditional courts but by the ICC ... You cannot expect someone who caused the death of 100 people to be tried in a traditional court if you are looking for justice to be done ... You must convince the international community that justice was done and that the punishment is proportionate with the crime.[20]

Similarly, international human rights NGOs argued that '[w]hile traditional justice processes may provide an important complement to prosecutions, they are not a substitute for them'.[21] They stressed that traditional justice fails to meet 'international benchmarks',[22] comprising:

> consistent with the Rome Statute, other international standards, and international and domestic practice ... impartial and independent investigation capable of leading to the identification of those responsible, and a determination of liability before an independent tribunal, during which an accused benefits from fair trial guarantees ... and, if convicted, [receives] appropriate punishment.[23]

Ugandan justice practices were thus discussed and evaluated in the language of and according to the standards of international criminal law. Most external actors took the invocation of traditional justice as an alternative to the ICC literally, and thus, in the context of the ICC's complementarity, jumped on the research of traditional mechanisms with a view to analysing their legal merits and shortcomings. However, the Acholi community had in the past never used these mechanisms with

---

[20] J. Maseruka, 'Traditional Justice Not Applicable to War Suspects', *New Vision* (30 June 2009). www.newvision.co.ug/new_vision/news/1241289/traditional-justice-applicable-war-suspects accessed 8 January 2018.

[21] Human Rights Watch, 'Thomas Kwoyelo's Trial before Uganda's International Crimes Division, Questions and Answers' (July 2011) 6–7. www.hrw.org/node/100283 accessed 8 January 2018.

[22] See O. L. Ogora, 'Traditional Justice: A Significant Part of the Solution to the Question on Accountability and Reconciliation in Northern Uganda: A Case Study of the Acholi Local Justice Mechanism of *Mato Oput*', *Uganda Living Law Journal*, 5 (2007), 282–96 at 289, observing a 'tendency to downplay the significance of traditional justice, with the main argument that they do not conform to international benchmarks manifested in formal justice processes'.

[23] Human Rights Watch, 'Benchmarks for Assessing Possible National Alternatives to International Criminal Court Cases against LRA Leaders' (May 2007), available at: http://hrw.org/backgrounder/ij/icc0507/icc0507web.pdf accessed 8 January 2018, p. 6.

a legal objective in mind. While the Amnesty Act 2000 did contain references to these mechanisms,[24] in reality, up to then, they had hardly been used for amnesty seekers. But apparently aware of the 'somewhat tragic reality that resistance must work, to some extent, within the parameters established by that which is being resisted',[25] the Acholi had phrased their resistance to the Court in the language of criminal law. The real explanation for the call for *mato oput* was not adoration for a domestic practice, but a call for autonomy and agency. As Barney Afako has observed, for most Acholi praise for *mato oput* was simply shorthand for saying: 'Please leave us alone and let us address these problems ourselves.'[26] This reading of *mato oput*, however, was lost on most international observers involved in the evaluation of Acholi justice practices.

## Marching to The Hague

A visit of Acholi community leaders to the ICC in 2005 is illustrative of the challenges faced by the Acholi in convincing the ICC of the value of its alternative approach. In March 2005, six Acholi community leaders from northern Uganda went to The Hague to try and persuade the ICC prosecutor to discontinue his proceedings in northern Uganda. There was a meeting between the Acholi leaders and the ICC Prosecutor, which ended with both parties issuing separate press statements. The Acholi leaders stated that they had asked the Prosecutor 'that he is mindful of our traditional justice and reconciliation process and that he is also mindful of the peace process and dialogue'.[27] On his part, the Prosecutor echoed that he was 'mindful of traditional justice and reconciliation processes and sensitive to the leaders' efforts to promote dialogue between different actors in order to achieve peace'.[28] But he also reiterated that he had 'a clear policy to focus on those who bear the greatest responsibility for the atrocities committed'.[29]

---

[24] Amnesty Act 2000, s. 8 (c).
[25] B. Rajagopal, *International Law from Below: Development, Social Movements and Third World Resistance* (Cambridge: Cambridge University Press, 2003), 10.
[26] Afako paraphrased in N. Waddell and P. Clark, 'Peace, Justice and the ICC in Africa' (2 March 2007), 10. www.lse.ac.uk/international-development/Assets/Documents/PDFs/csrc-background-papers/Peace-Justice-and-the-ICC-series-report.pdf accessed 8 January 2018. See also Allen, *Trial Justice*, 27.
[27] ICC-OTP, 'Statements by ICC Chief Prosecutor and the Visiting Delegation of Acholi Leaders from Northern Uganda', Press Release, ICC-OTP-20050318–95, 18 March 2005.
[28] Ibid.
[29] Ibid.

The Acholi delegation returned to Uganda to find an upset government. The Government of Uganda argued that it was not the role of community leaders internationally to take political positions that went against that of the government.[30] At the government's insistence, another mission went to The Hague in April 2005. This delegation was four times the size of the first one and included, in addition to Acholi community leaders, many people affiliated with the government. This time the parties could agree on a joint statement. It proclaimed: 'The Lango; Acholi; Iteso and Madi community leaders and the Prosecutor of the ICC have agreed to work together as part of a common effort to achieve justice and reconciliation, the rebuilding of communities and an end to the violence in Northern Uganda.'[31]

Seemingly similar to the first statement, this statement was fundamentally different in that it no longer referred to the one issue on which the ICC and the local leaders disagreed: the importance of a peace process. Three months after the Acholi visit, the ICC issued arrest warrants for the leadership of the LRA.[32]

This 'dialogue' is illustrative of other dialogues between the ICC and its international proponents on the one hand, and local communities on the other hand. Local leaders were invited to confer at meetings, seminars, and workshops all over the world, but only lip service was paid to their advice. Their presence served merely to validate decisions and to satisfy international donors' need to appear to be 'in dialogue with locals'.[33]

## The Juba Process (2006–2008): The Struggle between Local and International Voices

At the instigation of the Acholi civil society leaders, the Government of Southern Sudan invited Uganda in May 2006 to come to Juba, the capital of Southern Sudan, for peace talks with the LRA. To the surprise of many, President Museveni accepted the invitation. The following one and a half years of on-and-off negotiations eventually generated agreements

---

[30] Nouwen's interview with a representative of a donor government, May 2008 (on file with the author).

[31] ICC-OTP, 'Joint Statement by ICC Chief Prosecutor and the Visiting Delegation of Lango, Acholi, Iteso and Madi Community Leaders from Northern Uganda', Press Release, ICC-OTP-20050416-99-En, 16 April 2005.

[32] 'Decision on the Prosecutor's Application for Warrants of Arrest under Article 58', ICC-02/04-01/05-1, Pre-Trial Chamber II, 8 July 2005.

[33] Nouwen's interview with a representative of a donor government, May 2008 (on file with the author).

between the Government of Uganda and the LRA on the five adopted agenda items, as well as on implementation matters. However, eventually LRA leader Joseph Kony refused to sign the Final Peace Agreement, citing fears for his personal security; he did not seem to trust that the Ugandan government would save him from the ICC.

## Internationalisation of the Juba Peace Process as a Result of the Arrest Warrants

The Juba peace process was not an affair of only the Ugandan government, the LRA, and the Government of Southern Sudan; it attracted a large number of international actors who wished to observe the negotiations. This internationalisation was to a large extent due to the involvement of a party that was not even present at the table: the ICC. First, many international ICC-supporting actors wanted to ensure that the outcome of the negotiations would not undermine the ICC. Secondly, international buy-in, in particular support from states members of the UN Security Council, was necessary because part of the strategy was to ask the Security Council to defer ICC proceedings while the Government of Uganda prepared for domestic proceedings[34] (a prerequisite for any successful challenge on grounds of complementarity).[35]

The increase in foreign voices at the negotiation table made the talks in several ways more complicated. First, internationalisation brought formalisation, but for a group such as the LRA, isolated and without any diplomatic experience, it was a huge challenge to participate in such a formal peace process. A simpler and more local process, taking place 'under the mango tree', would perhaps have been more manageable for them. Secondly, some observers in fact tried to participate, inserting their own preferences into the process. For instance, having vehemently opposed the Juba peace process in the first place, the United States sent a representative to the talks and, as a result, the process changed in character: time lines were inserted, competing solutions proposed, and preparations for military action initiated.[36] Finally, the mantra 'that the

---

[34] See Agreement on Implementation and Monitoring Mechanisms, Juba, 29 February 2008, clause 37.
[35] See Rome Statute, arts. 17 and 19.
[36] S. Browning, 'Uganda: A/S Frazer discusses LRA, Congo and Somalia with President Museveni', Ref: 07KAMPALA1449 (14 September 2007). www.scoop.co.nz/stories/ WL0709/S00012.htm accessed 8 January 2018; S. Rice, 'A/S Frazer's June 13 meeting with Ugandan President Museveni', Ref: 08STATE65820 (18 June 2008). www.scoop.co

peace agreement had to be in line with international law' was repeated time and again to the mediators and the parties.[37] This limited the room for manoeuvre by the mediation team.

One international voice in particular threatened the peace process. When discussions about the make-or-break agenda item 'Accountability and Reconciliation' were about to begin, the United Nations Office of the High Commissioner for Human Rights sent out the following statement: 'Discussions concerning those persons [the LRA leadership sought by the ICC] should be focusing on the terms and circumstances of their surrender so they can go and address the charges against them before the ICC.'[38]

While the negotiations in Juba were working towards domestic proceedings as an alternative to the ICC, this statement suggested that the discussions had to focus on handing over the LRA leadership to the ICC. There is no such requirement in international law, but the statement did cause considerable confusion and apprehension on the side of the LRA. The statement undermined the lawyers at the peace process who had been trying to explain the principle of complementarity to the LRA delegation. Hearing the contradictory voices of lawyers in Juba and of international actors, the LRA's trust in the process decreased.[39]

### Consultations with the Ugandan Population

Initiating the peace process at the explicit request of Acholi leaders, the chief mediator was well aware of the crucial role that the Acholi community had played in promoting peace and would have to play in any reintegration process in the future. Accordingly, the mediation involved representatives of affected local communities in the talks. Between 2006 and 2008, several northern Ugandan community leaders participated in the talks, ensuring that the concerns, interests, and views of northern Ugandans were taken into account in the negotiations. Moreover, both the LRA and the Ugandan government, for the first time in its long

.nz/stories/WL0806/S00081/cablegate-as-frazers-june-13-meeting-with-ugandan.htm accessed 8 January 2018.

[37] Nouwen's interview with a person involved in the negotiations, May 2008 (on file with the author).

[38] UN News Centre, 'UN Official Urges Ugandan Parties to Put Human Rights at Centre of Talks' (11 May 2007). http://www.un.org/apps/news/story.asp?NewsID=22524&Cr=uganda&Cr1=#.UdlDK_lll0Q accessed 8 January 2018.

[39] Nouwen's interview with a person involved in the negotiations, May 2008 (on file with the author).

history of negotiating with rebel movements, went on extensive consultation missions throughout Uganda.

However, the imposition of international criminal law severely limited
the scope of the consultations. While local communities could give their
views on all kinds of issues, ranging from disarmament to development
and from reparations to reintegration,[40] one very contentious issue,
critical to the entire peace agreement, was not subject to consultations:
the need for domestic criminal investigations and prosecutions. That
such proceedings were imperative had been decided by the ICC's involvement: the prevailing, and probably correct, legal view was that the use
of traditional justice and reconciliation mechanisms would not render
the ICC case inadmissible on grounds of complementarity. Noticing that
they were not allowed to give their views on one of the most contentious
elements of the entire peace process, some participants in the consultations questioned the genuineness of the consultation exercise.

## Post Juba (2008–2014): a Legalistic Approach towards a Peace Agreement

In the context of the Juba peace process, the Accountability and
Reconciliation Agreement and the Annexure reflected the classical bal-
ancing of transitional justice aims: peace, justice, and reconciliation.
However, Joseph Kony never signed the Final Peace Agreement and, in
practice, there never was a transition. Nonetheless, the Government of
Uganda stated that, to the extent possible, it would implement the
agreements.[41] Accordingly, the Ugandan Justice Law and Order Sector
(JLOS)[42] began implementing the transitional justice elements of
the Accountability and Reconciliation Agreement and its Annexure.
The idea was that even without Kony's signature, implementation of

---

[40] Akijul, National Consultation Process on the Implementation of Agenda Item Number
Three, *Accountability and Reconciliation*, Juba Peace Talks, 29 October 2007 (on file with
authors).

[41] J. Gatdet Dak, 'Uganda's Peace Deal Implementation Begins without Signature', *Sudan
Tribune* (25 September 2008). www.sudantribune.com/spip.php?article28747 accessed 8
January 2018.

[42] JLOS is a coordinating forum bringing together senior officials in government agencies
working in the areas of justice, law, and order, including the Ministry of Justice and
Constitutional Affairs, the Ministry of Internal Affairs, the Judiciary, the Uganda Police
Force, the Uganda Prison Service, the Directorate of Public Prosecution, the Judicial
Service Commission, the Uganda Law Reform Commission, the Uganda Human Rights
Commission, and the Uganda Law Society.

the Final Peace Agreement could be beneficial to justice for northern Uganda.

The Agreement and Annexure had left important issues for resolution to the executive, legislative, and, where necessary, judiciary. For instance, it remained to be decided under which laws the persons before the Special Division of the High Court would be tried, how possible issues of retro-activity would be addressed, which alternative sanctions would apply, how the Amnesty Act 2000 would be dealt with, how formal and tradi-tional justice would relate to each other, and how cooperation of indivi-duals with transitional justice mechanisms would be rewarded.[43] But in the absence of Kony's signature, politicians were uninterested in taking these decisions. Instead, they allowed JLOS to go ahead with partial implementation, encouraged by the interest – and funding – of interna-tional donors and advocacy groups.

A range of transitional justice activists, supported by donor money, went to Uganda to advise on implementation of the transitional justice components of the Agreement. The heavy involvement of transitional justice advisors and limited interest of politicians led to a shift in focus from transitional justice as a political compromise, as reflected in the Juba agreement, to transitional justice as a practice of technical instru-ments (truth commissions, trials, reparations), with particular attention for the instrument of trials for special international crimes in special courts. Approached in this way, transitional justice was not an alternative to ordinary criminal justice (recognising the need to balance peace, justice, and reconciliation), but a toolbox of instruments in which the criminal justice tool lies on top. This approach ignored the political character of the Juba Agreement and thus undermined its relevance for any possible future transition.

Illustrative of this approach to transitional justice was the creation of a Ugandan War Crimes Court, modelled on the ICC, to investigate and prosecute serious international crimes. The Accountability and Reconciliation Agreement and the Annexure had envisaged this special

---

[43] See Agreement on Accountability and Reconciliation between the Government of the Republic of Uganda and the Lord's Resistance Army/Movement, clauses 3.6, 5.6, 6.3, 14.3, and 14.4; and Annexure to the Agreement on Accountability and Reconciliation, Juba, 19 February 2008, clauses 2 and especially 9: 'For the proper functioning of the special division of the court in accordance with the agreed principles of accountability and reconciliation, legislation may provide for: (a) The constitution of the court; (b) The substantive law to be applied; (c) Appeals against the decisions of the court; (d) Rules of procedure; (e) The recognition of traditional and community justice processes in proceedings.'

60     THE GLOBALISATION OF JUSTICE

division of the High Court in order to make it possible to successfully challenge the admissibility of the case before the ICC on grounds of complementarity. The War Crimes Court, however, was established in the absence of an agreement and thus of LRA suspects. Moreover, if any LRA suspect was to abandon the struggle, he or she would still be able to qualify for amnesty, as the Amnesty Act continued to apply.

Proponents of the War Crimes Court (mostly international transitional justice actors, donors, and donor-funded transitional justice advisors 'embedded' in the Ugandan Ministry of Justice) therefore increased the lobby to have the Amnesty Act abolished. They argued that there could not be amnesty for international crimes, thereby radically departing from donors' own pro-amnesty lobbying in the past. This lobby became particularly strong when there suddenly was a defendant who could be tried before the War Crimes Court: Thomas Kwoyelo. When the LRA commander, who had been arrested by the UPDF in the Democratic Republic of the Congo in March 2009,[44] applied for amnesty, the Director of Public Prosecutions refused to grant the required go-ahead for the Amnesty Commission to issue an amnesty certificate. The legal reasons for this refusal changed over time, but the most radical argument came when the Attorney General's representative, reading a script based on advice of the donor-sponsored transitional justice advisors, argued that the entire Amnesty Act was, and had always been, unconstitutional. The Constitutional Court found that there was no general prohibition on amnesties in international law and rejected the Attorney General's argument.[45] Kwoyelo, however, remained in prison, court orders notwithstanding.[46]

Meanwhile, international pressure increased to abolish the Amnesty Act in another way. The Minister of Internal Affairs succumbed and unilaterally amended the Amnesty Act, so that after twelve years of operation, there was no more amnesty in May 2012.[47] Ultimately, after parliamentary action, the Amnesty Act was reinstated.[48] In 2015, the

[44] R. Baguma, 'LRA's Kwoyelo Flown to Entebbe on Drip', *New Vision* (4 March 2009).
[45] *Thomas Kwoyelo Alias Latoni (Applicant) and Uganda (Respondent)*, Constitutional Court, Constitutional Petition No.036/11, 22 September 2011.
[46] See also *Thomas Kwoyelo Alias Latoni (Applicant) v. The Attorney General (Respondent)*, High Court (Civil Division), HCT-00-CV-MC-0162–2011, Order by Judge Vincent T. Zehurikize, 25 January 2012.
[47] Amnesty Act (Declaration of Lapse of the Operation of Part II) Instrument, 2012, Statutory Instruments 2012 No. 34, Statutory Instruments Supplement No. 15, 23 May 2012.
[48] Amnesty Act (Revocation of Statutory Instrument No. 34 of 2012) Instrument 2013, Statutory Instruments Supplement No. 11, *Uganda Gazette* (24 May 2013); and Amnesty

Supreme Court, feeling the pressure from donors who wanted to see the War Crimes Court work, reinterpreted the Amnesty Act so that Kwoyelo could not benefit from it: it argued that his types of crimes were never covered by the Amnesty Act.[49]

The story of attempts to end the applicability of the Ugandan Amnesty Act thus reveals how after the ICC's intervention and the adoption of a peace agreement with transitional justice components inspired by the need to find an alternative to the ICC, the voice of transitional justice activists and JLOS was amplified, to the detriment of parliament, the judiciary, and the Acholi. The international lobby against the Ugandan amnesty was costly to the rule of law. Those who favoured the argument that the entire Amnesty Act was unconstitutional were willing to put at risk the legal certainty of the over 26,000 people who had benefited from the amnesty with a view to making it possible to prosecute one man before the War Crimes Court. The Parliamentary Committee that had recommended the revocation of the instrument by which the Minister had ended the amnesty's applicability explicitly reflected upon the influence of international actors on Ugandan legislation when it stated:

> The Committee must report that in the course of its work, it became concerned by a failure of due diligence on the part of the Executive in appraising claims about [the] status of international law. In particular there was a notable failure on the part of officials to distinguish between generally recognised international law obligations and aspirational positions promoted by norm entrepreneurs ... The Committee notes that the situation in Uganda is complicated by the fact that external actors, including some development partners funding the JLOS, appeared to have exerted a disproportionate influence on the executive's approach to the amnesty issue, by promoting their own policy preferences.[50]

## Conclusion

The above examples show how, following the ICC's intervention in northern Uganda, international criminal law became one of the dominant languages in which the conflict was analysed, discussed, and addressed. This led to the amplification of the voices of those who

---

Act (Extension of Expiry Period) Instrument, 2013, Statutory Instruments Supplement No. 11, *Uganda Gazette* (24 May 2013).

[49] *Uganda v.Thomas Kwoyelo*, Supreme Court of Uganda, Constitutional Appeal No 01/2012, 8 April 2015.

[50] Report of the Parliamentary Committee on Defence and Internal Affairs on the Lapsing of Part II of the Amnesty Act, 2000, May 2013, paras. 9.37 and 9.38.

favoured that language, while silencing those who adopted different, non-legal languages that did not fit the paradigm of international criminal justice and the fight against impunity.

The above examples have also illustrated that it is not just the ICC that, intentionally or not, silences some voices and amplifies others. This process of silencing and amplification has been intensified by a large group of international actors (international organisations, NGOs, and donor states) that promote the ICC agenda.

The amplification of some voices and the silencing of others is a result that almost any intervention has, whether judicial, economic, or military. However, the process of amplifying some voices and silencing others is different in the event of an ICC intervention, for two reasons. First, particularly in the early years of the Court's existence, the agenda underlying the Rome Statute – the global fight against impunity using international criminal justice as the mechanism – became an ideology, i.e. an agenda that is presented as so self-evidently necessary that it cannot be contested. The popularity and strength of this ideology decreased the space for local dissenting voices.

Secondly, in addition to the political character that a judicial intervention shares with an economic or military intervention, an intervention by the ICC also has a normative character. It is often argued that the Court's actions, even when they do not serve certain policy objectives, for instance promoting peace or the experience of justice, are nonetheless justified because they are required by international law. Rebutting that argument requires mastering the language of international law. In the early years of the ICC's intervention, only very few Ugandans mastered the language of international law. Most Ugandans were thus either easily persuaded or overpowered by it. Against this background, it is promising that the Ugandan Parliamentary Committee, reviewing the abolishment of the Amnesty Act, as referred to above, called for a more critical approach of Ugandan state actors towards what international law actually says. As if endorsing Koskenniemi, the Committee wrote: 'Unlike national legislation, the development of international law is a contested field of claim and counter claim, where assertions do not always reflect reality, and in which it behoves state actors to have a clear grasp of the politics of international law.'[51]

---

[51] Ibid. para. 9.38.

# 4

# Justice through Direct Action: The Case of the Gaza 'Freedom Flotilla'

CLAUDIA SABA

## Introduction

This chapter explains how social movement actors, in the pursuit of justice, can work together, mobilising international law in a way that has a direct relationship with politics. This is illustrated through an examination of what became known as the Freedom Flotilla (FF), a campaign that has repeatedly attempted, by sea, to breach an Israeli-imposed blockade on the occupied Palestinian territory of Gaza.

The campaign's most high profile mission took place in May 2010, when six boats carrying 700 activists sailed in tandem towards Gaza, only to be attacked by Israeli commandos in international waters.[1] At approximately 4 a.m. on 1 June 2010, Israeli helicopters and military boats, including zodiacs and frigates, attacked the FF boats, firing plastic and live ammunition from the air.[2] At the end of the attack, nine activists had been killed and fifty others had been injured.[3] The attack garnered extensive international media attention and helped highlight the situation in Gaza to global audiences and expose Israel's intransigence to international law.

Following this particular violent incident, activists continued their campaign and organised further missions to Gaza, most notably in

---

[1] Initially the May 2010 FF comprised eight vessels. However, the Irish vessel, the *Rachel Corrie*, was delayed and the *Challenger II* suffered engine trouble, so the FF comprised only six boats at the time of the Israeli attack.

[2] Interviews were conducted with: Ehab Lotayef, national coordinator of Canada Boat to Gaza, by Skype call on 21 August 2012; Fintan Lane, national coordinator of Irish Ship to Gaza, in Dublin, Ireland, on 23 August 2012.

[3] United Nations Human Rights Council, 'Report of the International Fact-Finding Mission to Investigate Violations of International Law, Including International Humanitarian and Human Rights Law, Resulting from the Israeli Attacks on the Flotilla of Ships Carrying Humanitarian Assistance', *UN Doc.* A/HRC/15/21, 27 September 2010.

2011, which became known as Freedom Flotilla II.[4] This chapter explains why the FF campaign emerged and how it was executed, with special attention to the way in which activists utilised legal discourse combined with direct, political action to advance their aims. The aims of the FF activists were grounded in a belief that what the people of Gaza were enduring was a gross injustice that the extant political regime had been unable or unwilling to address. The terrible predicament of Gaza, a territory stricken by poverty and de-development due to the effects of a military occupation in place since 1967, demonstrates the impotency of international law alone to liberate an occupied population, or even to deter occupying forces from committing crimes in the occupied territory.[5] As will be discussed in this chapter, this impotency stems from the toothlessness of international law vis-à-vis the existing political order, as well as its susceptibility to misuse by the occupier.

Nonetheless, international law has formed the backbone of arguments used to defend the Palestinians and continues to be employed in their defence. This was reiterated by the then UN Special Rapporteur for Occupied Palestine, Richard Falk, who argued that international law supports Palestinian claims on all the major issues of contention between them and Israel, even if this had not been put to optimum use by the Palestinian leadership.[6] The implication of these arguments was that international law, as a tool for political action, could be put to better use. As will be discussed throughout this chapter, that was precisely what the FF attempted to do. It

---

[4] According to observations by the author, who was involved in this campaign, boats attempted sailing to Gaza again in June 2011 but were prevented from leaving Greek ports. In November 2011, two boats, Irish and Canadian, managed to reach fifty kilometres from Gaza's shores before they were attacked by Israeli forces. The boats were seized and the activists imprisoned for six days before being deported back to their countries. The author was a member of the coordinating committee of Irish Ship to Gaza, some of whose members had been aboard the 2010 FF and regrouped to sail to Gaza again on two occasions (in June 2011 and November 2011). She attended dozens of coordination meetings as a representative of the Irish contingent to the international coalition of the FF.

[5] For a discussion of the 'de-development' of Gaza see: S. Roy, *Failing Peace: Gaza and the Palestinian-Israeli Conflict* (London: Pluto Press, 2007).

[6] Richard Falk, 'Israel's Politics of Deflection: Theory and Practice' (30 September 2013). http://richardfalk.wordpress.com/2013/09 accessed 28 February 2018. See also Richard Falk, 'No Peace without Rights: Why International Law Matters' *Transnational Law & Contemporary Problems*, 21 (2012), 31–48; Richard Falk, 'Why Have Palestinians Neglected International Law?', SOAS Palestinian Society Annual Conference (5 October 2013), transcript emailed to the author by Richard Falk. For a wider discussion of how international law supports Palestinian claims see Susan A. Akram et al., eds, *International Law and the Israeli–Palestinian Conflict: A Rights-Based Approach to Middle East Peace* (New York: Routledge, 2011).

did so by framing a political-cum-humanitarian crisis in legal and ethical terms, while simultaneously employing direct action to give real life relevance to those claims. In this way, the FF activists to some extent emulated notable social justice campaigners such as Martin Luther King, who observed that: 'Nonviolent direct action seeks to create such a crisis and foster such a tension that a community which has constantly refused to negotiate is forced to confront the issue. It seeks so to dramatise the issue that it can no longer be ignored.'[7] Moreover, as will be discussed in this chapter, the dissonance between legal talk and political talk intensified following the start of a blockade on Gaza in 2007. Israel looked at Gaza and saw a security threat, while the UN looked at Gaza and saw a humanitarian crisis. Israel advanced a rationale for its closure of Gaza that was shrouded in threats to its security, whereas pleas by the Palestinian Centre for Human Rights that the blockade be lifted were grounded in principles of international humanitarian law (IHL).[8] Western media reporting on Gaza largely reflected Israel's security discourse by prioritising the dangers of Hamas and Palestinian internal struggles. These themes dominated, whereas the suffering resulting from Israel's blockade of Gaza was largely ignored. Where hardships were acknowledged, they were explained as a consequence of the so-called takeover of Gaza by Hamas, with minimal attention to Israel's role in the hostilities.[9] The gap between the reality about the suffering on the ground and what had been deemed politically expedient by Israel grew larger. In this chapter, it will be demonstrated how activists aimed to bridge that gap by combining legal and political discourse in their public framing of the FF campaign, thereby compelling the two discourses to 'talk' to each other. This analysis will culminate in the conclusion that the way in which law is instrumentalised in the context of Israel's occupation of Gaza reveals what Koskenniemi has referred to as 'the indeterminacy of international law'.[10]

---

[7] Martin Luther King, 'Letter from a Birmingham Jail' (16 April 1963). www.africa.upenn .edu/Articles_Gen/Letter_Birmingham.html accessed 28 February 2018.

[8] Palestinian Centre for Human Rights, 'Gaza Strip Is Threatened by Unprecedented Humanitarian Crisis: Economic Siege and Closure of Border Crossings Is Leading to an Imminent Humanitarian Crisis' (27 June 2007). www.pchrgaza.org accessed 28 February 2018.

[9] See for example Isabel Kershner, 'Israel Lets Food and Medicine Enter Gaza to Avert Crisis', *New York Times* (20 June 2007); Mark MacKinnon, 'A Tense and Desperate Sense of Order Settles In: There's No Doubt Hamas's Brigades Have a Firm Hold on Tiny Gaza: But a Humanitarian Crisis Looms', *The Globe and Mail* (20 June 2007).

[10] Martti Koskenniemi, *From Apology to Utopia: The Structure of International Legal Argument* (New York: Cambridge University Press, 2005), 590.

## Methodology

To probe the aims of the FF and how activists prioritised their campaign, interviews were conducted with the national coordinators of the Canadian and Irish campaigns of the FF mission.[11] Primary research also drew on participant observation by the author who at the time was an organiser and media spokesperson for the Irish contingent of the FF.[12] The websites and press releases of four participating FF organisations were used for documentary analysis as an illustrative sample of the various campaigns that constituted the FF coalition.[13]

To observe the effect of the 2010 FF on the media, a content analysis of news articles was conducted for four periods in which Gaza could be expected to have received media coverage.[14] The first period studied was the week following Israel's closure of the Gaza Strip in June 2007, which coincided with the peak of the crisis between the Palestinian factions of Fatah and Hamas. The second period covered the week immediately following Israel's Cast Lead assault on Gaza in 2008–2009 which killed over 1400 Palestinians and devastated much of Gaza's infrastructure.[15] The third period was the week immediately following the fatal attack on the FF boats in the early hours of 1 June 2010. The fourth period covered the week following the Palestinian Authority's successful UN bid for statehood through its designation as a non-member observer state at the United Nations on 29 November 2012. Each of those periods contained some reference to Gaza. The purpose of studying the news from those periods was to understand how Gaza was reported on and whose voices were being represented during each period. Accordingly, the density of news coverage about the blockade was identified, with attention to the language used to describe it. The publications looked at were: the *New York Times, USA Today*, the *Daily Telegraph*, the *Times*, the *Globe and Mail*, and the *Irish Times*. These mainstream publications were

---

[11] Ehab Lotayef, national coordinator of *Canada Boat to Gaza*, by Skype call, 21 August 2012; Fintan Lane, national coordinator of *Irish Ship to Gaza*, in Dublin, Ireland, 23 August 2012.

[12] See n. 4.

[13] Free Gaza Movement: www.freegaza.org accessed 28 February 2018; Canada Boat to Gaza: www.tahrir.ca accessed 28 February 2018; Irish Ship to Gaza: www.irishshiptogaza.org (website decommissioned); US Boat to Gaza: www.ustogaza.org (website decommissioned).

[14] Only news articles and editorials were studied; op-eds were excluded.

[15] United Nations Human Rights Council, 'Human Rights in Palestine and Other Occupied Arab Territories: Report of the United Nations Fact-Finding Mission on the Gaza Conflict', 'Goldstone Report', UN Doc. A/HRC/12/48, 25 September 2009.

chosen since the mainstream press is the primary forum used by political elites for self-representation, and the main media platform for state policy debates.[16]

Finally, in order to examine the effect of the FF on the blockade itself, data from the UN Office for the Coordination of Humanitarian Affairs (OCHA) was studied for variations in the volume of goods allowed into Gaza before and after the 2010 FF.[17]

### The Context of the Freedom Flotilla and Gaza's Legal Status

The Gaza Strip, like the West Bank, came under Israeli occupation in 1967. Under international law, both Gaza and the West Bank are regarded as occupied territory despite subsequent agreements between Israel and the Palestinians (including the Oslo Accords). This still applies since 'the Palestinian self-governing entity in the West Bank and the Gaza Strip does not constitute a state'.[18] Moreover, the occupation remains intact in Gaza despite the fact that Israel unilaterally withdrew its settlers and soldiers from Gaza in 2005. The effective control of Gaza has continued from afar through the control of fuel provision, telecommunications networks, the population registry, and the movement of people, and through Israel's recurrent incursions into the territory by land, sea, and air. Such a situation fulfils numerous aspects of effective control over civilian life, which are characteristic of occupation, and any claims to the contrary are 'legally incongruous'.[19]

The occupation of Gaza increased in severity when Israel imposed an effective blockade on the territory in 2007. From that point on, Israel banned a host of goods which had previously passed into Gaza. Although the list of banned goods was never made public, it was known to the United Nations to have been extensive and to have included items ranging from lentils to pasta and tomato juice, and even batteries for

---

[16] Ronald N. Jacobs and Eleanor Townsley, *The Space of Opinion: Media Intellectuals and the Public Sphere* (USA: Oxford University Press, 2011).

[17] The findings from OCHA were echoed by Shane Middleton, a project director of CHF International, a charity working in Gaza, whom the author interviewed in Gaza on 16 January 2013.

[18] Feras Milhem and Jamil Salem, 'Building the Rule of Law in Palestine: Rule of Law Without Freedom', in Akram et al., *International Law and the Israeli–Palestinian Conflict*, 253.

[19] Ibid. 254. See also John Dugard, 'Report of the Special Rapporteur on the Situation of Human Rights in the Palestinian Territories Occupied since 1967', 29 January 2007, UN Doc. A/HRC/4/17.

hearing aids used by deaf children.[20] Medical supplies were generally limited, a development which became all the more acute following a twenty-three day Israeli assault on the territory in 2008–2009. The assault left thousands injured and in need of physical and psychological treatment.[21] Restrictions imposed by the blockade were particularly concerning since 43 per cent of Gaza's population was at that time under the age of fifteen.[22]

It should be noted that the blockade was not announced openly by Israel at the time it was imposed.[23] Instead, in September 2007, Israel declared Gaza to be 'hostile territory' and announced that restrictions on the movement of goods would apply for security purposes and in order to pressure Hamas 'as part of the State of Israel's operations against continuous terrorism'.[24] A study by the Israeli human rights organisation 'Gisha' into the timing of border openings and closings and into the items banned from Gaza suggested that this policy amounted to 'economic warfare' which prevented economic development and was designed to pull political strings.[25] The Israeli government's argument for its closure of Gaza, as articulated in 2010 by the Israeli Defense Minister, Ehud Barak, was that it was necessary 'to prevent the strengthening of Hamas in Gaza [in order to] create the conditions for negotiating [Israeli tank gunner] Schalit's release, and [more broadly, to] frustrate terrorist attacks from Gaza'.[26] In other words, the Israeli state's primary rationale for maintaining a blockade affecting an entire population was that it was a measure necessary to secure Israel from terrorist attacks.

---

[20] Kevin M. Cahill, 'Gaza – Destruction and Hope: Letter of Chief Advisor on Humanitarian Affairs to the President of the United Nations General Assembly, H.E. Miguel D'Escoto Brockmann' (22 February 2009), www.un.org/ga/president/63/news/GazaReport.pdf, p. 5., accessed 28 February 2018.

[21] United Nations Human Rights Council, 'Human Rights in Palestine', paras. 1254, 1259.

[22] *The World Factbook*, 'Gaza Strip'. https://www.cia.gov/library/publications/the-world-factbook/geos/gz.html accessed 28 February 2018.

[23] Knowledge about the blockade was first highlighted by Palestinian sources in Gaza. See: Palestinian Centre for Human Rights, 'Gaza Strip'.

[24] UNHRC, 'Report of International Fact-Finding', para 30.

[25] Sari Bashi, 'Remarks by Sari Bashi' in 'Proceedings of the 105th Annual Meeting', *American Society of International Law*, 105 (2011), 463–6 at 463.

[26] Rebecca Anna Stoil, 'Government Easily Survives No-Confidence Vote over Flotilla', *The Jerusalem Post* (8 June 2010). Jilad Schalit was a captive IDF soldier held by Hamas at the time and often used as an anti-Gaza totem by the government of Israel. He was released in October 2011 in exchange for over 1000 Palestinian prisoners held by Israel.

This argument rests on the idea that a sovereign country may seal its borders to defend itself from external threats. Israel, however, does not simply control its own land border with Gaza, but also prevents Palestinians from traveling or trading by land, air, or sea in all directions. Israel has exercised control over Gaza's border with Egypt through agreements with that country, thereby placing its own security above Palestinian rights to freedom of movement and trade.[27] As the occupying power, Israel has a legal responsibility to provide for the occupied population, and by imposing the blockade, with all its restrictions on items necessary to sustain life and development, it has instead 'violated the prohibition on collective punishment of an occupied people contained in article 33 of the Fourth Geneva Convention'.[28]

In the midst of Israel's 2008–2009 assault on Gaza, on 3 January 2009, Israel abruptly declared that a naval blockade applied to the area, meaning that no vessels would be allowed to leave or enter Gaza. This declaration made public an existing, forty-two year policy of preventing Palestinians from freely using their sea port for travel or trade.[29] Activists engaged in the campaign to sail to Gaza believed this particular announcement was a response to direct actions that had succeeded in landing six small boats in Gaza in the six months prior to the declaration, and to the continued efforts by activists to sail other boats to Gaza in early January 2009.[30] A further study of the timing of the naval blockade announcement revealed that it was advocated by the Israeli Military Advocate General Mandelblit, who understood that an official naval blockade would help legitimate the use of force against boats attempting entry into Gaza.[31]

Meanwhile, the international community's response to Israel's escalating blockade on Gaza included voices of condemnation, but fell short of concrete action to lift the blockade or to ease it. For example, the United Nations Human Rights Council (UNHRC), which led an inquiry into the 2008–2009 military assault on Gaza, concluded that the blockade had severely affected the economy and

---

[27] Amnesty International, 'Israel/Occupied Palestinian Territories: Suffocating, the Gaza Strip under Israeli Blockade', *Amnesty International* (18 January 2010), 3. https://ilgraf fionews.files.wordpress.com/2010/02/rapporto-amnesty.pdf accessed 28 February 2018.

[28] Dugard, 'Report of the Special Rapporteur', para 22.

[29] Bashi, 'Remarks', 464.

[30] Bill Dienst and Greta Berlin, *Freedom Sailors: The Maiden Voyage of the Free Gaza Movement and How We Succeeded in Spite of Ourselves* (USA: Free Gaza Press, 2012), 15.

[31] Alan Craig, *International Legitimacy and the Politics of Security: The Strategic Deployment of Lawyers in the Israeli Military* (United Kingdom: Lexington Books, 2013), 225–6.

well-being of its inhabitants, and had 'amounted to a violation of Israel's obligations as an occupying power under the Fourth Geneva Convention'.[32] In June 2009, a group of forty United Nations agencies and non-governmental organisations called for Israel to lift the blockade.[33] Neither of these condemnations translated into action on the ground. Even the Palestinian Authority, tied up as it was with US-brokered negotiations with Israel, obstructed the implementation of the UNHRC's report at the UN after its issuance in September 2009.[34] To date, the findings of the 2009 UNHRC report have not been acted upon in any meaningful way, despite the General Assembly's vote to endorse the findings of the report. Instead it was left to Israel and the Palestinian Authority to address its recommendations, a move that perpetuated the imbalance of power between the two sides.[35] Ultimately, while the report had concluded that the blockade was illegal, it was rendered a dead letter when, in February 2010, the Secretary-General of the United Nations concluded that 'no determination can be made on the implementation of the resolution by the parties concerned'.[36] The UN, in effect, failed to endorse the conclusions of its own fact-finding mission on the situation in Gaza.

In this context of condemnation without enforcement, the FF emerged. Activists were of the view that the international legal regime had long failed to address the continuing suffering of those in Gaza due to a lack of political will, and that there was a need to shake up the status quo by way of direct political action.[37] Specifically, they felt that, by sailing to Gaza in defiance of Israel's blockade on the area, the media's attention would be drawn to the issue and political actors would be pressured to respond.

[32] UNHRC, 'Human Rights in Palestine', para. 1931.
[33] UN News Centre, 'UN, Aid Agencies Call for End to Israel's Two-Year Blockade of Gaza' (17 June 2009). www.un.org/apps/news/story.asp?NewsID=31174&Cr=gaza&Cr1#.Un0DXShEP8w accessed 28 February 2018.
[34] S. Farhan Mustafa, 'PA Stonewalled the Goldstone Vote', *Al Jazeera* (26 January 2011). www.english.aljazeera.net/palestinepapers/2011/01/2011126123125167974.html accessed 28 February 2018.
[35] United Nations General Assembly, 'Follow-Up to the Report of the United Nations Fact-Finding Mission on the Gaza Conflict: Report of the Secretary-General', 4 February 2010, UN Doc. A/64/651.
[36] Ibid. para. 11, p. 3.
[37] Based on interviews and participant observation.

## Direct Action

The FF's antecedent campaign was an organisation of human rights activists called the Free Gaza Movement, which began sailing small boats to Gaza at the beginning of 2008.[38] Activists managed to reach Gaza on four missions between August and December 2008 before Israel began interfering with their boats, a development that mobilised an even greater number of activists to try and 'break the blockade'.[39] By 2010, several organisations had come together to synchronise sailing missions to the Palestinian coastal territory. The first such international collaboration came in the form of what was called Freedom Flotilla I, which saw six vessels sail together in May 2010.[40]

The six campaigns involved were the Free Gaza Movement, the European Campaign to End the Siege in Gaza, the International Committee to End the Siege in Gaza, Ship to Gaza Greece, Ship to Gaza Sweden, and IHH of Turkey.[41] The member organisations in these campaigns were coalitions, consisting of Palestine solidarity groups and human rights organisations, which in some cases also had the support of leftist parliamentary parties.[42] Although many of the activists and component organisations within the FF coalition were veteran Palestine solidarity activists and thereby knowledgeable about the larger military occupation by Israel of Palestinian territories, the FF campaign was to be Gaza-specific and specifically highlight the injustice of the blockade and its illegality under international humanitarian law.

Many of the boats carried prominent individuals with a public profile in their respective countries to act as international witnesses to the effects of the blockade. This strategy was designed to circumvent a potential media blackout on the campaign, since Israel had a history of barring international journalists from Gaza.[43] For this reason, the boats also carried sixty accredited journalists, including journalists from the Al Jazeera satellite television network, who broadcasted footage from one

---

[38] Dienst and Berlin, *Freedom Sailors*.

[39] Interview with Fintan Lane.

[40] Originally these had been eight vessels, but only six were sailing together when intercepted by the Israeli forces at dawn on 1 June 2010.

[41] Interview with Fintan Lane.

[42] Participant observation. For example, Irish Ship to Gaza was openly supported by Sinn Fein and the United Left Alliance and carried party members aboard its boat.

[43] For example, Israel barred journalists from Gaza beginning six weeks before its 2008–2009 assault on the territory, giving it monopoly over the narration of developments. See UNHRC, 'Human Rights in Palestine', para. 116.

of the boats.[44] Flotilla organisers emphasised the presence of journalists together with the cross-national character of mission participants in order to demonstrate that the campaign enjoyed widespread support.

From the perspective of the FF organisers, the blockade on Gaza was both illegal and morally wrong. When interviewed, Ehab Lotayef, a participant of the 2010 FF and national coordinator of the Canadian arm of the 2011 FF mission Freedom Flotilla II, explained that his group had been formed on the conviction that the situation imposed on Gaza was 'inhumane and unjust' and that 'the international community's lack of action was immoral and had to be challenged'.[45] Specifically, the Canadian arm of the campaign sought 'to challenge the Canadian government's position' on the issue.[46] Lotayef explained that the group 'did not expect the Canadian government to take a strong stand with Gaza as a result of this direct action', but 'expected to make the government feel challenged, uncomfortable and exposed'.[47] The way to do this was to raise public awareness about the effects of the blockade. Lotayef further explained:

> We were running a political campaign with humanitarian goals, but the campaign was political. Our physical action may have been on the waters of the Mediterranean, but we were challenging our own government and spreading information to build a base of support [for the Palestinians]. We were not fixated on reaching Gaza, raising public awareness was the major priority.[48]

On how the message was propagated Lotayef stated: 'We used both alternative and mainstream media, we used everything at our disposal, including some progressive print media.'[49] When interviewed, the national coordinator of the Irish arm of the 2011 FF campaign, Fintan Lane, who had been aboard one of the boats attacked on 1 June 2010, echoed Lotayef's reasoning:

> The situation [in Gaza] became normative as far as most of the international community was concerned. Yes, Israel's behavior continued to attract condemnation, but nothing tangible was done. It was this failure by international bodies such as the UN and governments that forced

[44] Anne de Jong, 'The Gaza Freedom Flotilla: Human Rights, Activism and Academic Neutrality', *Social Movement Studies: Journal of Social, Cultural and Political Protest*, 11 (2012), 193–209 at 203.
[45] Interview with Ehab Lotayef.
[46] Ibid.
[47] Ibid.
[48] Ibid.
[49] Ibid.

concerned individuals to take direct action to challenge the siege. Our view was that if governments won't act in defense of the lives and human rights of Palestinians in Gaza, then civil society would.[50]

Although aid cargo was carried on FF boats, both the FF interviewees emphasised that ultimately what Gaza needed was not aid, but the freedom to connect with the outside world through trade and travel. They understood that sailing to Gaza would attract media attention and that this would provide an opportunity to publicise conditions in Gaza. It was also understood that politicians studied news content as a proxy for public opinion.[51] Therefore, the campaign's interaction with the media was of central importance. Essentially, campaigners sought to reframe understandings of the Israel–Gaza impasse in the public arena.

The framing of an issue by social movement actors is a strategic effort to shape understandings of a problem in a way that legitimises collective action. Human rights activists engage in the reframing of issues in order to advance an alternative understanding of a particular problem.[52] Reframing works by engaging citizens in a rational debate, and some-times includes an attempt to change the topic of conversation or the way a conversation is approached to reset the terms of debate around a given issue.[53] A central aim of the FF campaign was that of challenging the security narrative proposed by Israel, and in turn changing the way the blockade was understood and spoken about in the media.

Activists wanted to highlight the dysfunctional international political regime, which maintained the status quo and Israel's intransigence to the will of the international community. FF organisers emphasised that, since Israel controlled the population registry, natural resources, and entry and exit points of Gaza, it occupied the territory. This allowed them to demonstrate that political pressure was needed to make Israel meet its obligations under IHL, thereby employing legal arguments alongside humanitarian appeals. The underlying message was that international institutions had been complicit in the strangulation of Gaza, as both governments and organs like the United Nations had failed to act on legal conclusions regarding Israel's conduct.

For example, campaign websites focused on the debilitating aspects of the blockade, frequently referred to as a 'siege', and explained that these

---

[50] Interview with Fintan Lane.
[51] Jacobs and Townsley, *Space of Opinion*.
[52] David A. Snow and Robert D. Benford, 'Framing Processes and Social Movements: An Overview and Assessment', *Annual Review of Sociology*, 26 (2000), 611–39.
[53] Jacobs and Townsley, *Space of Opinion*, 149.

had a political objective, and that it was 'Israel [that had] refused the 1.5 million people of Gaza the right to rebuild their homes, schools, mosques, hospitals, as well as fixing their drinking water, sewage installations and systems'.[54] It was explained that, although Gaza was 'one of the most densely populated places on Earth', Israel had permitted less than 20 per cent of needed supplies to enter the area, leading to 'massive shortages that . . . rippled through the economy and society'.[55] When the 2011 FF boats were prevented from sailing out of Greek ports on their way to Gaza, the US arm of the FF campaign blamed the Israeli and US governments for having thwarted that mission.[56] Activists invited the Greek and international media to inspect their boats, so as to demonstrate that they posed no security threat, and thereby to expose the political order that, they believed, was working diligently to maintain the status quo in Gaza.[57] Activists also appealed to the Secretary-General of the United Nations, Ban Ki-moon, through a press release asking that the UN cease bowing to pressure from Israel and its allies, thereby publicising their view that the UN was complicit with the unjust blockade.[58]

Moreover, through the media, activists wanted to remind Israel that the world was watching and monitoring its human rights violations.[59] Highlighting the situation in Gaza, it was thought, would curb Israel's violence against the Palestinian population. Finally, activists hoped that their actions would cause some people in Israel to challenge their government's Gaza policy and would move people in the West to challenge their own governments' complicity in the blockade.[60]

FF activists were careful to ensure that they themselves operated within the law. Beginning with the first boats of the Free Gaza Movement in 2008, campaigners took care to sail in international waters and Gaza territorial waters only, never entering Israeli waters.[61] Other precautions

---

[54]  www.freegaza.org accessed 28 February 2018.
[55]  www.freegaza.org/about-us/why-we-care accessed 28 February 2018.
[56]  Press release on file with the author.
[57]  Annie Robbins, 'Irish Flotilla Ship Will Not Sail to Gaza Due to Extensive Sabotage', *Mondowiess* (29 June 2011). mondoweiss.net/2011/06/irish-flotilla-ship-will-not-sail-to-gaza-due-to-extensive-sabotage.html accessed 28 February 2018.
[58]  Greta Berlin, 'Dear Ban Ki-moon, Your Concern for Our Safety Is Touching', Free Gaza Movement (29 May 2011). www.freegaza.org/dear-ban-ki-moon-your-concern-for-our-safety-is-touching accessed 28 February 2018.
[59]  Interview with Fintan Lane.
[60]  I personally participated when these aims were discussed internally within Irish Ship to Gaza and the steering committee of the international coalition of the FF. These aims were also verified in the interview with Fintan Lane.
[61]  Dienst and Berlin, *Freedom Sailors*.

included training campaign participants on the theory and practicalities of non-violent resistance.[62] During all sailing missions, FF campaigns consistently communicated to the media (via interviews and press statements) that their campaign operated within the confines of the law.[63]

## News Coverage and International Responses to the FF

The focus of the mainstream media in the aftermath of the 2010 FF attack was on international condemnation of Israel for its handling of the aid mission and the rift that this incident had created between Israel and Turkey (since the nine activists killed on 1 June 2010 were Turkish citizens). A comparison of news coverage of the FF campaign and subsequent Israeli attack with news coverage of other newsworthy events about Palestine shows that the FF campaign highlighted the blockade on Gaza more than any other event. Media coverage in the period following the blockade imposition in 2007 focused almost exclusively on the internal fighting taking place between Palestinian factions at the time. In the period following the end of the 2008–2009 assault on Gaza, news coverage focused mainly on the destruction of life and property resulting from that war. Following the Palestinian bid for statehood at the UN in 2012 there was almost no news coverage of Gaza at all.

The FF, on the other hand, helped write many column inches about the blockade and its effects. In an editorial, the *New York Times* urged that 'there can be no excuse for the way that Israel completely mishandled the incident' and asked 'is the blockade working? . . . or just punishing Gaza's 1.4 million residents[?]'. The editorial went on to cite the shortages of supplies in the strip which it said were 'severely lacking' before ultimately calling on the US administration to urge Israel 'to permanently lift the blockade'.[64] In *USA Today*, Israel was described as having imposed a 'severe embargo that left Gazans short even of medical supplies', resulting in the world being 'sympathetic to their plight'.[65] Another article spoke of the high unemployment rate in Gaza and quoted Eyad Al Saraj, a founder of the *International Campaign to End the Siege of Gaza* (part of the FF coalition), citing figures from the World Bank relating to water, food, and sanitation deficiencies resulting from the embargo.[66]

---

[62] See de Jong, 'Gaza Freedom Flotilla'.
[63] Participant observation.
[64] 'Israel and the Blockade' [editorial], *New York Times* (2 June 2010).
[65] 'Israel's Assault on Flotilla Hands Its Enemies a Victory', *USA Today* (2 June 2010).
[66] 'Gaza Flotilla Clash Prompts Backlash', *USA Today* (4 June 2010).

Canada's *Globe and Mail* published a lengthy interview with a FF activist documenting the Israeli military's disproportionate force against the boat and its refusal to take care of the wounded.[67] Elsewhere, a FF activist was quoted in an article which cast doubt on Israel's account of the Flotilla raid.[68] The overall narrative was that Israel had committed a regrettable mistake which might cost it friends regionally and internationally and damage its relations with Turkey. In addition to quotations from activists, Turkey's then Foreign Minister, Ahmet Davutoglu, was quoted calling Israel's raid 'an act of barbarism', while the EU High Commissioner called for the 'immediate, sustained and unconditional opening of the crossing' with Gaza.[69]

In the UK, *The Times* reported extensively on the several dozen UK nationals who had been aboard the boats and were taken to Israeli prisons following the attack on the FF. It was said that the boats had been in 'international waters over which the Israelis have no jurisdiction'.[70] The names of prominent activists were listed, such as the Northern Irish Nobel peace laureate Mairead Corrigan-Maguire. This affirmed what FF organisers had anticipated: that the Western press would be more interested in reporting on the plight of its own citizens; that is why the presence of Westerners aboard the boats was pivotal. Elsewhere, it was explained that the FF had been delivering '10,000 tonnes of supplies, from building materials to electric wheelchairs'.[71] Another UK paper, the *Daily Telegraph*, reported that 'Israel says it allows humanitarian aid into Gaza, but critics, including the UN, say the flow of aid is inadequate'.[72]

The coverage in the *Irish Times* displayed an even more strident tone against Israel's policies. The raid on the FF was described as an attack on a peaceful aid convoy. The paper reported that boats carrying '10,000 tonnes

---

[67] Patrick Martin, 'Inside the Flotilla Raid', *Globe and Mail* (4 June 2010): 'Farooq Burney, the Canadian director of al-Fakhoora, a Qatar-based charity for fostering education in Gaza, was among the passengers aboard the *Mavi Marmara*, the Turkish ship boarded by Israeli commandos on Monday. He tells *Globe and Mail* Middle East correspondent Patrick Martin what he saw.'

[68] Patrick Martin, 'Veracity of Flotilla Audio Recording Debated', *Globe and Mail* (7 June 2010).

[69] Patrick Martin, 'After Deadly Raid, Israel Stands Alone', *Globe and Mail* (1 June 2010).

[70] Mary Bowers et al., 'Concern Grows for the Britons Who Sailed to Beat the Blockade', *The Times*, London (1 June 2010).

[71] Catherine Philp and James Hider, 'Death on the High Seas: Attack by Israel on Gaza Aid Flotilla Leaves at least 9 Dead, UN Holds Emergency Session amid International Outcry', *The Times*, London (1 June 2010).

[72] James Kirkup and Richard Spencer, 'Israel Holds 41 Britons after Flotilla Raid', *Daily Telegraph* (2 June 2010).

of aid, mainly construction material, medicines, paper for school books, wheelchairs and chocolate, which Israel does not allow into Gaza' had been 'stormed' in 'international waters well outside the exclusion zone'.[73] Leading Irish politicians, such as then Foreign Affairs Minister Micheál Martin, 'condemned Israel's unacceptable and disproportionate use of force' and accused Israel of 'essentially kidnapping Irish citizens' who had been aboard the FF.[74] It was also reported that the then Irish prime minister, Brian Cowen, had called for 'an international inquiry' and said that 'Israel had violated international law by imposing a blockade against humanitarian assistance to Gaza'.[75]

The Irish press also reported on Israel's mainstream press during this time, which noted that the botched raid would cause Israel 'astronomical damage in innumerable spheres'.[76] The international fallout for Israel was unremitting. For example, two months after the 1 June attack, the UK prime minister, in an unprecedented tone, accused Israel of turning Gaza into a 'prison camp' and characterised its attack on the FF as 'piracy', echoing the FF activists' depiction of the situation.[77]

Accordingly, the FF organisers, at least for a brief window, succeeded in influencing media discourse on Gaza, through both their actual attempt to sail to Gaza and speaking about Gaza in interviews with the media and through their press releases.[78] When compared with the other three flashpoint periods for Israel–Palestine news coverage, which had focused on the security discourse surrounding the blockade of Gaza, news coverage following the FF drew unprecedented attention to both ethical concerns relating to the people of Gaza and legal concerns.

## The UN and Israel

The previous sections demonstrated how FF activists made reference to international humanitarian law, and particularly the crucial fact that Gaza was occupied territory, to defend their position for intervening against the blockade. Similarly, defenders and detractors of the blockade

---

[73] Michael Jansen and Mary Fitzgerald, 'Seven Irish Citizens Detained in Israel after Raid on Aid Flotilla', *Irish Times* (1 June 2010).
[74] Mary Fitzgerald and Deaglán De Bréadún, 'Martin Accuses Israel of "Kidnapping" Irish Citizens', *Irish Times* (1 June 2010).
[75] Ibid.
[76] Mark Weiss, 'Newspapers Criticise 'Fiasco' over Aid Flotilla', *Irish Times* (2 June 2010).
[77] Rosa Prince, 'Gaza Is Like a Prison Camp, says PM', *Daily Telegraph* (28 July 2010).
[78] The Irish campaign, of which the author was an organiser, regularly briefed Irish parliamentarians on the progress of the campaign.

summoned legal arguments to lend legitimacy to their respective positions after the media fallout from the FF killings. These came in the form of four high profile inquiries, two from the United Nations, one from Turkey, and one from Israel.[79] An examination of the two reports from the United Nations and that of Israel reveals the manner in which these two actors reacted to the intervention of the FF: at first in diametrical opposition and finally in a reconciliatory manner aimed at healing the diplomatic rift between Israel and Turkey while maintaining the blockade on Gaza. Through an examination of these three inquiries, the frailty of the United Nations in addressing issues of justice relating to Gaza becomes clear.

First, against a background of negative publicity, Israel announced that it would conduct an investigation into the actions of its soldiers, to determine whether any laws had been breached in the Israeli navy's handling of the FF. The inquiry first reported in July 2010 that Israel had operated within the law and quickly exonerated the military from any misconduct related to the killing of the nine FF activists.[80] Furthermore, the inquiry painted a picture of a campaign comprised of peace activists on the one hand and allegedly violent activists on the other by drawing a distinction between different FF organisations.[81] The FF campaigners rejected such characterisations and maintained that Israel lied to cover for the killing of the nine activists while confiscating cameras and other evidence in the immediate aftermath of the incident so as to destroy evidence that would corroborate the FF campaign's version of events.[82]

Perhaps even more astonishing than Israel's self-exoneration for the shooting of the activists was the finding by its inquiry that there was no humanitarian crisis in Gaza.[83] This conclusion flew in the face of findings

---

[79] In chronological order: A UNHRC report 'Report of International Fact-Finding', published in September 2010; an Israeli report, 'The Public Commission to Examine the Maritime Incident of 31 May 2010' (January 2011). www.legal-tools.org/doc/f2aae4/pdf accessed 28 February 2018; a Turkish report, 'Report of Turkish National Commission of Inquiry' (11 February 2011). www.mfa.gov.tr/data/Turkish%20Report%20Final%20-%20UN%20Copy.pdf accessed 28 February 2018; and another UN report, the Palmer Report, 'Report of the Secretary-General's Panel of Inquiry on the 31 May 2010 Flotilla Incident' (September 2011). www.un.org/News/dh/infocus/middle_east/Gaza_Flotilla_Panel_Report.pdf accessed 28 February 2018.

[80] Craig, *International Legitimacy*, 217–20.

[81] 'Public Commission to Examine' [Israeli report], 218.

[82] Participant observation.

[83] 'Public Commission to Examine' [Israeli report], Chapter A, paras. 71–3.

by several reputable agencies in the preceding period that had detailed conditions of food insecurity and medical negligence in Gaza.[84] These included the findings by the high profile inquiry of the United Nations Human Rights Council into the circumstances surrounding the attack on the FF on 1 June 2010, which did attest to a humanitarian crisis in Gaza.[85] The UNHRC had invited Israel to cooperate with its inquiry, but the latter refused, just as it had refused to engage with the UNHRC's inquiry a year earlier into the 2008–2009 war on Gaza.[86] The UNHRC's mission found Israel's conduct towards the FF campaign to be illegal, and moreover found that the blockade amounted to the collective punishment of a population and was therefore also illegal. It was further said that the closure regime constituted collective punishment of the population and violated article 33 of the Fourth Geneva Convention.[87] This was because the mission, concurring with the consensus of international legal opinion, found that Israel did in fact occupy Gaza despite having no ground troops inside its perimeter.[88] Moreover, the mission concluded that 'a series of violations of international law, including international humanitarian and human rights law, were committed by the Israeli forces during the interception of the flotilla and during the detention of passengers in Israel prior to deportation'.[89] Finally, the inquiry was satisfied 'not only that the flotilla presented no imminent threat but that the interception was motivated by concerns about the possible propaganda victory that might be claimed by the organizers of the flotilla'.[90]

The findings of the UNHRC mission also revealed that Israeli plans for a naval blockade had not been approved prior to the phenomenon of boats attempting to reach Gaza '"on grounds of legitimacy" and the possibility of ... "severe criticism" at the international level'.[91] In other words, Israel's policy makers thought that a publicly declared naval blockade would have come under international criticism and consequently postponed taking an official position vis-à-vis a maritime closure

---

[84] UNHRC, 'Human Rights in Palestine'; ICRC, 'Gaza Closure: Not Another Year!', News Release 10/103 (14 June 2010); Amnesty International, 'Palestinian Authority', in *Amnesty International Report 2010*.

[85] UNHRC, 'Report of International Fact-Finding', paras. 37–44.

[86] Ibid. para 16. The UNHRC report did, however, include testimonies from Israel's own inquiry into the incident.

[87] Ibid. para. 54.

[88] Ibid. para. 63.

[89] Ibid. Summary, 1.

[90] Ibid. para. 57.

[91] Ibid. para. 33.

until it became necessary due to the persistent arrival of Free Gaza Movement boats to Gaza between August and December 2008. It should be recalled here that Israel's land blockade was not declared when it came into effect in mid 2007. Indeed, it remains undeclared, as it would be difficult to prove its legality under international law, which allows for blockades only in times of international armed conflict.[92] It is therefore unsurprising that the government of Israel, after refraining from declaring a blockade on Gaza in any form, later sought to disaggregate its closure of Gaza by declaring a naval blockade only and addressing it separately from the undeclared land blockade.[93] The benefits of bifurcating the two blockades would serve Israel well a year later when another UN report, the 'Palmer Report', was commissioned.

The Palmer Report, released in September 2011, was the result of a Panel of Inquiry established by the UN Secretary-General to investigate the circumstances of the FF attack.[94] Relying on the Israeli and Turkish inquiries into the same, with the former alleging that Israel's blockade was legal and the latter maintaining that the occupation of Gaza rendered any blockade on the territory illegal, the panel sided with the Israeli position and found the naval blockade to be legal. This represented a turnaround in the position of the United Nations in so far as this conclusion was opposite to the findings of the UNHRC's fact-finding mission a year earlier.

The conclusions of the Palmer Report were striking because they used fragments of legal principles which, when put together, did not constitute a coherent legal argument. For example, although the Palmer Report was careful to state that 'the Panel is not a court [and] was not asked to make determinations of the legal issues or to adjudicate on liability', this did not stop it from doing just that. Specifically, the report found that 'the naval blockade was imposed as a legitimate security measure in order to prevent weapons from entering Gaza by sea, and that its implementation complied with the requirements of international law'.[95] The report concluded that since

---

[92] Ibid. e.g. para. 51.

[93] IDF Chief Military Advocate-General (Avichai Mandelblit's) testimony to the Turkel Committee: Public Commission to Examine the Maritime Incident of May 31, 2010, Session Number 4, 26 August 2010, 41. As cited in UNHRC, 'Report of International Fact-Finding, 8.

[94] Palmer Report, so named because the inquiry was headed by Sir Geoffrey Palmer. The report notes that the panel was established by the Secretary-General 'in the light of the Statement of the President of the Security Council dated 1 June 2010 (S/PRST/2010/9)'.

[95] Ibid. paras. 5, 82.

foodstuffs came via land and not by sea, this situation 'militate[d] against a finding that the naval blockade itself has a significant humanitarian impact'.[96] The issue of Gaza's ports being ill-equipped for large cargo ships as a direct result of Israel's occupation did not arise.[97] Similarly, Israel's prevention of tiny fishing boats from fishing beyond a few miles into the sea was left unaddressed, obscuring the broader humanitarian impact of the naval blockade against the entire fishing community of the coastal territory of Gaza.[98] Consequently, the panel accepted Israel's position that the naval blockade was a separate measure from the land blockade in order to escape the accusation that a naval blockade adversely affected the population by disallowing the transfer of goods. By bifurcating the blockade into separate land and sea closure policies, Israel could successfully claim that the naval blockade alone did not result in the collective punishment of the population.

In addition to the disingenuous bifurcation of the blockade policy, the laws employed to justify the naval blockade did not stand up to legal scrutiny. To reach its conclusion that the naval blockade was legal, the Palmer Report relied on customary international humanitarian law, and specifically on the San Remo Manual on International Law Applicable to Armed Conflicts at Sea (1994), which requires that a number of principles be fulfilled in order to render a naval blockade legal. Among these principles are the requirements that an international armed conflict exists between two or more states and that a blockade must be in accordance with the principle of humanity.[99] Since Gaza is occupied territory that is nominally administered by the Palestinian Authority and is not recognised as a state by the Government of Israel, the first principle is clearly unfulfilled. It is legally incorrect to claim that an international armed conflict exists between Israel and a non-state territory which the former occupies.[100] Second, and perhaps more importantly, international humanitarian

---

[96] Ibid. para. 78.
[97] For a discussion on Gaza's underdevelopment, see Sara Roy, *Failing Peace*.
[98] The author met with fifteen fishermen in Gaza in January 2013 and was briefed on the effect of the blockade and its enforcement, often with live ammunition, on the livelihoods and safety of the fishing community. See also: ICRC, 'Gaza Closure'.
[99] Russell Buchan, 'The Palmer Report and the Legality of Israel's Naval Blockade of Gaza', *International and Comparative Law Quarterly*, 61 (2012), 264–73 at 266. See also San Remo Manual on International Law Applicable to Armed Conflicts at Sea (1994), paras. 102–4.
[100] Dugard, 'Report of the Special Rapporteur', 21–2.

law requires that a naval blockade does not result in the collective punishment of a population, something to which the blockade on Gaza as a whole had led.[101]

In an apparent attempt to reinvent international humanitarian law, an Israeli legal academic, Ruth Lapidoth, suggested the following formulation: 'in those areas in which Israel still has control – which means sea and airspace – Israel is responsible'.[102] According to this argument, Israel could 'distinguish between full control of the territory and control only of the sea and airspace' in executing its duties of responsibility as the occupying power.[103] This formulation would relieve Israel's military commanders of any responsibility towards the people of Gaza since Israel would implicitly no longer be responsible for harm that came about as a result of the land blockade. As observed by Koskenniemmi, such attempts at reinventing IHL in this way conflict with the principle that 'no rule is more important than the reason for which it is enacted' and forgets that IHL exists to protect civilian life.[104] Once again, as was the case with the Palmer Report, Lapidoth's reasoning overlooked that 'international law is not just some haphazard collection of rules and principles', but rather 'it is about their use in the context of legal work'.[105] Sadly, the intentions behind the legal reasoning in the Palmer Report and by Israeli lawyers like Lapidoth seemed aimed at legitimising a continuation of the status quo.

The legal incoherence of the Palmer Report was not lost on the activists of the FF. The website of Canada Boat to Gaza published a response to Israel's defence of the naval blockade in which it cited Ambassador Craig Murray, a former Alternate Head of the UK Delegation to the United Nations Preparatory Commission on the UN Convention on the Law of the Sea, who challenged Israel's invocation of the San Remo Manual as flawed. Murray argued:

> It falls completely on one fact alone. San Remo only applies to blockade in times of armed conflict. Israel is not currently engaged in an armed conflict, and presumably does not wish to be. San Remo does not confer any right to impose a permanent blockade outwith times of armed

---

[101] Ibid. 11.
[102] Ruth Lapidoth, 'The Legal Basis of Israel's Naval Blockade of Gaza', Jerusalem Center For Public Affairs (18 July 2010). http://jcpa.org/article/the-legal-basis-of-israel's-naval-blockade-of-gaza
[103] Ibid.
[104] Koskenniemi, *Apology to Utopia*, 591.
[105] Ibid. 567.

conflict, and in fact specifically excludes as illegal a general blockade on an entire population.[106]

Elsewhere, the executive director of the Israeli human rights organisation 'Gisha' noted that since Israel had been blocking boats from reaching Gaza since 1967, 'it is not the declaration of a naval blockade, but rather the law of occupation that authorizes Israel to prevent ships from reaching Gaza'.[107]

How then did a report containing legally incoherent conclusions, albeit conclusions that were not legally binding, emerge from a panel sanctioned by the Secretary-General of the United Nations? The answer may lie in the widely regarded view that the Palmer Report was aimed at healing diplomatic tensions between Israel and Turkey rather than addressing the blockade itself.[108] It has also been suggested that the Palmer Panel of Inquiry 'changed the context of the legal analysis from Israel–Palestine to Israel–Turkey and the analysis of IHL from civilian rights to state rights'.[109] Ultimately, the rights of the FF participants that had been attacked and the rights of the people living under the blockade of Gaza were cast to the background while Israel worked to remedy the negative image that the FF had exposed to the media in an attempt to improve its relations with Turkey.

## Effect of the FF on the Actual Blockade

Apart from eliciting a series of investigations by the United Nations, Israel, and Turkey, and in addition to its demonstrable influence on media discourse as presented earlier in this chapter, did the FF's interventions have any impact on the blockade itself? A possible indicator could be the extent to which the blockade changed in scope. On 17 June 2010, less than three weeks following the attack on the FF, Israel announced that it was going to 'ease' the blockade on Gaza.[110]

---

[106] 'The Blockade is Illegal No Matter What Israel Claims', Canada Boat to Gaza. www .tahrir.ca/content/blockade-illegal-no-matter-what-israel-claims

[107] Sari Bashi, 'U.N.'s Gaza Flotilla Report Adrift at Sea' *Foreign Policy*, 2 (September 2011). http://mideast.foreignpolicy.com/posts/2011/09/02/flotilla_report_adrift_at_sea accessed 28 February 2018.

[108] Daragh Murray, 'The UN Palmer Inquiry and Israel's Attack on the *Mavi Marmara*', *Jadiliyya* (7 September 2011).

[109] Craig, *International Legitimacy*, 227.

[110] Harriet Sherwood, 'Israel to Ease Gaza Blockade', *The Guardian* (17 June 2010). www .guardian.co.uk/world/2010/jun/17/israel-to-ease-gaza-blockade accessed 28 February 2018.

According to the Office for the Coordination of Humanitarian Affairs (OCHA), 'following the tragic results of the flotilla's attempt to break the blockade, Israel announced a package of measures to ease the access restrictions it had imposed on Gaza since June 2007'.[111] These measures followed a gradual expansion in the variety of items that had been allowed to enter in late 2009 but showed a marked improvement in the latter half of 2010.[112] Israel committed itself to expanding the import capacity of the Kerem Shalom Crossing from 90 to 250 truckloads a day for five days a week, and of the conveyer belt at Karni Crossing, used for the transfer of bulk aggregates and grains, from 80 to 120 truckloads a day twice a week.[113] Data provided by OCHA revealed that the number of truckloads of goods entering Gaza through Kerem Shalom, the checkpoint through which goods were transferred between Israel and Gaza, increased after the 2010 FF incident, as shown in Table 1.

Israel also allowed a small number of exports, as shown in Table 2. These provided a negligible boost to the economy of Gaza. However, these modest concessions made Israel less vulnerable to criticism by rendering the blockade less visible.

OCHA concluded that: 'the June 2010 relaxation of the blockade resulted in mild improvement in the access of inputs needed to upgrade and expand existing infrastructure ... [although] this improvement has remained very limited compared with the huge challenges generated by

Table 1. *Truckloads entering Gaza through Kerem Shalom*[114]

| | |
|------|-------|
| 2007 | 3901 |
| 2008 | 5091 |
| 2009 | 22806 |
| 2010 | 30901 |
| 2011 | 46399 |
| 2012 | 57370 |

---

[111] OCHA, 'Easing The Blockade: Assessing the Humanitarian Impact on the Population of the Gaza Strip. Palestinian Territories', Special Focus Report, East Jerusalem (March 2011), 2.

[112] Ibid. 5.

[113] Ibid. 4.

[114] Data adapted from OCHA, *Gaza Crossings Activities Database*. www.ochaopt.org/loca tion/gaza-strip accessed 28 February 2018

Table 2. *Truckloads*
*leaving Gaza through*
*Kerem Shalom*[115]

| 2007 | 414 |
| --- | --- |
| 2008 | 33 |
| 2009 | 42 |
| 2010 | 215 |
| 2011 | 268 |
| 2012 | 210 |

three years of blockade'.[116] This 'easing' of the blockade, in addition to being demonstrable through the increase in truck consignments coming into Gaza, was documented by Alan Craig, who noted that following the 2010 FF 'Israel moved rapidly to ease restrictions by technical changes to the identification of items to be allowed through border checkpoints'.[117]

## Conclusion

Israel has historically used its military superiority over the Palestinians to enforce its policies, at the same time claiming the rights that flow from its position as a sovereign state to legitimise these policies in the eyes of international audiences. This may be likened to what Martti Koskenniemi has called the concrete or 'sovereign' approach to international law that reveals the indeterminate nature of international legal rules and becomes simply an apology for extant power relations.[118] In contrast, Palestinian actors and human rights organisations have relied heavily on generating reports and sending appeals to international institutions to implement international law in the 'utopian' sense. The various sides participated in the crisis surrounding Gaza but seemed to speak different languages. The FF activists understood that international humanitarian law is not an objective, independent norm, but must be employed as a tool of struggle. In this regard, the campaign forced the UN, the media, and Israel to deal with new immediate facts of maritime movement between Gaza and the outside world, thereby compelling legal

---

[115] Data adapted from OCHA, *Gaza Crossings Activities Database*. www.ochaopt.org/loca
tion/gaza-strip accessed 28 February 2018
[116] Ibid. 17.
[117] Craig, *International Legitimacy*, 216.
[118] Koskenniemi, *Apology to Utopia*.

and political discourse on Gaza to intersect. The campaign thus forced a crucial conversation between legal, humanitarian, and security claims.

However, this chapter has also shown that principles of international law, while capable of providing a guide to what is ethical, are largely powerless when a political order exists for which implementation of the law may undermine an existing arrangement that suits power-holders. Power-holders can employ fragments of international law to defend policies in fragments, which however clumsily or incoherently employed can nevertheless impart a veneer of respectability to the otherwise questionable actions of their military. This is what the Palmer inquiry succeeded in doing. It did not do so in the manner associated with the inherent indeterminacy of law that may reasonably be expected of a partisan side employing robust legal argument to defend a partisan position.[119] Rather, the Palmer Report simply disregarded the principles contained in a single body of law, in this case the San Remo Manual on International Law Applicable to Armed Conflicts at Sea. Both before and after the FF missions of 2010 and 2011, Israel managed to escape punitive juridical action for its collective punishment of the population of Gaza. Moreover, no individual from among the soldiers or commanders of the Israeli forces that executed the fatal attack on the 2010 FF has to date been tried for the lives lost that day. Attempts to bring about ICC involvement in the *Mavi Marmara* case (and other aspects of the Israeli occupation of Palestine) so far have not changed this picture.[120]

Overall, although unsuccessful in ending the devastating blockade on Gaza, by instrumentalising international law in combination with a skilful media strategy, the FF campaign succeeded in achieving two important results. The first of these was highlighting of the Gaza situation to international audiences. The second, which flowed from the first, was the pressuring of Israel to increase, however slightly, the amount of goods

---

[119]  Ibid. 590–6.

[120]  In May 2013 the Comoros referred the '31 May 2010 Israeli raid on the Humanitarian Aid Flotilla bound for [the] Gaza Strip' to the ICC. In November 2014 the Prosecutor announced that the preliminary examination had been closed. While 'there is a reasonable basis to believe that war crimes under the jurisdiction of the International Criminal Court … were committed on one of the vessels, the *Mavi Marmara*, when Israeli Defense Forces intercepted the "Gaza Freedom Flotilla" on 31 May 2010' the Prosecutor concluded that 'the potential case(s) likely arising from an investigation into this incident would not be of "sufficient gravity" to justify further action by the ICC'. See https://www.icc-cpi.int/Pages/item.aspx?name=otp-statement-06-11-2014 (accessed 28 February 2018). In January 2015 Palestine acceded to the Rome Statute (in force 1 April 2015).

allowed into Gaza. The exact causal mechanism which brought about this development is worthy of further study, both to confirm the effect of the FF on this positive, though grossly inadequate, development and to further understand the workings of the political order that has thus far allowed the blockade to persist.

Beyond the direct effect on the blockade's restrictions, the first achievement of the FF highlighted the Gaza situation to the international media. Campaigners tackled a major problem that has been avoided by the Palestinians for decades, that of framing and narrative. Although it is the Palestinians that have been perpetually dispossessed of land and freedoms since 1948, Israel has presented itself as a victim throughout the history of the conflict.[121] In the case of the Gaza blockade, Israel perpetuated the victimhood narrative by prioritising political discourse that placed security needs ahead of an acknowledgement of an occupier's obligations under international law, or indeed the Palestinians' security needs. This resulted in the alienation of legal discourse from political discourse, particularly in media coverage of Gaza, which largely reflected Israel's security discourse rather than legalistic and humanitarian appeals from human rights organisations to end the blockade. The FF sought to highlight the essential validity of the legal claims made by and in the name of the Palestinians by organising a political action that made the closure of Gaza and the inability of Palestinians to enter or leave it impossible to ignore. In doing so, and by skilfully engaging with the media, the FF forced legal concerns to become worthy of news coverage. Consequently, the FF shifted the focus from Israel's security concerns to the rights of the Palestinians. The FF campaign furthermore demonstrated, through the heinous killing of nine Turkish citizens, that Palestinian claims about Israel's disproportionate use of violence against civilians were well founded.

These accomplishments notwithstanding, at the time of writing, the outlook for Gaza's inhabitants was bleak. Israel's July 2014 Operation Protective Edge incursion yet again caused many Palestinian casualties, including the death of 501 children, and further damaged basic infrastructure, including power and water supplies.[122] If a 2012 UN report is a

---

[121] Rashid Khalidi, 'The 2010 Edward Said Memorial Lecture', The Palestine Center, Washington DC, 7 October 2010. https://www.youtube.com/watch?v=DCB76sDcZvk accessed 28 February 2018.

[122] See e.g. OCHA, 'Occupied Palestinian Territory: Gaza Emergency Situation Report (as of 4 September 2014, 08:00 hrs)'. https://www.ochaopt.org/content/occupied-palestinian-territory-gaza-emergency-situation-report-4-september-2014–0800-hrs accessed 28

reliable indicator of what is to come, Gaza could become 'unliveable' by 2020 unless current sanitation and health conditions are improved.[123] This sombre outlook should compel legal scholars to pay heed to the unique manner in which Israel has instrumentalised legal language, exceeding the apologetic tradition of international law and departing from good legal 'grammar'.[124] In any case, as Richard Falk has argued:

> the presuppositions of IHL are addressing a belligerent occupation of short duration, and so it is not adequate to address a situation of prolonged occupation of the sort that the Palestinian people have been subject to for decades; also, IHL does not even pretend to deal with such developments as annexation, apartheid, ethnic cleansing, [and] settler colonialism that are at the core of Israel's mature occupation policy.[125]

Indeed, the political intervention by the FF demonstrated that a resolution to the continuing crisis in Gaza cannot come from legal battles conducted through impotent conventional channels, but requires determined and imaginative direct action.

February 2018; and DCI Palestine, *Operation Protective Edge: A War Waged on Gaza's Children*, Ramallah (April 2015). www.dci-palestine.org/operation_protective_edge_a_war_waged_on_gaza_s_children accessed 28 February 2018.
[123] United Nations Country Team, 'Gaza in 2020: A livable place?' Jerusalem (2012).
[124] Koskenniemi, *Apology to Utopia*, Epilogue.
[125] Falk, 'Why Have Palestinians'.

# 5

# The Hague Conventions: Giving Effect to Human Rights through Instruments of Private International Law

MAJA GROFF*

## Introduction

A range of modern Hague Conventions give effect to important aspects of broader international human rights norms, in particular in cross-border settings.[1] These Conventions furthermore establish multilateral legal structures within which states may support and actualise these commitments.[2] A number of provisions of the 1989 United Nations Convention on the Rights of the Child[3] have been implemented through Hague Conventions addressing international child abduction,[4] inter-

---

* The views expressed in this chapter are those of the author alone and do not reflect the views of the Permanent Bureau or the Hague Conference on Private International Law. The author would like to thank Hans van Loon, former Secretary General of the Hague Conference, and Philippe Lortie, First Secretary at the Permanent Bureau, for comments on this chapter.
1 This refers to conventions negotiated under the auspices of the Hague Conference of Private International Law. The Hague Conference on Private International Law (the 'Hague Conference) is a permanent intergovernmental organisation, currently comprised of 83 Members (82 states and one regional economic integration organisation, the European Union). A full list of Hague Conventions can be found at the Hague Conference website, www.hcch.net, under 'Conventions, Protocols and Principles' (see also under 'The old Conventions' for the Hague Conventions adopted before 1945).
2 It should be noted that the focus of the Hague Conventions is on cross-border issues, which may not be at the centre of traditional human rights instruments. Yet, with regional cooperation and globalisation on the rise, these transnational issues are increasingly important, and global and regional human rights instruments increasingly call for international cooperation in cross-border situations.
3 Convention on the Rights of the Child (CRC), New York, 20 November 1989, in force 2 September 1990, 1577 *UNTS* 3.
4 Convention on the Civil Aspects of International Child Abduction, The Hague, 25 October 1980, in force 1 December 1983. See Arts. 11 and 35 of the CRC.

country adoption,[5] the international protection of children,[6] and the international recovery of child support and other forms of family maintenance.[7] The 2000 Hague Convention on the International Protection of Adults[8] provides a complement to one of the most recent comprehensive United Nations human rights treaties, the 2006 United Nations Convention on the Rights of Persons with Disabilities.[9] In addition, a potential new international instrument on the cross-border recognition and enforcement of foreign civil protection orders addressing, inter alia, cases of domestic and interpersonal violence has recently been on the work agenda of the Hague Conference.[10] If developed, such a global instrument, like a range of existing Hague Conventions, would reinforce a number of state obligations found in important regional and international human rights treaties.

This chapter seeks to respond to critiques that international law may be predominantly, or always, an (unconvincing) 'apology' for the exercise of entrenched state self-interest and power.[11] To the contrary, there are examples in which international law exhibits strong trends towards a genuine rule of law,[12] and transcendence of the vicious circle

---

[5] Convention on Protection of Children and Co-operation in Respect of Intercountry Adoption, The Hague, 29 May 1993, in force 1 May 1995. See Art. 21 of the CRC.

[6] Convention on Jurisdiction, Applicable Law, Recognition, Enforcement and Co-operation in Respect of Parental Responsibility and Measures for the Protection of Children, The Hague, 19 October 1996, in force 1 January 2002. See Arts. 3, 21(e), 22, 34, and 35 of the CRC.

[7] Convention on the International Recovery of Child Support and Other Forms of Family Maintenance, The Hague, 23 November 2007, in force 1 January 2013. See Art. 27 of the CRC.

[8] Convention on the International Protection of Adults, The Hague, 13 January 2000, in force 1 January 2009.

[9] Convention on the Rights of Persons with Disabilities (CRPD), New York, 13 December 2006, in force 3 May 2008, 2515 UNTS 3. See Arts. 3, 12, 13, 18, 25, and 32 of the CRPD, setting forth a range of rights and obligations to be supported by the 2000 Protection of Adults Convention, for certain adults with disabilities implicated in cross-border situations falling within the scope of the 2000 Convention.

[10] This means that Members of the Hague Conference, at the annual meeting of the Organisation's principal governing body, the Council on General Affairs and Policy, have formally requested that the Permanent Bureau undertake work or monitoring in these areas.

[11] M. Koskenniemi, 'The Politics of International Law', European Journal of International Law, 1 (1990), 4–32 at 8.

[12] Koskenniemi has suggested that notions of law or the rule of law can be defined as rules which should apply 'regardless of political preferences of legal subjects'. If this is not the case, then the legal discourse simply consists of 'an apology for the legal subject's political interest'. (Ibid.)

established by the polarities of apology and utopia described in well-known critiques of (public) international law.[13]

Contemporary international law can manifest determinant outcomes for the individuals or groups intended to be served (for example, for the intended beneficiaries of certain human rights entitlements), rather than merely representing a reflection of political sovereign interest.[14] This chapter describes several such instances by focusing, in some detail, on three case examples of work related to the Conventions and projects of the Hague Conference on Private International Law. These Conventions and projects, in effect, work to facilitate tangible access to justice for individuals across international boundaries, often taking as their inspiration 'higher level' human rights norms established by the international community.

The case examples focused on below describe the newest (2007) Hague Convention in the area of child support, the Hague Conference work related to the practical operation of the 1980 Hague Convention on international child abduction and, third, preliminary Hague Conference work towards a possible new international instrument or other cooperation mechanisms in the area of protection orders. Bearing these case examples in mind, the chapter will conclude by offering further thoughts in response to contemporary critiques of international law both as an intellectual discipline and as a practice.

## Case Example 1: The 2007 Hague Child Support Convention

### Overview of the Convention

The 2007 Hague Child Support Convention seeks to ensure the effective cross-border recovery of child support and other forms of family maintenance for individual creditors and single parent families.[15] The Convention's provisions seek to establish, in detail, an efficient and responsive system of cooperation between contracting states to process

---

[13] Ibid. See also M. Koskenniemi, *From Apology to Utopia: The Structure of International Legal Argument* (Cambridge: Cambridge University Press, 2005).

[14] For a definition of what might be considered politics (the assertion of subjective interests) as opposed to genuine law, see n. 12.

[15] Applicable law issues in relation to international maintenance cases are addressed by the Protocol on the Law Applicable to Maintenance Obligations, The Hague, 23 November 2007, in force 1 August 2013. The Protocol is complementary to the 2007 Child Support Convention.

international applications for maintenance. They also introduce expedited and simplified procedures for the recognition and enforcement of foreign maintenance decisions issued in contracting states. Currently, there are at least five other global multilateral treaties in force, including a number of older Hague Conventions, which address the cross-border recovery of family maintenance.[16] The 2007 Convention and its Applicable Law Protocol are intended to replace the existing treaties, offering one comprehensive and up-to-date global system for the international recovery of maintenance, building upon and improving the older instruments in this field.[17]

The 2007 Convention entered into force on 1 January 2013, subsequent to its second ratification.[18] The European Union is a party to this Convention. The United States, another major economic player and significant geographic entity, completed ratification in 2016.

Negotiation of the 2007 Convention spanned a number of years and included the involvement of practitioners in the field of child support and maintenance, including specialised national caseworkers with cross-disciplinary knowledge. The objective of these negotiations was to design a practical and effective instrument in line with modern best practices in this field of law.[19] Members of the Hague Conference who participated in negotiations of the Convention included states from all regions of the

---

[16] See the Convention on the Recovery Abroad of Maintenance, New York, 20 June 1956, in force 25 May 1957, 268 *UNTS* 3 and 649 *UNTS* 33; Convention on the Law Applicable to Maintenance Obligations towards Children, The Hague, 24 October 1956, in force 1 January 1962; Convention concerning the Recognition and Enforcement of Decisions Relating to Maintenance Obligations towards Children, The Hague, 15 April 1958, in force 1 January 1962; Convention on the Recognition and Enforcement of Decisions Relating to Maintenance Obligations, The Hague, 2 October 1973, in force 1 August 1976; and Convention on the Law Applicable to Maintenance Obligations, The Hague, 2 October 1973, in force 1 October 1977.

[17] See e.g. a description of structural, operational, and other issues concerning existing Conventions in the maintenance field in W. Duncan, 'Towards a New Global Instrument on the International Recovery of Child Support and Other Forms of Family Maintenance', Preliminary Document No 3, Permanent Bureau of the Hague Conference on Private International Law (April 2003).

[18] As of 15 January 2018, 37 states and the European Union (binding 27 European Union member states) were contracting parties to the 2007 Convention.

[19] A mandate to develop a new instrument in this field was given in 1999, after which the Permanent Bureau commenced background research in advance of formal negotiations initiated in May of 2003 (see Duncan, 'New Global Instrument'). One manifestation of the Convention's embrace of national best practices that are by no means globally widespread is Art. 34, which lists a range of innovative maintenance enforcement measures that have been pioneered in certain jurisdictions.

world,[20] with a significant number of non-member states taking part as observers, which added further regional, legal, and cultural diversity to the process.[21]

Barriers to the recovery of child support and other forms of family maintenance within national legal systems have traditionally included expensive court-based legal procedures. These procedures often are not user friendly, tend to be very slow, and generate concerns over the protection of confidential and personal information. Such problems are magnified when a creditor seeks the recovery of child support or family maintenance internationally, an increasingly common scenario given the reality of international travel and migration.[22]

The 2007 Convention addresses these barriers in a variety of ways, with provisions that: (a) invite domestic reform to develop more efficient national systems for the recovery of maintenance; (b) oblige the provision of free legal assistance for child support applications concerning children under the age of 21 (with minor exceptions); (c) establish a Central Authority[23] for an international administrative cooperation system; and (d) specify the protection of personal information. A new

---

[20] Participating members from greater Europe and Eurasia included Albania, Austria, Belgium, Bulgaria, Croatia, Czech Republic, Denmark, Estonia, Finland, France, Germany, Greece, Hungary, Ireland, Italy, Latvia, Lithuania, Luxembourg, Monaco, Netherlands, Norway, Poland, Portugal, Romania, Russian Federation, Serbia, Slovakia, Slovenia, Spain, Sweden, Switzerland, the former Yugoslav Republic of Macedonia, Ukraine, United Kingdom of Great Britain and Northern Ireland, and the then-European Community (as a regional economic integration organisation); Latin American members included Argentina, Brazil, Chile, Ecuador, Mexico, Peru, Uruguay, and Venezuela; Asia-Pacific members included Australia, China, Japan, Republic of Korea, Malaysia, New Zealand, and Sri Lanka; North American members included Canada and the United States of America; and Middle Eastern and African members included Egypt, Israel, Jordan, Morocco, and South Africa.

[21] Non-members at the time included Algeria, Burkina Faso, Colombia, Costa Rica, Dominican Republic, El Salvador, Guatemala, Haiti, Holy See, India, Indonesia, Iran, Philippines, and Vietnam. Five of these states have become members of the Hague Conference since (i.e. Burkina Faso, Costa Rica, India, Philippines, and Vietnam).

[22] Trends in the ever-greater mobility of persons across international borders continue to intensify. Recent United Nations statistics show that more people than ever are living abroad, with some 232 million (3.2 per cent of the world's population) living outside of their countries of origin, in contrast to 174 million in 2000 and 154 million in 1990. See United Nations Department of Economic and Social Affairs, 'The Number of International Migrants Worldwide Reaches 232 Million', *Population Facts No. 2013/2* (September 2013).

[23] Each contracting state must designate a national Central Authority (Art. 4) in order to discharge a number of specified duties and to assist generally with the operation of the Convention.

global case management system (iSupport) has been developed to employ information technology to promote the swift and effective cross-border recovery of family maintenance payments. A number of these features are described in more detail below, followed by a description of important economic and social rights which may be addressed by this Convention.

## Access to Justice Provisions

The package of provisions enshrined in the 2007 Convention aims to facilitate concrete access to justice in this important area of law.[24] Central to the facilitation of access to justice are novel provisions which address the right of applicants under the Convention to have 'effective access to procedures'. Such provisions are not found in any previous international instruments related to maintenance, but are considered to be 'a 'fundamental principle' of the 2007 Convention.[25] Article 14 of the Convention obliges contracting states to provide all applicants with effective access to procedures (including access to enforcement and appeal procedures), defined as the ability of an applicant to put his or her case as fully and as effectively as possible, with the assistance of relevant authorities and the goal that 'a lack of means should not be a barrier'.[26]

A crucial element of this general obligation concerning effective access to procedures for all applicants under the Convention, be they creditors or debtors of a maintenance obligation, is the requirement to provide further assistance to a special group of maintenance creditors, namely children under the age of 21 years.[27] Subject to some minor exceptions,[28]

---

[24] The Hague Conference has a general instrument to facilitate access to justice, the Convention on International Access to Justice (The Hague, 25 October 1980, in force 1 May 1988). This Convention aims to ensure that the mere status of being a foreigner or the lack of residence or domicile in a contracting state is not a ground for discrimination with respect to access to justice in that contracting state.

[25] A. Borrás and J. Degeling (with the assistance of W. Duncan and P. Lortie), 'Explanatory Report on the Convention on the International Recovery of Child Support and Other Forms of Family Maintenance', Permanent Bureau of the Hague Conference on Private International Law (2009), 72, para. 356.

[26] Ibid. 73, para. 358.

[27] See Art. 15, 'Free legal assistance for child support applications'.

[28] Art. 15(2) allows states to refuse to provide free legal assistance for certain applications if it is judged that they are 'manifestly unfounded', and Art. 16 allows states to make a formal declaration that some types of child support applications may be subject to a child-centred means test. It is anticipated that only a handful of states will make a declaration in accordance with Art. 16.

the Convention obliges states to provide free legal assistance for these creditor child support applications without subjecting applicants to a means or merits test for the receipt of such legal aid. 'Legal assistance' is defined broadly in the Convention as 'the assistance necessary to enable applicants to know and assert their rights and to ensure that applications are fully and effectively dealt with in the requested State ... The means of providing such assistance may include as necessary legal advice, assistance in bringing a case before an authority, legal representation, and exemption from costs of proceedings.'[29] Accordingly, the vast majority of international child support creditors will be able to apply for the recovery of child support from another country free of charge. Such a system is particularly important in this field of law, as many applicants will be of lesser or modest economic means and may rely upon the child support or other maintenance payments for the fulfilment of basic needs and living expenses.

As contracting states must provide free legal assistance to certain classes of applicants under the Convention, and this will have financial implications, it is anticipated that these obligations may lead to domestic reform within contracting states. It is expected that there may be a move towards employing cheaper, simpler, and more effective procedures for the establishment, modification, and enforcement or recovery of maintenance obligations domestically, such as procedures which do not in general require the assistance of a lawyer and do not involve unwieldy and expensive court proceedings.[30]

Additionally, it is important to note that the Convention's specific provisions on effective access to procedures and free legal assistance are supplemented with a comprehensive Central Authority system in which each contracting state must designate a national body to provide for a range of specified functions in the service of applicants. These functions must, as a rule, be provided at no cost to individuals.[31]

During the course of the negotiations of the Convention, it was considered that providing generous access to justice provisions was

---

[29] Art. 3(c).
[30] The availability of such systems is foreseen in Art. 14(3) of the Convention. National child support and maintenance systems which are considered to be relatively efficient and are of a predominantly administrative rather than court-based character already exist in countries such as Australia and Norway. Discussions of such systems were part of the comparative policy exercise which took place in the course of the background research and negotiations of the 2007 Convention.
[31] See Art. 6, detailing specific functions, and Art. 8, which sets out the costs to be borne by Central Authorities.

crucial to ensuring that the largest possible number of maintenance beneficiaries experience the full benefits of the new treaty. The policy rationale is stated as follows: 'Applicants for maintenance generally have very limited resources, and even small financial barriers may inhibit use by them of the opportunities otherwise provided by the new Convention. The costs for the applicant should not be such as to inhibit the use of, or prevent effective access to, the services and procedures provided by the Convention.'[32]

## Information Technology Features

Evidence of interdisciplinary and pragmatic thinking behind the development and planned implementation of the 2007 Convention can be found in its provisions on, and engagement with, information technology (IT) solutions to modernise the field of international maintenance recovery. The Convention's preamble states that signatories to the Convention seek 'to take advantage of advances in technologies and to create a flexible system which can continue to evolve as needs change and further advances in technology create new opportunities'.[33]

Article 13 of the Convention enshrines a 'medium neutral' standard for the operation of the instrument, which means that the 'medium or means' of communication used in making applications between Central Authorities cannot be challenged by a respondent. This provision was included in order to ensure that the operation of the Convention could benefit from swift electronic communications and electronic (paperless) documentation of applications.

Second, an electronic country profile (the 'eCountry profile') has been developed for the Convention, using a web-based, multilingual electronic form with which states can, in a systematic and accessible way, fulfil the information-sharing obligations enshrined in the treaty.[34] The eCountry profiles of individual contracting states are publically available on the Hague Conference website, which greatly facilitates access to legal information, procedures, and requirements under the Convention for the benefit of individual applicants, lawyers, caseworkers, judges, and others.

Third, the global electronic case management and secure communication system, 'iSupport', should further reinforce the practical operation of

---

[32] Borrás and Degeling, 'Explanatory Report', 73, para. 357.
[33] Para. 4.
[34] In particular under Art. 57.

the 2007 Convention.[35] The iSupport system provides a tailored platform for Central Authorities within states to manage international cases, securely communicate with each other, and collect and process data. If widely used by contracting states,[36] iSupport will add significant efficiencies to the operation of the Convention. It will contribute to a more consistent fulfilment of state obligations under the instrument through the use of tailored software following the text of the Convention,[37] and generally facilitate the rapid and effective cross-border recovery and transfer of maintenance sums for the benefit of children and families relying on such payments.

Thus, beyond the traditional private international law mechanisms found in the 2007 Convention, such as those which standardise an expedited recognition and enforcement procedure for foreign maintenance decisions (i.e. Arts. 23 and 24), the technology solutions developed around the Convention text can, if fully employed, revolutionise the international recovery of maintenance payments. Traditional barriers in this area which have frustrated access to justice and respect for fundamental economic rights will be overcome.[38] Furthermore, these measures will give effect to a ruling of the European Court of Human Rights that national authorities have a positive obligation to assist diligently and in a timely manner with the enforcement of a foreign maintenance decision for the benefit of a creditor.[39]

---

[35] See e.g. 'Development of an International Electronic Case Management and Communication System in Support of the Future Hague Convention on the International Recovery of Child Support', Information Document No. 1, Permanent Bureau of the Hague Conference on Private International Law (June 2006).

[36] Thanks to a substantial grant from the European Union and other states, the iSupport project started as of September 2014, and successive iterations of the system have been launched. For more information see www.hcch.net/en/instruments/conventions/isupport1.

[37] For example, by limiting the range of responses or fields allowed in the case management system (and by guiding users to a certain set of predetermined data fields) based on an authoritative interpretation of the text of the Convention.

[38] It has been noted that a creditor of support attempting to obtain maintenance from a debtor located in a foreign nation may be 'faced with almost insuperable legal obstacles, and the cost involved is such as to discourage most claimants from even attempting to commence proceedings in a foreign country'. See P. Contini, 'The United Nations Convention on the Recovery Abroad of Maintenance', *St. John's Law Review*, 31/1 (1956), 1–48, at 1–2.

[39] See Case No. 7618/05, *Romańczyk* v. *France* [18 November 2010]. The court found a violation of Art. 6(1) of the Convention for the Protection of Human Rights and Fundamental Freedoms, Rome, 4 November 1950, in force 3 September 1953, *ETS* 5; 213 *UNTS* 221.

### Anticipated Economic Benefits and Support for International Economic Rights

By becoming a party to this Convention, contracting states give effect to a clear international obligation under Article 27(4) of the Convention on the Rights of the Child to 'take all appropriate measures to secure the recovery of maintenance for the child from the parents or other persons having financial responsibility for the child . . . In particular, where the person having financial responsibility for the child lives in a State different from that of the child, States Parties shall promote the accession to international agreements.' Article 27(1) and (2) of the Convention on the Rights of the Child, quoted in the preamble of the 2007 Convention, more generally specify a right to 'a standard of living adequate for the child's physical, mental, spiritual, moral and social development', with the primary responsibility of the parent(s) or others responsible for the child to secure, within (financial) abilities, 'the conditions of living necessary for the child's development'.

In addition, the 2007 Convention reinforces a number of obligations enshrined in the United Nations 1966 International Covenant on Economic, Social and Cultural Rights,[40] in particular Article 10(1) and Article 11(1), which address, respectively, obligations of protection and assistance to a family, 'particularly while it is responsible for the care and education of dependent children', and the right of everyone 'to an adequate standard of living for himself and his family, including adequate clothing and housing'.

The Convention thus may support important aspects of one of the two fundamental pillars pertaining to economic, social, and cultural rights of the modern, post-World War II international human rights system. Regular maintenance payments to children, and, indeed, also to single parent families and others, can be a factor in avoiding poverty or insecure economic circumstances. Further, the cross-border transfer of maintenance payments, in particular from economically developed countries to developing countries (for instance, when one parent has relocated abroad to take advantage of employment opportunities), may act as a form of international remittance.[41] It is interesting to note that a number of countries on the Official Development Assistance (ODA) list of the

---

[40] International Covenant on Economic, Social and Cultural Rights, New York, 16 December 1966, in force 3 January 1976, 993 *UNTS* 3.

[41] Benefits of international migrant remittances have been noted to include: stable and counter-cyclical income for a nation; macroeconomic multiplier effects and poverty

OECD[42] were early signers of this Convention (including Albania, Burkina Faso, Bosnia and Herzegovina, and Ukraine).

### Case Example 2: the 1980 Hague Child Abduction Convention

The 1980 Hague Child Abduction Convention seeks primarily to combat international parental child abduction[43] by providing a system of cooperation between Central Authorities designated by states parties to the Convention and a rapid procedure for the return of a child to the country of his or her habitual residence after the child's wrongful removal or retention abroad. The principal objective of the Convention is to protect children from the harmful effects of such wrongful cross-border removals and retentions; an issue of great contemporary relevance given the reality of transnational couples and families. Under Article 11 of the Convention on the Rights of the Child, states parties must 'take measures to combat the illicit transfer and non-return of children abroad' and '[t]o this end ... promote the [accession] to existing [multilateral] agreements'. Article 35 of the Convention on the Rights of the Child also affirms that states parties must 'take all appropriate national, bilateral and multilateral measures to prevent the abduction of, the sale of or traffic in children for any purpose or in any form'. Furthermore, the Hague 1980 Child Abduction Convention reinforces Articles 9(3) and 10(2) of the Convention of the Rights of the Child, relating to a child's right to maintain 'personal relations and direct contact' with both parents, including when parents reside in different states.[44] The 1980 Child

---

reduction in the receiving economy; associations with increased household investments in education, entrepreneurship, and health (areas of high social return); and other benefits. See D. Ratha, 'Leveraging Remittances for Development' *Policy Brief: Program on Migrants, Migration and Development* (Washington: Migration Policy Institute, 2007). There have previously been proposals on the agenda of the Hague Conference to explore generally 'the application of certain private international law techniques to aspects of international migration', including issues of circular or temporary migration which also cover remittances.

[42] See the OECD Development Assistance Committee (DAC) List of ODA recipient states for 2012–2013, available on the OECD DAC web page (www.oecd.org/dac/stats).

[43] The Convention seeks to remedy the wrongful removal or retention of a child in a foreign country in contravention of the custody rights of another person or body, in practice usually a parent (see Art. 3).

[44] In addition to the procedure under the Convention for the return of a child to the jurisdiction of his or her habitual residence, the Convention provides for the arrangement of 'effective exercise of rights of access' in relation to a child in cross-border circumstances (Art. 21).

Abduction Convention is one of the most widely ratified Hague Conventions.[45]

Subsequent to the coming into force of the instrument, a series of Special Commissions have been held to review the practical operation of the Child Abduction Convention, as is common with widely ratified Hague Conventions. Contracting states, scholars, judges, and practitioners have noted a number of challenges with respect to the operation of the Convention. First, states have noted that the 'safe return' of a child to his or her place of habitual residence is important, but can pose some complicated cross-border challenges for judges and other system actors who handle Convention cases, which must be processed expeditiously.[46] Second, academic researchers as well as judges and other practitioners have indicated that domestic and family violence issues were being raised as exceptional defences to the return of a child to the state of his or her habitual residence (namely, under the article 13(1)(b) 'grave risk' defence). The raising of these exceptional defences in this context can involve a number of sensitive and important safety considerations.[47] Some of these operational challenges may be intensified due to changes in the underlying social patterns of families affected in these circumstances. Of particular note, in the majority of countries for which statistical data is currently available, most 'taking parents' have been found to be mothers.[48]

The 2012 Sixth Special Commission held to review the 1980 Child Abduction Convention recommended that a new 'Guide to Good Practice' on the Convention be developed in order to address a more consistent interpretation and application of the Convention's 'grave risk'

---

[45] As at 15 January 2018, this Convention had 98 contracting states (www.hcch.net/en/instruments/conventions/status-table/?cid=24).

[46] See, for instance, Conclusion and Recommendation 1.1.12, 'Ensuring the safe return of children' of the 'Conclusions and Recommendations of the Fifth Meeting of the Special Commission on the practical operation of the 1980 and 1996 Hague Conventions', Hague Conference on Private International Law (2006), reaffirming Recommendation 1.13 of the Fourth Meeting of the Special Commission of 2001.

[47] See e.g. research cited in 'Domestic and Family Violence and the Article 13 "Grave Risk" Exception in the Operation of the Hague Convention of 25 October 1980 on the Civil Aspects of International Child Abduction: A Reflection Paper', Preliminary Document No. 9 for the attention of the Special Commission of June 2011, Hague Conference on Private International Law (May 2011).

[48] N. Lowe, 'A Statistical Analysis of Applications Made in 2008 under the Hague Convention of 25 October 1980 on the Civil Aspects of International Child Abduction—Part I, Global Report', Preliminary Document No. 8 A for the attention of the Special Commission of June 2011 (November 2011), 14.

defence, including issues of domestic and family violence. The Special Commission furthermore recommended that an international 'Working Group composed of judges, Central Authorities [designated under the Convention] and cross-disciplinary experts' be established to this end.[49] The Guide will build upon the conclusions of past Special Commission meetings and existing Guides to Good Practice on the 1980 Child Abduction Convention.[50] The new Guide will also support and assist judges, and other practitioners around the globe, who must deal with complex family matters in cross-border settings, grappling with language barriers and a diversity of legal orders and cultural norms, as well as other practical challenges. While the new Guide to Good Practice will not be considered as binding on states parties to the 1980 Child Abduction Convention, it will be a practical tool that can be widely disseminated internationally, to assist judges and other practitioners in promoting a more consistent application of the Convention, in the interests of children and families.[51]

The work to develop the Guide to Good Practice is inevitably set against a backdrop of evolving human rights norms which have developed since the original negotiations of the 1980 Child Abduction Convention, and in particular international norms concerning violence against women and children.[52] For example, in relation to the United Nations 1979 Convention on the Elimination of All Forms of Discrimination against Women (CEDAW),[53] the Committee on the Elimination of Discrimination against Women's commentary on CEDAW has noted the obligations of states parties to protect women against violence, including violence within the family.[54] The 1993 United

---

[49]  See Conclusion and Recommendation No. 82 of Part II of the Special Commission on the practical operation of the 1980 and 1996 Hague Conventions, Hague Conference on Private International Law (25–31 January 2012). The Recommendation to form the Working Group was subsequently approved by the Council of General Affairs and Policy of the Hague Conference at its annual meeting in April 2012.

[50]  See https://www.hcch.net/en/instruments/conventions/publications1/?dtid=3&cid=24.

[51]  More recent Hague Conventions, such as the 2007 Child Support Convention, contain a 'Uniform Interpretation' provision (Art. 53) that stipulates that in relation to the interpretation of the Convention 'regard shall be had to its international character and to the need to promote uniformity in its application'.

[52]  See Lowe, 'Statistical Analysis', Annex II.

[53]  Convention on the Elimination of All Forms of Discrimination against Women, New York, 18 December 1979, in force 3 September 1981, 1249 *UNTS* 13.

[54]  See General Recommendation No. 12, Eighth Session (1989), and General Recommendation No. 19, Eleventh Session (1992). There are also notable regional instruments in this field, such as the Inter-American Convention on the Prevention,

Nations General Assembly Declaration on the Elimination of Violence against Women (Resolution 48/104) and subsequent declarations and campaigns by United Nations agencies and bodies have further developed international consensus on this topic.[55] The Convention on the Rights of the Child also obliges states parties to protect children from various forms of violence, physical or mental, including violence within the family.[56] Further, a significant 2006 report of an independent expert on violence against children including violence within the family, appointed by the United Nations Secretary-General, delineated the scope and prevalence of violence against children globally. This led to the appointment of a Special Representative of the Secretary-General on Violence against Children.[57]

Another practical tool developed under the auspices of the Hague Conference to improve the operation of the 1980 Child Abduction Convention is the International Hague Network of Judges (IHNJ). The IHNJ is a global network of sitting judges specialised in family matters, currently comprised of 124 judges from 81 countries.[58] This network is a powerful mechanism for the cross-border sharing of professional knowledge and experience on good practices in the operation of 1980 Child Abduction Convention (and other Hague children's Conventions) and, crucially, for the resolution of practical matters in individual cross-border cases involving children by judges engaging in 'direct judicial communications' across national boundaries.[59] The IHNJ

---

Punishment and Eradication of Violence against Women, Belem do Para (Brazil), 9 June 1994, in force 5 March 1995, A-61, and the recent Council of Europe Convention on preventing and combating violence against women and domestic violence, Istanbul, 11 May 2011, *ETS* 210.

[55]  For example, General Assembly resolution 'Elimination of Domestic Violence against Women', *UN Doc.* A/RES/58/147 (22 December 2003), and the campaign of the United Nations Secretary-General, 'UNiTE to End Violence against Women' (http://endviolence.un.org).

[56]  Art. 19.

[57]  'Report of the Independent Expert for the United Nations Study on Violence against Children', *UN Doc.* A/61/299 (29 August 2006), transmitted to the General Assembly of the United Nations by the Secretary-General.

[58]  As of August 2017, see https://assets.hcch.net/docs/18eb8d6c-593b-4996-9c5c-19e4590ac66d.pdf.

[59]  See 'Emerging Rules regarding the Development of the International Hague Network of Judges and Draft General Principles for Judicial Communications, including Commonly Accepted Safeguards for Direct Judicial Communications in Specific Cases, within the Context of the International Hague Network of Judges', Preliminary Document No. 3 A for the attention of the Special Commission of June 2011 on the practical operation of the 1980 Hague Child Abduction Convention and the 1996 Hague Child

is a significant and novel advance in the development of a functioning international legal system in the area of international family law, and responds to the concrete needs of individual children and families who are (increasingly) faced with legal matters which encompass more than one state.[60]

## Case Example 3: Preliminary Work on the Recognition and Enforcement of Foreign Civil Protection Orders

In April 2011 the governing body of the Hague Conference, the Council on General Affairs and Policy of the Hague Conference ('the Council'), added to the Agenda of the Conference 'the topic of the recognition of foreign civil protection orders made, for example, in the context of domestic violence cases'.[61] The Permanent Bureau of the Hague Conference was requested to prepare 'a short note on the subject to assist the Council in deciding whether further work on this subject is warranted'.[62]

At the Sixth Meeting of the Special Commission on the practical operation of the 1980 Child Abduction Convention and the 1996 Child Protection Convention, the Special Commission, in its conclusions and recommendations, welcomed the addition of the recognition and enforcement of foreign protection orders as a topic to the Hague Conference's work agenda. The Special Commission recommended that 'account should be taken of the possible use of such orders in the context of the 1980 Convention'.[63] Accordingly, this new Hague Conference agenda

---

Protection Convention, Permanent Bureau of the Hague Conference on Private International Law (March 2011).

[60] The Hon. Justice D. Baragwanath, 'Who Now Is My Neighbour? Cross-Border Co-Operation of Judges in the Globalised Society' (June 2004) *The Inner Temple*, 22–36. Justice Baragwanath notes that issues of access to justice are of pre-eminent importance in the cross-border context and urges judges to play a constructive role in the globalisation process by actively engaging in procedural and other reforms to respond to internationalised circumstances.

[61] Conclusion and Recommendation No. 23 of the Conclusions and Recommendations of the Council on General Affairs and Policy of the Conference, Hague Conference on Private International Law (5–7 April 2011).

[62] Ibid.

[63] Conclusion and Recommendation No. 43 of Part I of the Sixth Meeting of the Special Commission on the practical operation of the 1980 Hague Child Abduction Convention and the 1996 Hague Child Protection Convention, Hague Conference on Private International Law (1–10 June 2011).

topic revealed 'synergies' with practical experiences gained under the 1980 Child Abduction Convention.

In April 2012, the Permanent Bureau presented Preliminary Document No. 7, 'Recognition and Enforcement of Foreign Civil Protection Orders: a Preliminary Note'[64] to the Council in fulfilment of the previous year's mandate. This document provided comparative information on national legislation in this field, based on available information from a variety of sources. It also presented a description of existing or planned national and regional projects to address the cross-border recognition and enforcement of 'protection measures'.

The terms 'protection order', 'protection measure', or other similar terminologies are used under various national or regional legal instruments, denoting legal regimes which aim to protect victims or potential victims of domestic violence and/or other types of harmful or illegal interpersonal behaviour.[65] Specific types of protection orders under various national legal regimes may include what are known as restraining orders, 'stay away' or no contact orders, barring/eviction orders, various types of preventive or precautionary measures, and other types of civil or criminal injunctions.[66] Legislation on protection orders, whether targeted at victims of domestic violence or more general violence against women and others, stalking, forced marriage, or other types of harmful or criminal behaviour, is used in jurisdictions around the world as a legal tool to protect at-risk persons, seeking to offer a practical remedy to provide safety for individuals, formally backed by the enforcement power of the state.[67]

Preliminary Document No. 7 noted significant contemporary national and regional policy attention to the issue of cross-border recognition and enforcement of protection orders based on a growing awareness of '[t]he ease of international cross-border travel combined with the severe risk to an individual who cannot obtain immediate recognition and enforcement of a foreign protection order'.[68] The Council subsequently

---

[64] Preliminary Document No. 7 for the attention of the Council of April 2012 on General Affairs and Policy of the Conference, Permanent Bureau of the Hague Conference on Private International Law (March 2012).

[65] For example, types of harassment, sexual assault, stalking, and forced marriage.

[66] Prel. Doc. No. 7 (n. 64) gives examples of common protection order legal regimes and variations of these regimes in a variety of jurisdictions.

[67] Prel. Doc. No. 7 (n. 64) found protection order legislation in *at least* eighty-six states worldwide (see 7 and Annex I).

[68] 'Foreign Protection Orders: Joint ULCC/CCSO Working Group Report with Draft Act and Commentaries', Uniform Law Conference of Canada, Civil Law Section, Winnipeg, Manitoba (7–11 August 2011), 3, quoted in Prel. Doc. No. 7 (n. 64), 5.

instructed the Permanent Bureau to: (a) circulate a questionnaire to Hague Conference Members in order to assess the need and feasibility of an international instrument in this area and to obtain further information on existing legislation;[69] and (b) to convene an international experts' group, resources allowing, to assist in further exploration of the topic in order to report to the Council in April of 2014.[70] In 2015 the Council on General Affairs and Policy (Conclusion and Recommendation No. 6) mandated the Permanent Bureau to continue exploratory work on this topic, again subject to available resources.[71]

The work of the Hague Conference on protection orders is set against the backdrop of current international and national efforts to elaborate and consolidate human rights norms in the field of violence against women and children in particular, as referenced above under case example 2. Expert groups convened under the auspices of the United Nations have developed handbooks on legislation addressing violence against women, including recommendations to ensure that protection orders are available, noting that: '[p]rotection orders are among the most effective legal remedies available to complainants/survivors of violence against women... They were first introduced in the United States in the mid-1970s, offering an immediate remedy to complainants/survivors of domestic violence by authorizing courts to order an offender out of the home.'[72] The United Nations General Assembly has also adopted 'Updated Model Strategies and Practical Measures on the Elimination of Violence against Women in the Field of Crime Prevention and Criminal Justice', which reference the use and proper implementation of protection orders.[73] In addition, the Council of Europe Convention on Preventing and Combating Violence

---

[69] Conclusion and Recommendation No. 22 of the Conclusions and Recommendations of the Council on General Affairs and Policy of the Conference (17–20 April 2012). 'Questionnaire on the Recognition and Enforcement of Foreign Civil Protection Orders: Summary of Member Responses and Possible Ways Forward', Preliminary Document No. 4 B for the attention of the Council of April 2013 on General Affairs and Policy of the Conference, Permanent Bureau of the Hague Conference on Private International Law (March 2013).

[70] Conclusion and Recommendation No. 9 of the Conclusions and Recommendations of the Council on General Affairs and Policy of the Conference (9–11 April 2013).

[71] See https://www.hcch.net/en/projects/legislative-projects/protection-orders.

[72] See 'Handbook for Legislation on Violence against Women', Division for the Advancement of Women, Department of Economic and Social Affairs, United Nations, New York (2010), 44-50, citing international norms set out by the Committee on the Elimination of Discrimination against Women, General Recommendation No. 19 (1992) on violence against women (at para. 9).

[73] UN Doc. A/Res/65/228, adopted December 2010, paras 15 (h), 16 (h), and 18 (f) and (h).

against Women and Domestic Violence,[74] a comprehensive human rights instrument in this field, requires state parties to 'ensure that appropriate restraining orders or protection orders are available to victims of all forms of violence covered by the scope of [the] Convention'.[75]

Members of the Hague Conference have not yet decided whether or not to proceed with a new international Convention or other international work in this field. However the subject matter, as exemplified by the international and regional work of other organisations, responds to the very real safety needs of vulnerable individuals, in line with broader articulated human rights entitlements. Furthermore, the national legislation examined in this area to date reveals governmental efforts aimed at the fine-tuning of these legal regimes and their better enforcement, enabling individuals subject to forms of interpersonal violence or harmful behaviour perpetrated by other private individuals to receive the effective protection of the state.[76] If further work is undertaken at the Hague Conference in this area, it is hoped that the innovations pioneered at the national level in the field of protection orders will also be reflected at the international level (as has happened in the field of child support).

## A Response to General Critiques of International Law

Contemporary critiques of international law, as exemplified by the writings of a range of critical scholars, are numerous.[77] With respect to international human rights law, for instance, various avenues of modern criticism have been identified.[78] These include: the over-reliance of

---

[74] See n. 54.

[75] At Art. 53(1). See also Arts. 52 and 62, which also reference particular obligations with respect to protection orders.

[76] See national legal regimes and law reform noted in Prel. Doc. No. 7 (n. 64) and in Prel. Doc. No. 4 B (n. 69).

[77] See, e.g. M. Koskenniemi, *The Politics of International Law* (Oxford: Hart, 2011); M. Koskenniemi, 'The Politics of International Law: 20 Years Later', *European Journal of International Law*, 20/1 (2009), 7–19; Koskenniemi, *Apology to Utopia*; A. Anghie, *Imperialism, Sovereignty, and the Making of International Law* (Cambridge: Cambridge University Press, 2005); A. Anghie et al. eds, *The Third World and International Order: Law, Politics and Globalization* (Leiden: Martinus Nijhoff, 2003); D. Kennedy, 'International Human Rights Movement: Part of the Problem?' *Harvard Human Rights Journal*, 15 (2002), 101–26; D. Kennedy, *The Dark Side of Virtue: Reassessing International Humanitarianism* (Princeton, NJ: Princeton University Press, 2004).

[78] See, for example F. Mégret, 'Where Does the Critique of International Human Rights Stand? An Exploration of 18 Vignettes', Working Paper Series, Social Science Research Network (November 24, 2010). http://ssrn.com/abstract=1714484 or http://dx.doi.org/10.2139/ssrn.1714484

international law and/or international lawyers on formalistic rules to the detriment of appropriate interdisciplinary engagement;[79] excessive 'managerialism' in international institutions and the flourishing of opaque technical vocabularies in fields of international law;[80] the indeterminacy of international legal norms, including human rights as a body of law;[81] critiques of a dominant Eurocentrism in international law;[82] and finally, a liberal, normative tendency that sets discourses on the rule of law above serious engagement with politics.[83]

The three case examples introduced above provide interesting material for countering such criticisms. With respect to the interaction of international law with other disciplines, the three examples reveal a significant engagement with the theory and practice of other disciplines and technologies. The 2007 Hague Child Support Convention owes many of its novel features to the involvement of governmental officials who had extensive first-hand practical experience in this field (or who drew upon the knowledge of others with such expertise). The use of IT in support of this Hague Convention similarly adds to its functionality and effectiveness. The background to the planned work in support of the 1980 Child Abduction Convention also drew on multidisciplinary research, and the Working Group to develop a new 'Guide to Good Practice' was specifically mandated to include cross-disciplinary experts.[84]

Second, in the above-mentioned three case examples, and in particular by way of the establishment of dedicated Central Authority systems in the service of the Hague Conventions (as described above in relation to the 2007 Child Support Convention in case example 1), one can appreciate the practical value of technically specialised public officials who fulfil a functional role, often directly interacting with individuals who are confronted with challenging cross-border legal issues. A number of Hague Conventions in effect create an international administrative cooperation system, with specified obligations of these Central Authorities to assist both each other and individuals in the operation of the Hague Conventions, thereby facilitating individuals' access to justice across

---

[79] See Koskenniemi, *Politics of International Law* (2011), 32.
[80] Koskenniemi, 'Politics of International Law: 20 Years Later',15 and *seq.*
[81] Ibid.; Koskenniemi, *Politics of International Law* (2011).
[82] See, for example, M. Koskenniemi, 'Histories of International Law: Dealing with Eurocentrism', *Zeitschrift des Max-Plank-Instituts für Europäische Rechtsgeschichte*, 19 (2011), 152–76.
[83] See Koskenniemi, *Politics of International Law* (2011).
[84] See cross-disciplinary research cited in Prel. Doc. 9 (n. 47).

borders.[85] Contact details for all Central Authorities are publically listed on the website of the Hague Conference (and usually on national websites), and states have an obligation to keep this information current.[86]

In these administrative cooperation systems are networks of specialised national professionals from various governmental bodies who negotiate, operate, and review Hague Conventions.[87] In addition to the IHNJ described as part of case example 2, there are processes at work that confirm some of the observations that have been made by Anne-Marie Slaughter with respect to a paradigm shift in the traditional understanding of international politics and international relations.[88] According to Slaughter, decentralised and practically focused intergovernmental networks are adding an extremely important (if largely underappreciated) dimension to global problem-solving, beyond rigid traditional definitions of sovereignty and the formalistic practices of supranational authorities, which have traditionally been the hallmark of international law.[89] Slaughter has further noted the increasing reality and practical effectiveness of transnational networks of public officials and judges (among others), representing 'disaggregated state institutions' that 'translate paper principles into individual and organizational action', all in the service of better global governance.[90] She has noted that:

> A new world order is emerging, with less fanfare but more substance than either the liberal internationalist or new medievalist visions. The state is not disappearing, it is disaggregating into its separate, functionally distinct parts. These parts – courts, regulatory agencies, executives, and even legislatures – are networking with their counterparts abroad, creating a dense web of relations that constitutes a new, transgovernmental order.[91]

---

[85] See, for example, Chapter II of the 1980 Convention, Chapter V of the 2000 Convention, and Chapter III of the 2007 Child Support Convention.
[86] See the Hague Conference website, www.hcch.net, under 'Authorities'.
[87] The Hague Conference practices review and monitoring of its Conventions through, among other things, 'Special Commission' meetings of contracting states generally held every four to five years to discuss one or more specific Conventions, other post-Convention services, and the provision of technical assistance to individual states, which further supports the fine-tuning and realisation of the goals of the Conventions.
[88] See A. Slaughter, 'The Real New World Order', *Foreign Affairs*, 76/5 (1997), 183–97; A. Slaughter, *A New World Order* (Princeton, NJ, and Oxford: Princeton University Press, 2004).
[89] Slaughter, 'Real New World Order', 95–197.
[90] Slaughter, *New World Order*, 271.
[91] Slaughter, 'Real New World Order', 184.

In response to critiques of indeterminacy in international law, one can in fact find examples of a number of specified, determinant procedures within the Hague Conventions that are to be replicated in the national law of contracting states. Examples relate to the recognition and enforcement provisions for foreign judgments in Articles 23 and 24 of the 2007 Child Support Convention, or the return procedures when a child is wrongfully removed or retained abroad under Chapter III of the 1980 Child Abduction Convention. More generally, Hague Conventions, as instruments regulating private international law matters, include provisions that interlink particular national private law systems. Hague Conventions may designate the law applicable to various issues (i.e. specific and determinant national or foreign law)[92] and/or enable the recognition and enforcement of specific foreign decisions in national courts.[93] Further, the concrete provisions contained in these Conventions are either implicitly or explicitly framed by, and/or pushed forward by, modern human rights developments, which leads to a tangible expression of these norms in the course of the operation of the Hague Conventions.

Indeterminacy is also addressed through the procedures found in Hague Conventions for monitoring and review of the practical operation of widely ratified Conventions. Monitoring and review can add considerable focus and detail to shared understandings of specific provisions of the Hague Conventions.[94] Additionally, as with the case of the 2007 Child Support Convention, the elaboration of a new treaty kept in mind older incarnations of related instruments,[95] adding more detail and specificity to provisions or concepts of the older instruments that were considered to be too vague to provide adequate guidance, for example concerning the extent of reciprocal obligations or with respect to important operational matters.[96]

---

[92] See e.g. Chapter III of the Hague 2000 Convention.

[93] See e.g. Chapter IV of the Hague 2000 Convention and Chapter V of the 2007 Hague Child Support Convention.

[94] E.g. noting that in the context of 'the protection' of children under the Hague 1980 and 1996 Conventions, 'regard should be given to the impact on a child of violence committed by one parent against the other', in line with modern human rights norms (under the CRC, Art. 19). Conclusion and Recommendation No. 42 of Part I of the Sixth Meeting of the Special Commission on the practical operation of the 1980 Hague Child Abduction Convention and the 1996 Hague Child Protection Convention, Hague Conference on Private International Law (1–10 June 2011).

[95] See n. 16.

[96] See n. 17.

Critiques of pervasive Eurocentrism are not unique to the field of international law, but concern a range of academic fields and practices. Modern global political life and international legal inquiry should include, logically, efforts to 'unpack' a global historical record marked by colonialism.[97] However, while it is valid to take this historical context into account in the further development and refinement of international law, it is important not to underestimate the opportunities for sincere intercultural dialogue at a number of international venues. A wide range of countries participated in the negotiations of the 2007 Child Support Convention and ratified the 1980 Child Abduction Convention, not to mention the 148 states that were party to one or more Hague Conventions at the end of 2015.[98] The diverse representation of states in these negotiations illustrates the potential of truly international legal dialogue and exchange. The Hague Conference itself is indeed emblematic of the history of international law. Beginning in 1893 as an ad hoc conference of thirteen European states,[99] in 2018 it has 83 members (82 states and one regional economic integration organisation, the European Union) from every region of the world, with regional offices in both Latin America and in Asia. As early as 1980, the Hague Conference formally 'granted that non-Member States may participate in the work of the Conference where, by virtue of the subject treated, it is felt that such participation is necessary'.[100]

Traces of progressive intercultural awareness and dialogue on the Hague Conventions and other instruments can also be seen, for example, with the inclusion of the *kafala* legal regime in the 1996 Child Protection Convention[101] and in the ongoing 'Malta Process' with a range of states with or influenced by Islamic legal traditions in the context of the various Hague children's Conventions.[102] Accordingly, the approach of the

---

[97] See Koskenniemi, 'Dealing with Eurocentrism'. Koskenniemi noted the important work of a number of modern 'postcolonial' and other critical authors working to delineate and unpack the historical development of international law and strategies to overcome historical biases.

[98] Hague Conference on Private International Law, *Annual Report 2015* (The Hague, 2016), Foreword. https://assets.hcch.net/docs/9af8b39d-b699-4249-a997-41c9fdbb7a4d.pdf

[99] Austro-Hungary, Belgium, Denmark, France, Germany, Italy, Luxembourg, Netherlands, Portugal, Romania, Russia, Spain, and Switzerland.

[100] 'Final Act of the Fourteenth Session', *Actes et documents de la quatorzième session*, Proceedings of the Hague Conference on Private International Law, i (1980),1–63.

[101] See Arts. 3 and 33.

[102] See 'Malta Process' at www.hcch.net/en/publications-and-studies/details4/?pid=5214.

Hague Conference aims to be 'a melting pot of legal traditions' and to build bridges between disparate legal systems.[103]

Finally, as to the suggestion that international law by and large avoids the political, if one accepts the twentieth-century adage that 'the personal is political', the constructive nature of the Hague Conventions in supporting tangible individual rights of historically disenfranchised groups (and in particular women and children), who have been traditionally overlooked by policymakers, is not insignificant.[104] As shown in the above three case examples, the Hague Conventions and projects have sought to address the legal and very practical needs of individuals, for example, to collect child support across international borders, to resolve cross-border child custody issues and disputes over access, and to protect certain vulnerable individuals from interpersonal violence when moving between countries. In a range of the Hague Conventions and projects described, one can see the crystallisation of progressive dialogues concerning fundamental human rights, which have taken place at both the national and international levels.

In relation to case example 3, civil society and grassroots women's organisations in individual countries have played a crucial role in the development and progressive refinement of protection orders as a preventive tool in circumstances of domestic violence in particular. In relation to case example 1, significant national policy dialogues in the area of the recovery of child support for the benefit of children and single parent families have preceded recent developments at the international level. Political processes played out at various levels of government have been integral to policy development in a number of legal fields addressed by Hague Conventions or projects.

## A Greater Focus on the Individual in International Law

Public international law, in its classical incarnation, has been exemplified by a system that has focused 'exclusively on inter-state relations'.[105] Critiques of international law have sometimes focused on a sceptical analysis of such a system, in which nation states jockey for relative

---

[103] See www.hcch.net/en/about.
[104] All three case examples prominently evidence an awareness of the specific needs of these groups, within the context of human rights developments arising principally in the latter half of the twentieth century, as described above.
[105] K. Parlett, *The Individual in the International Legal System: Continuity and Change in International Law* (Cambridge: Cambridge University Press, 2011), 343.

power among themselves, as the sole bearers of international legal prerogative.[106]

However, this classical system of international law has evolved in the course of the twentieth and early twenty-first centuries to become 'a system of law which covers a wider range of entities, including individuals', in which individuals, rather than being considered mere objects, are allocated a certain measure of status and capacity under international law.[107] Rights and obligations granted to individuals under international law, however, remain attenuated and lopsided in contrast to the privileges accorded to states as the main actors in the international legal order.[108] Indeed, in the case of Hague Conventions, individuals are not afforded direct standing to sue states for non-compliance with their treaty obligations under the Conventions.[109]

However, the case examples above of Hague Conventions and other Hague Conference work arguably pave the way for more progressive incarnations of the individual as an actor and/or subject in the international legal order. Under a range of modern Hague Conventions, private individuals have access to tailored legal procedures and/or cross-border administrative cooperation systems enshrined in instruments of classical public international law. The very favourable access to justice provisions of the Hague 2007 Child Support Convention offer a particularly striking

---

[106] See Koskenniemi, *Politics of International Law* (2011).

[107] Parlett, *The Individual*, 343. See also A. Cassesse, *International Law* (2nd edn, Oxford: Oxford University Press, 2005), 142–50.This shift has been noted in particular by those pursuing international claims via the classical mechanisms of state-based diplomatic protection of individuals, and later through more direct individual rights claims against states established by treaty. The latter are particularly manifest in international humanitarian law, international criminal law, and international human rights law.

[108] Cassesse, *International Law*, 150.

[109] States may raise a claim at the International Court of Justice (ICJ) against another state in relation to a Hague Convention, although this is an option very rarely exercised. In practice, Hague Conventions are subject to a system of peer review, monitoring, and discussion for better compliance with obligations under the Conventions. Such peer review may be particularly detailed due to many of the reciprocal operational obligations states have under Hague Conventions that are necessary for the Conventions to be functional. Individuals affected by the Conventions may also be able to petition a regional human rights court, such as the European Court of Human Rights, for review of aspects of operation of a Convention domestically. For a description of the relationship between the ICJ and private international law, and suggestions for further developments, see H. van Loon and S. De Dycker, 'The Role of the International Court of Justice in the Development of Private International Law', in *Preadviezen, Mededelingen van de Koninklijke Nederlandse Vereniging voor International Recht (140): One Century Peace Palace, from Past to Present* (The Hague: TMC Asser, 2013), 73–119.

example in this respect, revealing the power of a 'remote' international instrument (negotiated within the framework of traditional international diplomatic and legal norms) to reach the recipients of international child support or other family maintenance and to effect concrete material change in the living circumstances of these individuals.[110] Interestingly, it was suggested in a 2012 International Court of Justice decision (albeit in a dissenting opinion) that the principle of an individual's right of access to justice might properly form part of the *jus cogens* of international law.[111] The 2007 Child Support Convention is an interesting example of how strong principles of access to justice can be enshrined in an international legal instrument.[112]

Finally, it has been noted that the 'international legal system has experienced a structural transition [towards the greater role or visibility of the individual] as a result of the need to manage and address practical problems rather than resulting from any deliberate attempt to effect a structural transformation'.[113] The Hague Conventions, which are creations of classical public international law, respond to practical cross-border legal problems that are in need of a solution. The Conventions furthermore bring into focus the needs of individuals or distinctive groups of individuals (e.g. the needs of children, women, parents, families, certain adults with disabilities, and others caught in cross-border circumstances), forming part of the evolving story of individuals gaining greater ground as participants in international legal processes.[114]

## Conclusion

As briefly illustrated by the above case examples, potential and existing Hague Conventions are international legal instruments that primarily address the private international law or national private law sphere. These

---

[110] Indeed, in the course of negotiations for the 2007 Convention, there was concern among some negotiators that the very generous international legal assistance provisions of the new Convention would be more favourable than those already available for domestic maintenance creditors.

[111] *Jurisdictional Immunities of the State (Germany v. Italy: Greece Intervening)* (Judgment) [2012] ICJ General List No. 143. See the dissenting Opinion of Judge Cançado Trindade, at para. 214 et seq.

[112] As mentioned, see also the 1980 Hague Convention on International Access to Justice (n. 24).

[113] Parlett, *The Individual*, 367.

[114] See e.g. R. Higgins, *Problems and Process: International Law and How We Use It* (Oxford: Oxford University Press, 1994).

Conventions seek to provide concrete legal remedies in international or cross-border circumstances for private persons whose needs would otherwise be caught between two or more systems of national private law. As evident in the case examples, a number of modern Hague Conventions address subjects who have traditionally not had optimal access to national legal systems (for example, women, children, and persons with disabilities), let alone been recognised as subjects under international law. Specifically addressing the needs of such individual actors is far from what have been criticised as the classical obsessions of sovereign entities acting on the international legal and political stage, under the broad, general categories of 'honour' or 'vital interest',[115] or in relation to more tangible topics such as the international use of force by states, international boundary disputes,[116] or humanitarian intervention.[117]

As noted in the case examples, a number of Hague Conventions also give effect to or are framed by well-accepted norms found in comprehensive human rights treaties, potentially indicating a sort of 'cascade effect' caused by the putative 'human rights revolution'.[118] In the negotiation and operation of the Conventions, overarching human rights norms can be seen woven into or at least reflected in the technical private international law and international cooperation systems embodied in the Hague Conventions.[119] Also, as new Hague Conventions are negotiated,

---

[115] See Chapter 2 of this book, in which M. Koskeniemmi discusses the work of Hans Morgenthau.

[116] See, for example, the territorial disputes of sovereign states discussed by Koskenniemi in *Politics of International Law* (2011).

[117] Of course, international humanitarian intervention, and the Responsibility to Protect (RtoP) doctrine, have as their stated theoretical underpinnings the respect for individual human rights. Whether or not the doctrine is deployed 'apologetically' for traditional balance of power/state interest purposes is a matter of analysis (and controversy) in each distinctive case. See, for example, Chapter 7 by Kersten in this book.

[118] As e.g. articulated in M. Ignatieff, *The Rights Revolution* (Toronto: House of Anansi, 2007).

[119] Indeed, such patterns at the international level are supported by trends seen at the national level. Recent theoretical discussions and court practices in relation to what has been termed the 'horizontal effect' of fundamental rights, when national constitutional and regional or international human rights norms interpenetrate and substantially influence the national private law sphere, also show the permeation of a culture of fundamental rights in private law systems. See e.g. G. Brüggemeier, A. Colombi Ciacchi, and G. Comandé, eds, *Fundamental Rights and Private Law in the European Union* (Cambridge: Cambridge University Press, 2010) and also O. Cherednychenko, 'Fundamental Rights and Private Law: A Relationship of Subordination or Complementarity?' *Utrecht Law Review*, 3/2 (2007), 1–25.

an opportunity is presented for a comparative policy exercise among individual states, which may lead to important domestic private law reforms.[120] Understandings of existing Conventions can be periodically refreshed and calibrated in order to ensure that their operation is adapted to an evolving global legal landscape, shaped by evolutions in human rights thinking and sociological shifts.[121] Such processes can be argued to be in contrast with noted trends of fragmentation in international law,[122] and rather may suggest meaningful convergences in parts of the international legal order. If well-designed and subsequently well-implemented, with sufficient monitoring and review, the Hague Conventions can be seen as helpful vehicles to actualise relevant aspects of the global *acquis* of human rights law.

Of course, one could also argue that the area of private international law, as reflected in Hague Conventions, is unique, representing an interface between more developed national legal orders and the (less-developed) international legal order. Although the field of private international law is indeed a unique area, scholars have argued that a conceptual bridge should be built between the fields of private and public international law to transcend 'outdated norms' that tend to sharply divide the fields.[123] Accordingly, it is argued that private international law should be regarded as part of a more generalised 'law of nations' encompassing the spheres of both public and private international law.[124]

[120] For example, national law reforms to allow for legal regimes relating to 'durable powers of attorney' for individuals to plan their representation in advance of future potential incapacity were catalysed by negotiations and ratifications of the 2000 Protection of Adults Convention. Under the 2007 Child Support Convention, as mentioned above, it is anticipated that contracting states may reform their domestic family maintenance systems in connection with joining the Convention.

[121] See e.g. case example 2 in this chapter.

[122] See M. Koskenniemi, 'Fragmentation of International Law: Difficulties Arising from the Diversification and Expansion of International Law', Report of the Study Group of the International Law Commission (13 April 2006), *UN Doc.* A/CN.4/L.682.

[123] A. Mills, *The Confluence of Public and Private International Law: Justice, Pluralism and Subsidiarity in the International Constitutional Ordering of Private Law* (Cambridge: Cambridge University Press, 2009), 2. Private international law, according to Mills, has traditionally been conceived of as a concern of national legal systems, addressing 'issues of jurisdiction, applicable law and the recognition and enforcement of foreign judgments in international private law disputes before national courts' (at 1).

[124] Ibid. 28. Mills noted: '[t]he sharp distinction between the public and the private in international legal theory does not accurately reflect the real character of these subjects – it does not correspond with a clear separation in their effects, their social products, or their practice. Public and private international law are increasingly facing the same

Regardless of one's position in these theoretical debates, the work of the Hague Conference also reveals avenues for the progressive development and refinement of international law emanating from one of the oldest intergovernmental organisations in the world.[125] It may illustrate ways that international law in various areas can follow a certain path of maturation over the course of decades and over the course of negotiation of successive instruments in a given field,[126] systematically drawing upon legal innovations and praiseworthy aspects of established legal regimes at the national and international levels.[127]

While this chapter has sought to point to positive trends and opportunities, there is of course much long-term work that must be sustained at the Hague Conference and on Hague Conventions if trends are to continue, and to be consolidated and developed further. The range of Conventions and projects depends on intensive, continuous interstate collaboration among an array of professionals and agencies working in the relevant fields for the progressive refinement and realisation of global policy aims. Hague Conventions, as instruments of public international law, are also challenged by some of the traditional problems associated with international law: states must go through individual lengthy ratification or accession processes to join the Conventions; 'compulsory adjudication and enforcement procedures' are not complete;[128] adequate, sustainable funding for the work associated with the Conventions is often difficult to secure;[129] and a range of other practical

problems and issues – reconciling the traditional role and impact of the state with the legalization of the international system, and balancing universal individual rights against the recognition of diverse cultures, under the shadow of globalization' and 'serving a public constitutional function' (at 2 and 309).

[125] The Hague Conference was established in 1893, with a first meeting before the two Hague Peace Conferences of 1899 and 1907, and well before the establishment of the League of Nations and the United Nations.

[126] E.g. in the maintenance field (see n. 17).

[127] The Statute of the International Court of Justice, of course, includes as one of the sources of international law 'the general principles of law recognized by civilized nations' (Art. 38(1)(c)). This clearly notes the pathway from established, salutary domestic law as influential on the international plane.

[128] See Koskenniemi, *Politics of International Law* (2011), 9. See also the suggestions for future improvement by van Loon and De Dycker, 'Role of the International Court of Justice', 118–19.

[129] With respect to the implementation and operation of Conventions, technical assistance to individual states (particularly developing nations) and the securing of adequate funding for the same remain very important issues. The Permanent Bureau regularly receives many more requests for technical assistance in relation to Hague Conventions than it is able to fulfil with current resources.

issues. Furthermore, the operation of the Conventions is only as robust as the national systems of state parties. If a national legal system is not functioning well or optimally for various reasons, the Conventions will not realise their aims.[130]

There is still much work to be done in the field of international law generally, and many critiques of international law are valid and should be used as a source of learning. However, criticism should also be accompanied by types of systematic analysis that is then linked to concrete problem-solving efforts and coordinated action. Criticism can become a self-fulfilling prophecy if a certain *status quo* is presumed and there is not engagement with the difficult work of pushing the substance and conditions of international law forward.

The progress of international law will only come about after sustained and painstaking work. Those involved in the 100 days of intense negotiation and drafting of the 2007 Child Support Convention, for example, describe the process as particularly noteworthy for its gruelling and precarious nature, as is undoubtedly the case for much successful treaty negotiation. The challenging work to further develop concrete international legal norms, procedures, and enforcement mechanisms that can meaningfully transcend 'politics' may also involve challenging engagements with forces that might be termed 'political' by legal professionals and other experts involved in this process, in the interests of establishing a more coherent international legal order.[131]

The post-World War II international legal and international human rights 'project' can be considered utopian in the sense that it is extremely ambitious.[132] Because this is the case, efforts to build the international

---

[130] For example, the Hague Conference has often worked with UNICEF in connection with various Hague children's Conventions in order that very general and fundamental child protection principles and systems are established before the Hague children's Conventions are implemented.

[131] See n. 12 and n. 14.

[132] If one takes a step back, the modern human rights project, exemplified by post-World War II documents arising from the United Nations system (e.g. the 1948 Universal Declaration of Human Rights and the subsequent two binding Covenants), is truly astounding in its scope and vision. The declared human rights are both universal, i.e. embracing the entire human race, and very particular, i.e. they are applicable to each individual as the intended beneficiary of these rights, and there are a range of discrete (albeit often interdependent) rights that apply to each individual. Such a broadly ambitious and particularised project embracing all of humanity, by its nature, must follow an incremental path towards the achievement of the stated goal of universal respect for human rights. Further innovations, likely far beyond those witnessed to date, will be necessary to achieve the aims of the modern human rights project.

legal system must be made over the long term, and will inevitably involve a multitude of challenges and disheartening reversals. What is needed is 'less fanfare and more substance',[133] with a focus on the difficult work of institution-building and proper international institutional governance, ensuring bureaucratic and technocratic effectiveness and relevance, serious and sustained work on effective and innovative enforcement mechanisms in relation to international law, and conscious efforts by international legal professionals to transcend colonial dynamics, among other aspects, in ways that respond to the important critiques that have been levelled. Such work is often not glamorous. However, with sound leadership and vision, there is no doubt that there can be further meaningful and practical advances in the building of a more functional global justice and a more effective system of international law. If we are to be fair, such efforts may have to follow a parallel path to the difficult (and often long) processes followed in developing national legal systems that exhibit something akin to an actual 'rule of law'. These efforts are ongoing, and, once established, the implementation of measures requires constant vigilance.[134] As we continue along this path, we can recall the words attributed to Tobias Asser, founder of the Hague Conference, who was a noted pragmatist and idealist: '*avec patience et courage*'.[135]

[133] See n. 91.

[134] For this reason, contemporary critiques of international law could be seen as premature if one looks to the incremental progress of national legal systems over centuries, for example the legal/constitutional 'innovations' starting with early versions of the Magna Carta in the early thirteenth century, its subsequent iterations and re-interpretations, and its more general influence across centuries to inspire or serve as a symbol for modern constitutional protections in the United Kingdom and in other legal systems throughout the world. However, given modern advancements in learning and technology, contemporary progress in the international legal order should theoretically be much more quickly achievable.

[135] G.J.W. Steenhoff, *Avec patience et courage (T.M.C. Asser): A History of the Foundation of the Hague Conference on Private International Law* (Den Haag: Ministry of Justice of the Netherlands, 1993).

# 6

# Current Developments in the Fight against Corruption

ABIOLA MAKINWA

## Introduction

The last two decades have witnessed the emergence of global rules criminalising corruption in international business transactions.[1] Also emerging is a global model of anti-corruption enforcement that encourages private-public collaboration.[2] This paper examines these developments in the light of Koskenniemi's analysis of politics and international society in relation to international law.[3] Does the international framework of rules criminalising business corruption and the sanctioning processes for international corruption offences represent the realisation of an ideal of international justice or are these developments simply the disappointing result of an interplay between economic power and politics?

Koskenniemi cautions against overreaching in any attempt to give a response. He speaks of a gap that represents the 'space of the politics of international law within which different actors and institutions try to speak in the voice of all, and then come to be seen, or are made to appear, as merely representatives of particular interests as biased as their rivals'.[4] Koskenniemi's writings suggest that sector-specific solutions, such as the solutions emerging in the fight against business corruption, must be viewed critically. This does not lessen the veracity of such sector-specific solutions, but rather emphasises the fact that a particular sector's response may have no natural link to the responses of other sectors.

---

[1] A. Makinwa, 'The Rules Regulating Transnational Bribery: Achieving a Common Standard?', *International Business Law Journal*, 1 (2007), 7–39.

[2] A. Makinwa, 'Good Governance: Negotiated Settlements for FCPA Violations as a Model', *Applied Research Today*, 3 (2013), 108–20.

[3] M. Koskenniemi, 'The Politics of International Law', *European Journal of International Law*, 1 (1990), 4–32, and 'The Politics of International Law: 20 Years Later', *European Journal of International Law*, 20/1 (2009), 7–19.

[4] M. Koskenniemi, 'International Community: From Dante to Vattel', in V. Chetail and P. Haggenmacher, eds, *Vattel's International Law in a XXIst Century Perspective* [*Le droit international de Vattel vu du XXIe siècle*] (Nijhoff, 2011), 52.

As a unique response to the political currents that give rise to it, each sectoral response contributes to the complexity and fragmentation of international law. Strategic awareness of the interplay of law and politics provides useful insights into the development of anti-corruption laws and policies on a global stage.

### Bridging the Impunity Gap – Developing a Common Rule

Corruption is universally condemned in most national laws and cultures.[5] However, until relatively recently a major obstacle to developing a common global strategy to the problem of corruption was the lack of agreement on a common definition of what constitutes corruption. Corruption has been described as having a 'multitude of faces',[6] and as being 'limitless' in its scope.[7] Corruption is an 'umbrella term' that covers a varied spectrum of activities.[8] In addition to this, corruption is a value-rich, culturally complex phenomenon that interacts with different standards and values. One person's corruption is another person's gift.[9] The environment of international business is culturally complex. Despite the legal prohibitions of bribery in commercial activity, until quite recently bribery was accepted as an inevitable fact of doing business, and was even tax deductible in many countries.[10] The absence of one unifying and

---

[5] P. Nichols, 'Outlawing Transnational Bribery through the World Trade Organization', *Law and Policy in International Business*, 28/2 (1997), 305–81 at 318–22.

[6] E. Campos and S. Pradham, 'Introduction, Tackling a Social Pandemic', in E. Campos and S. Pradham, eds, *The Many Faces of Corruption: Tracking Vulnerabilities at the Sector Level* (World Bank, 2007), 1–25 at 9.

[7] Elliott pointed out that 'corruption involves many types of crimes. The extent to which people abuse their position for personal gains is limitless'. 'Corruption as an International Policy Problem: Overview and Recommendations', in K. Elliott, ed., *Corruption and the Global Economy* (Washington, DC: Institute for International Economics, 1996), 177.

[8] Corruption includes grand corruption, petty corruption, bribery, embezzlement, theft and fraud, extortion, abuse of a discretionary power, conduct creating or exploiting conflicting interests, and improper political contributions. See *UN Handbook on Practical Anti-Corruption Measures for Prosecutors and Investigators* (Vienna: UNODC, 2004) 23–4.

[9] S. Rose-Ackerman, *Corruption and Government: Causes, Consequences and Reform* (Cambridge: Cambridge University Press, 1999), 5.

[10] In response to this practice, the OECD passed the Recommendation on the Tax Deductibility of Bribes to Foreign Public Officials, which calls on member countries that allowed the tax deductibility of bribes to foreign public officials to reconsider. See OECD 'Recommendation on the Tax Deductibility of Bribes to Foreign Public Officials' C(96)27/FINAL (adopted by the Council on 11 April 1996). www.oecd.org/ctp/crime/oecdrecommendationonthetaxdeductibilityofbribestoforeignpublicofficials.htm

global rule condemning corruption in international business meant that there was no generally accepted baseline of legality to demarcate illegal corrupt activity from accepted business practice.

Yet, corruption in international business can be regarded as a threat to the stability of the global market. An orderly market is threatened when states act according to their own rules and interpretations. It is also threatened when there is a lack of effective enforcement of anti-corruption rules. The absence of a single standard of enforcement results in unequal treatment of competitors. It also encourages the proliferation of unethical business practices in a form of pragmatism that asserts: 'if you can't beat them, join them'. Avoiding the negative effect of corrupt practices on society requires binding, enforceable rules that generate a harmonising effect. Simply put, global markets need global governance. To overcome the impunity caused by diverse rules and inconsistent enforcement, the fight against corruption in the de-territorialised space of global contracting requires a common legal regime. However, the environment in which international business corruption occurs has no singular node of governance. There is no sovereign, or nexus of power, but rather a diffuse, multinodal assembly of public and private actors.[11] Furthermore, this environment is a mix of diverse legal traditions and cultures, as well as differing levels of political, social, and economic development.

For these reasons, one of the major achievements of the last few decades has been the development of a global standard criminalising corruption in international business transactions. This global standard is found in a collection of international, regional, and domestic instruments. In 1996, the Organization of American States adopted the Inter-American Convention against Corruption (IACAC).[12] In 1997, the Organization of Economic Co-operation and Development (OECD) adopted a Convention on Combating Bribery of Foreign Public Officials in International Business Transactions (OECD Convention).[13] Also in 1997, the Council of the European Union adopted the

---

[11] Dorn has argued that the vertical segmentation of 'multi-level' governance structures has been challenged by the more horizontal notion of 'multi-source' governance, in which states inhabit a broad policy arena alongside multilateral forums, powerful market interests, and cosmopolitan actors. See N. Dorn, *Conceptualizing Security: Cosmopolitan, State, Multilateral and Market Dynamics* (The Hague: Boom, 2008), 8.

[12] Inter-American Convention against Corruption, 29 March 29 1996, 35 ILM, p. 724, adopted at Caracas, Venezuela, in force 6 March 1997.

[13] OECD Convention on Combating Bribery of Foreign Public Officials in International Business Transactions, Paris, 27 November 1997, in force 15 February 1999, 1998, 37 ILM, p. 1.

Convention on the Fight against Corruption Involving Officials of the European Communities or Member States of the European Union (EU Convention).[14] In 1999, the Council of Europe adopted the Criminal Law Convention on Corruption as well as the Civil Law Convention on Corruption.[15] In 2000, the United Nations Convention against Transnational Organized Crime (UNCTC) was adopted.[16] This was followed by the adoption of the African Union Convention on Preventing and Combating Corruption (AUC) in 2003.[17] Finally, in 2003 the United Nations Convention against Corruption (UNCAC) came about.[18] At the domestic level, the US 1997 Foreign Corrupt Practices Act[19] and the UK Bribery Act[20] have universal application for multinational corporations. Some of the instruments leave the adoption of rules criminalising corruption in international business to the discretion of the state.[21] Others adopt a mandatory approach. The OECD convention, for example, provides that 'each Party *shall* take such measures as may be necessary to establish that it is a criminal offense under its law'.[22] The thirty-six state parties to the OECD Convention have enacted legislation criminalising corruption in international business.[23] The

---

[14] Convention drawn up on the basis of Art. K.3(2)(c) Treaty on European Union on the Fight against Corruption Involving Officials of the European Communities or Officials of Member States of the European Union, C 195, 25 June 1997, p.2 (not yet in force). In 2003, this prohibition was extended to private sector bribery with the Council Framework Decision on combating bribery in the private sector. See Council Framework Decision 2003/568/JHA of 22 July 2003 on combating corruption in the private sector, OJ L 192, 31 July, 2003 p. 54 (not yet in force).

[15] Criminal Law Convention on Corruption, Strasbourg, 27 January 1999, in force 1 July 2002, 173 CETS; Civil Law Convention on Corruption, Strasbourg, 4 November 1999, in force 1 November 2003, 174 CETS.

[16] United Nations Convention against Transnational Organized Crime, New York, 15 November, 2000, in force 29 September 2003, 2225 UNTS; (2000), 40 ILM, p. 353.

[17] African Union Convention on Preventing and Combating Corruption, in force 5 August 2006 43 (1) ILM, p.1.

[18] United Nations Convention against Corruption, New York, 31 October 2003, in force 14 December 2005, 2349 UNTS, p. 41; (2005), 43 ILM, p. 37.

[19] The Foreign Corrupt Practices Act 1977, 15 USC Sec. 78dd-1, et seq.

[20] Bribery Act 2010 (C.23).

[21] The UNCAC e.g. requires states to take measures establishing the act of corruption in international business as a criminal offence but makes this subject to the principle of sovereign equality and non-intervention in the domestic affairs of other states. Similar provisions are found in the IACAC and UNCTC.

[22] Art. 1 OECD Convention.

[23] See the OECD's website for details on the implementation of the OECD Convention. http://www.oecd.org/daf/anti-bribery/countryreportsontheimplementationoftheoecdanti-briberyconvention.htm

domestication of the provisions of the international rules in the national laws of OECD members states means that criminalisation of corruption in international business is now a principle of general application in the global market.

Actors involved in grand scale corruption are now circumscribed by the force of rules that are global in reach. The tendency towards impunity in which each party sets its own rules according to its own interests has been set aside for common rules of global reach criminalising international corruption. To some extent, these developments can be described as a triumph of international law, a world where the rule of law has triumphed over the rule of men. However, Koskenniemi has cautioned against such a conclusion. He warned that there is an essential arbitrariness inherent in rule-making and argued that: 'it is impossible to make substantive decisions within the law which would imply no political choice ... in the end, legitimizing or criticizing state behaviour is not a matter of applying formally neutral rules but depends on what one regards as politically right or just'.[24]

In other words, Koskenniemi summed up an essential aspect of international rule-making: it is biased against a set of particular interests. Filling a governance gap with a rule is ultimately a political choice. The question is, whose law will fill the gap?[25]

This analysis rings particularly true with regard to the politics behind the international framework of rules criminalising corruption in international business. The catalyst for this international framework of rules was domestic US law, the Foreign Corrupt Practices Act (FCPA)[26] that resulted from the political upheaval of the Nixon Watergate scandal in the 1970s.[27] The American public was outraged to learn about the corrupt practices of their corporations in international contracting.[28]

---

[24] Koskenniemi, 'Politics of International Law' (1990), 31.

[25] Koskenniemi, 'Politics of International Law' (2009), 17.

[26] Cohen and Marriot wrote that '[I]t is impossible to understand global anti-corruption efforts today without appreciating the FCPA's role in getting those efforts started. It is impossible to discuss the development of international anti-corruption instruments ... without understanding that the FCPA provided a spur to their enactment', P. Cohen and A. Marriot, eds, *International Corruption* (London: Sweet and Maxwell, 2010), 73.

[27] For detailed information of the Watergate scandal see M. Farnsworth, Watergate Info Database. http://watergate.info/background

[28] Lowell Brown, commenting on the Senate and Securities Exchange Commission (SEC) investigation, remarked that the investigation resulted in enforcement actions against United Brands, Gulf Oil Corporation, Ashland Oil Company, Boeing Company, and Lockheed Corporation, among others, and that in all more than 400 companies admitted to making overseas payments in excess of US$300 million, and 117 of these companies

The FCPA was the political response and it was groundbreaking. Under the FCPA, US corporations were barred from giving bribes to foreign officials to influence the acquisition of business. In the words of Justice T. Noonan: 'For the first time in the history of the world a measure for bribery was introduced into law that was universal as far as those subjected to the law were concerned. For the first time, a country made it criminal to corrupt the officials of another country.'[29]

However, this new FCPA standard applied only to US corporations. This put them at a competitive disadvantage. For US corporations, either the FCPA was repealed or the FCPA standard had to become the world standard. The FCPA, a domestic US law, thus became the first step towards an international binding legal framework.[30] A direct line can be traced from the FCPA to the international rules criminalising corruption in international business. This process took about two decades. The international instruments criminalising corruption in international transactions are the progeny of the FCPA.[31] The effect of this network of rules is that there is now a new 'hyper norm' repudiating corruption that 'transcends national boundaries' and criminalises transnational bribery.[32] US domestic politics required the response of American politicians, but the reality of an integrated global market compelled the internationalisation of the American response.[33]

---

were in the Fortune 500. H. Lowell Brown, *Bribery in International Commerce* (Eagen, MN: Thompson/West, 2003), 2. See also United States Senate, Securities and Exchange Commission, 'Report on Questionable and Illegal Corporate Payments and Practices' (12 May 1976). www.justice.gov/criminal/fraud/fcpa/history/1977/senaterpt-95-114.pdf

[29] J. Noonan, *Bribes: The Intellectual History of a Moral Idea* (Berkeley: University of California Press, 1987), 680.

[30] Pieth described the genesis and development of the international legal framework to combat corruption and noted that the local political agenda in the United States marked the first step in legislative action against transnational bribery. See M. Pieth, L. Low, and P. Cullen, eds, *The OECD Convention on Bribery: A Commentary* (Cambridge: Cambridge University Press, 2007), 6–9.

[31] B. Shaw, 'The Foreign Corrupt Practices Act and Progeny: Morally Unassailable', *Cornell International Law Journal*, 33 (2000), 688–709 at 706–9.

[32] P. Nichols, 'Regulating Transnational Bribery in Times of Globalization and Fragmentation', *Yale Journal of International Law*, 24 (1999), 257–303 at 302–3.

[33] See generally S. Sporkin, 'The Worldwide Banning of Schmiergeld: A Look at the Foreign Corrupt Practices Act on Its Twentieth Birthday', *Northwestern Journal of International Law and Business*, 18 (1997–1998), 269–81 at 271; S. Lochner, 'The Criminalization of American Extraterritorial Bribery: The Effect of the Foreign Corrupt Practices Act of 1977', *New York University Journal of International Law and Politics*, 13 (1980–1981), 645–74 at 645–53; J. Duncan, 'Modifying the Foreign Corrupt Practices Act: The Search for a Practical Standard', *Northwestern University Journal of International Law and Business*, 4 (1982), 203; D. Gantz, 'Globalizing Sanctions against Foreign Bribery: The

The international framework that has emerged represents a convergence of politics and market competition catalysed by the FCPA. The regulatory framework evidences a global consensus that defines, gives content to, and criminalises corruption in international business. The fact that the FCPA standard became the world standard is probably more a direct result of the determination and economic power of the US[34] than the growing recognition of states of the negative consequences of corruption on political, social, and economic development.

Yet, an international framework of anti-corruption rules triggered into existence by the internationalisation of a domestic standard cannot be said to represent the values of all the groups that interact in a global economy. Rather, this international standard represents the rule that has 'won the day'. A US-derived standard is the demarcating line between a gift and a bribe. This may seem a rather crude and uncomfortable admission. After all, objective rules rather than arbitrary politics would seem to be more consonant with the idea of international justice. However, at least in the case of the anti-corruption rules, the international standard embraced in the regulatory framework can be said to be arbitrary to the extent that it results from the choice of one political system's solution above another. If we view all international rule-making as inherently political then this is nothing strange. As Koskenniemi has argued: '[t]he fight for an [i]nternational rule of [l]aw is a fight against politics'.[35] The notion that a society could be organised based on the rule of law is based on 'the assumption that rules are objective in some sense that political ideas, views or preferences are not'.[36] The actual verifiable

---

Emergence of a New International Legal Consensus', *Northwestern Journal of International Law and Business*, 18 (1998), 466–8; B. Earle, 'The United States Foreign Corrupt Practices Act and the OECD Anti-Bribery Recommendation: When Moral Persuasion Won't Work, Try the Money Argument', *Dickson Journal of International Law*, 14 (1996), 207; L. Low, 'New Antibribery Rules Create New Compliance Responsibilities', *International Business Lawyer*, 26 (1998), 272.

[34] The US in its self-evaluation report on the implementation of the OECD Convention referred to its push to internationalise the FCPA standard and noted that '[S]ince 1977, the United States has outlawed bribery of foreign officials in commercial transactions by its nationals and companies organized under its laws. In addition, the United States has worked with other countries and in various international fora, including the OECD, the United Nations, the Council of Europe, and the Organization of American States, to encourage the enactment of similar prohibitions by other major trading countries.' See the 1998 US Response to Phase 1 Questionnaire DAFFE/IME/BR (98)8/ADD1/FINAL, Sec. 0.1.

[35] Koskenniemi, 'Politics of International Law' (1990), 5.

[36] Ibid. 7.

impact of the FCPA on the international framework of rules repudiating corruption and the leading role that the US continues to play in the development of the anti-corruption enforcement framework illustrates the political nature of the regulatory framework of rules fighting corruption in international business transactions. As Koskenniemi has pointed out, the need for normativity that is sought in distancing the rule from state behaviour is challenged by the simultaneous requirement for concreteness of the law as demonstrated in the actual, verifiable behaviour of states.[37] He argued that: '[a]n argument about concreteness is an argument about the closeness of a particular rule, principle or doctrine to state practice. But the closer to state practice an argument is, the less normative and more political it seems and just another apology for existing power.'[38] The FCPA and its progeny are a sector-specific response to the problem of corruption in international business. Political choice explains how, despite the cultural complexity of corruption, a baseline of legality has been drawn. In drawing this line, there was no elusive quest for the legitimacy of a voice that speaks for all nations. Rather it was fashioned out of a pragmatic need to have companies bound by the same standard that applied to American companies. By dint of economic power, the particular interests of US politics have crystallised into the global rule. There is no universal unifying principle of international law, but rather the deliberate adoption of one set of values and laws as the world standard.

Why should it matter that the international rules criminalising corruption are viewed as the result of an arbitrary political choice rather than as the reflection of objective rules of law? The answer, to paraphrase Koskenniemi, is that every general discussion about corruption and governance should be prefaced with a 'strategic awareness' of whose understanding of corruption ought to be preferred; once that preference is fixed, it should be clear what type of action will best support it.[39] This general discussion also provides a reality check as new legal rules and mechanisms emerge in the normative space created by the international framework of anti-corruption rules. Strategic awareness strikes a cautionary note about extending particular lessons from the fight against corruption to a more general discussion on global governance or international rule-making. While there are certainly lessons to be shared,

[37] Ibid. 8.
[38] Ibid.
[39] Koskenniemi, 'Politics of International Law' (2009), 14.

these are perhaps more useful when put in the context of the political subjectivism that underpins them.

## Enforcing the Rules – The Politics of Management

Despite the evolution of an international regulatory framework, corruption remains a real and pressing problem. The 2016 Corruption Perceptions Index, for example, shows that about two-thirds of the 176 countries and territories assessed in the index scored below fifty on a scale of zero (highly corrupt) to one hundred (very clean), which indicates a serious corruption problem. Denmark was rated the least corrupt and Somalia the most corrupt according to this perceptions index.[40] The regular appearances of large corporations in bribery scandals also raises questions about the real substance of the international regulatory framework.[41] On the one hand, the reports of corporations being investigated for corrupt practices are a positive

---

[40] The Transparency International Corruption Perceptions Index (CPI) ranks countries and territories based on how corrupt their public sector is perceived to be according to corruption-related data collected by a variety of reputable institutions. According to its compilers, '[t]he CPI reflects the views of observers from around the world, including experts living and working in the countries and territories evaluated'. More information, including the full index is available at the website. www.transparency.org/news/feature/corruption_perceptions_index_2016

[41] Telia Company AB (Sweden) paid $965 million in 2017 to resolve allegations that it paid at least $330m in bribes to break into the Uzbekistan market. Siemens AG (Germany) entered into a plea agreement in 2008 for allegations of managing a slush fund totalling more than €1.3bn in bribes used to win overseas contracts from 2001 to 2007 in Argentina, Bangladesh, and Venezuela. Coordinated enforcement actions by the DOJ, SEC, and German authorities resulted in penalties of $1.6 billion. VimpelCom (Holland) paid $795 million in 2016 in relation to an admission to a conspiracy to make more than $114 million in bribery payments to a government official in Uzbekistan between 2006 and 2012 to enable them to enter and continue operating in the Uzbek telecommunications market. Alstom (France) paid $772 million in 2014 to resolve charges relating to a widespread corruption scheme involving at least $75 million in secret bribes paid to government officials in countries around the world, including Indonesia, Saudi Arabia, Egypt, the Bahamas, and Taiwan. In 2014 KBR/Halliburton (United States) entered into a plea agreement for its participation in a decade-long scheme to bribe Nigerian government officials to obtain engineering, procurement, and construction contracts. Enforcement actions by the US DOJ and SEC resulted in penalties of $579 million. Teva Pharmaceutical (Israel) agreed to resolve criminal charges in 2016 and pay a criminal penalty of more than $283 million in connection with schemes involving the bribery of government officials in Russia, Ukraine, and Mexico. Teva and its subsidiary agreed to pay nearly $520 million in penalties. Full details of DOJ FCPA cases since 1977 are available at the US Department of Justice website. www.justice.gov/criminal-fraud/chronological-list; SEC case details since 1978 are available at the US Securities and Exchange Commission website. www.sec.gov/spotlight/fcpa/fcpa-cases.shtml. See also

indication of the change that is taking place in the business world. On the other hand, they mean that there is still an urgent need to develop strategies for effective enforcement. The management of enforcement strategy takes place within the normative space triggered by the internationalisation of the FCPA standard. This normative space, in which countries can fashion a common anti-corruption strategy, remains extremely vulnerable to the particular political interests and pressures of the US economy. The next section identifies the management problems that exist in the normative space created by the anti-corruption regulatory framework and how the US is at the forefront of emerging global enforcement mechanisms.

## Conflicts and Gaps Exacerbated by Criminalisation

The very process of criminalising corruption put in place by the international regulatory framework brings with it fundamental structural problems that can create inconsistencies in the sanctioning environment. Conflicts of interest and regulatory gaps impede the veracity of the enforcement environment. The act of criminalisation in most legal systems gives the state the sole right to initiate the criminal sanctioning process. However, since the principal actors in international business corruption are often corporations and governments, the monopoly on initiating a sanction held by the state can lead to a conflict of interest in which the state does not have the political will to commence a criminal prosecution. A good example of such a structural conflict of interest was the action taken by the Blair government to stop investigations into bribery payments made to a Saudi official as part of a £40bn al-Yamamah arms deal involving the UK BAE Systems Plc., a British defence, security, and aerospace company. The Blair government insisted that an investigation could upset UK diplomatic relations with Saudi Arabia and would pose a threat to national security. In 2006, the Serious Fraud Office (SFO) controversially stopped the investigation. The action of the UK government was challenged unsuccessfully in court.[42] However, in 2007 the US DOJ commenced its own inquiry into the BAE/Al Yamamah case and in 2010 BAE Systems Plc. pleaded guilty in the US District Court in the District of Columbia for conspiring to defraud the United States by impairing and impeding its lawful functions, to make false statements about its Foreign Corrupt

Richard Cassin, Top 10 List, FCPA Blog (December 26, 2017). www.fcpablog.com/blog/2017/12/26/keppel-offshore-lands-seventh-on-our-top-ten-list.html

[42] See *R* (On the Application of Corner House Research and Others) v. *Director of the Serious Fraud Office* [2008] UKHL 60.

Practices Act (FCPA) compliance program and paid a $400 million criminal fine described as 'one of the largest criminal fines in the history of the DOJ's ongoing effort to combat overseas corruption in international business'.[43]

The state, through its officials, is often an actor in grand scale international contracting tainted by corruption. In this role it can be simultaneously a primary beneficiary of contracts tainted by corruption as well as the primary enforcer of anti-corruption rules. The structural conflict of interest, which is inherent in the criminal process of sanctioning corruption, implies that effective strategies to tackle international corruption must address the monopoly on initiating sanctions held by the state under the criminal process, especially in those states most badly affected by corruption. Paul Carrington remarks that the weakness of enforcing anti-corruption laws lies in the use of the very public servants that are part of the problem.[44] There is consequently a need to develop strategies in the fight against corruption that can circumvent the compromised state. The problem is not the absence of a rule, but the absence of a willingness to enforce it. A lack of effective enforcement can set into motion a vicious cycle of impunity, resulting in the breakdown of order, preventing development. Increased regulation does not necessarily resolve this conundrum.

A major 'gap' that emerges from traditional criminal law formulations is the fact that they do not sufficiently address the contracts that result from successful acts of bribery. Bribery is a means to an end and not an end in itself. The contract that results from the corrupt exchange is the *raison d'etre* of the act of corruption. The focus of international regulations is on punishing the giver and taker of the bribe. Yet, the transaction to give and receive a bribe for the acquisition of business is an agreement (contract) between parties. If this bribery transaction is successful, it will result in another contract, i.e. the contract for business that the bribe was proffered to obtain. The laws criminalising corruption do not pay enough attention to the primary contract to give and receive a bribe or to the secondary contracts that result from a successful act of bribery. These

---

[43]  See US Department of Justice press release: 'BAE Systems PLC Pleads Guilty and Ordered to Pay $400 Million Criminal Fine' (1 March 2010). www.justice.gov/opa/pr/2010/March/10-crm-209.html

[44]  P. Carrington, 'American Law and Transnational Corruption: Is There a Need for Lincoln's Law Abroad?', in O. Meyer, ed., *Civil Law Consequences of Corruption* (Baden Baden: Nomos, 2009), 49. He writes, 'it is the integrity of governments that is the global problem in greatest need of a plausible threat of civil liability'.

contracts, and especially the secondary contract, remain largely outside the ambit of the criminal law, which leaves gaps that can be exploited by players in the corruption game.[45] This enforcement gap reduces the efficacy of criminalisation. In addition, international contracts tainted by corruption often fall under the jurisdiction of confidential systems of international arbitration that keep disputes relating to them outside of national courts.[46]

Finally, it must be noted that, apart from the above identified conflicts and gaps, few states possess the capacity to detect, investigate, and prosecute complex, multi-jurisdictional corrupt transactions. Simply put, the mechanics of the traditional, state-centred criminal law systems are a poor fit for the de-territorialised environment in which corruption in international business occurs.

Several developments are changing the tide as far as a smart environment, in the sense of being conducive to compliance with corruption regulations, is concerned. As discussed in the following three sections, these developments aimed at managing corruption include: frameworks that allow countries to regulate foreign-based corruption; extending the reach of the FCPA regulatory framework to non-US based corporations as well as promoting enforcement in other countries; and incorporating anti-corruption measures in contract law.

## Regulating Foreign-Based Corruption

Firstly, the international regulatory framework creates an important route to bypass compromised states by allowing countries to intervene in corruption occurring in other countries. The international rules

---

[45] A distinction should be made between the primary contract that arises when a person pays a bribe that undermines the recipient's duty to negotiate in the best interest of another (e.g. contracts for special fees, kickbacks, consultancies, or intermediary commissions) and the secondary contract that results from the successful bribery exchange. This secondary contract is between the bribe-giver and the principal or employer of the bribe-recipient. It is referred to as secondary to emphasise the fact that it is the direct result of the successful execution of the primary contract to give and receive a bribe. Both primary and secondary contracts should have a legal status that is consistent with the aims of criminalisation. The primary contract is unenforceable in most jurisdictions, however the secondary contract is generally considered a valid contract. See Makinwa, *Private Remedies for Corruption: Towards an International Framework* (The Hague: Eleven International Publishing, 2013), at 11–13 and 331–63.

[46] Ibid. 299–328.

require states to sanction acts of corruption involving their nationals and foreign officials.

By providing a basis for intervention into acts of corruption occurring in other countries, the international regulatory framework has shifted the momentum in the fight against corruption away from the so-called demand-side (typically the bribe receiving side where the consequences of corruption are most severe, with the accompanying breakdown in the capacity of governance and enforcement mechanisms) to the supply-side (typically, a more advanced economy, with the social and governance institutions to match). This shift arguably allows enforcement by countries that may have better resources to address the negative influences of corruption on the global stage. Furthermore, this system provides an important alternative modality of intervention when a national government is crippled by corruption.

*Enforcing Foreign-Based Corruption Regulations on a Global Scale*

Second, the enforcement of regulations concerning foreign-based corruption, whether through the FCPA in the US or the UK Bribery Act, has affected the operations of multinational corporations across the globe regardless of whether or not they are nationally based corporations.

Given the size of the US economy, it would be exceptional for a multinational corporation to have no dealings with the US market. Such dealings bring the corporation well within the reach of the FCPA prohibitions. Any corporation that offers, registers, or sells securities on a US stock exchange falls within the scope of the FCPA. A US listing is sufficient to establish jurisdiction over acts involving the listed company that take place entirely outside the US.[47]

A foreign corporation also falls within the scope of the FCPA if it takes any action in furtherance of a bribery transaction within US territory. This jurisdictional link is widely interpreted. Meetings involving discussions about payments,[48] the use of bank accounts in the United States,[49]

---

[47] 15 USC Sec. 78dd-1(a).
[48] See e.g. *United States* v. *Alcatel-Lucent France, S.A., et al.* Information, Court Docket Number: 10-CR-20907 S.D. FLA. (2010) 4.
[49] See e.g. *Securities and Exchange Commission* v. *Siemens Aktiengesellschaft*, Civil Action No. 08 CV 02167 D.D.C. (2008). Siemens AG was held accountable for the acts of Siemens Argentina, Siemens Venezuela, and Siemens Bangladesh, all of which were foreign subsidiaries headquartered in other countries. These companies, although organised under the laws of foreign countries, were caught in the FCPA web as a result of meetings

and the authorisation of bribery cash payments while traveling in the United States,[50] for example, are regarded as a sufficient link to bring foreign corporations within the jurisdictional reach of the FCPA. Furthermore, foreign subsidiaries of US companies fall within the reach of the FCPA when it can be established that the parent company or its employees authorised, directed, or controlled the activity in question.[51]

The US experience suggests that the possibility of negotiated settlements[52] can have a positive effect on the management of corruption. Multinational corporations that voluntarily disclose instances of corruption and set up effective internal control mechanisms are rewarded by the possibility of negotiated penalties. At the same time, such cooperation by corporations provides governments with access to the information necessary to detect, investigate, and prosecute corruption.[53]

Several factors are considered in a determination of whether to prosecute, defer prosecution, or not to prosecute a company for a violation of the FCPA. Under the Securities Exchange Act of 1934 (sec. 21), the Securities and Exchange Commission (SEC) has discretion concerning whether or not to investigate if a person has violated the provisions of the act. In return for voluntary disclosure and cooperation, corporations may benefit from deferred prosecution, no prosecution, or other plea bargain arrangements. The factors that the SEC takes into consideration when making this determination are listed in the SEC Report of Investigation Pursuant to Sec. 21 (a) of the Securities Exchange Act of 1934 and the Commission Statement on the Relationship of Cooperation to Agency Enforcement Decisions, 23 October 2001. This report lists self-policing,

---

in the US, where discussions were held about improper payments, as well as moneys paid via US bank accounts.

[50] See for example *United States* v. *Syncor Taiwan, Inc.*, No. 02-CR-1244-ALL C.D. Cal. (2002).

[51] See for example the case of *United States* v. *ABB Inc.* Court Docket Number: 10-CR-664, S.D. Tex. (2010). ABB Ltd was a corporation headquartered and incorporated in Switzerland with shares publicly traded on the New York Stock Exchange. ABB Ltd was held accountable to the US government for these activities by its subsidiary as an 'issuer', within the meaning of Sec. 78dd-1 (a) of the FCPA, for bribes paid by an indirect subsidiary. ABB Network Management (ABB NM), based in Sugar Land, Texas, paid bribes from 1997 to 2004 that totalled approximately $1.9 million to officials at Commission Federal de Electricidad (CFE), a Mexican state-owned utility company.

[52] Also referred to as structured criminal settlements or pre-trial diversion agreements.

[53] For the 'push for' and the 'push against' negotiated settlements, see A. Makinwa, 'Negotiated Settlements for Corruption Offences, Wither Europe', in A. Makinwa, ed., *Negotiated Settlements for Corruption Offences: A European Perspective* (Eleven International Publishing, 2015), 1–16 at 9–11.

self-reporting, remediation, and cooperation as factors that are taken into consideration when deciding whether or not to take enforcement action, to bring reduced charges, to impose lighter sanctions, or to use mitigating language in documents used to announce and resolve enforcement actions.[54]

Similarly, the Principles of Federal Prosecution of Business Organizations list factors that the US Department of Justice (DOJ) considers when determining whether to charge a corporation or enter into a negotiated plea or other agreements.[55] Included in this list are the corporation's timely and voluntary disclosure of wrongdoing; its willingness to cooperate in the investigation of its agents; the existence and effectiveness of the corporation's pre-existing compliance program; and the corporation's remedial actions, including any efforts to implement an effective corporate compliance program or improve an existing one, replace responsible management, discipline or terminate wrongdoers, pay restitution, or cooperate with the relevant government agencies. The practice of the US DOJ and SEC is summarised in the joint *Resource Guide to the U.S. Foreign Corrupt Practices Act.*[56] Together, these instruments create an advantage for corporations who take steps to curb corruption and establish internal controls and other compliance processes by placing them in a good position to negotiate more favourable settlements with the authorities if violations occur.

The practice of negotiated settlements is slowly gaining traction beyond the United States. The UK is particularly important in this respect. London is a hub of commercial transactions, finance, and dispute settlement. The UK Bribery Act has a jurisdictional reach that makes multinational corporations susceptible to its enforcement. The Bribery Act of 2010 applies if an offence under the act is committed within the UK.[57] The act also applies if the corrupt activity took place outside the UK and the corporation or person committing the activity has had a close connection to the UK.[58] Under the act, the failure by a commercial organisation to prevent bribery became a new offence.[59] The act applies

---

[54] Otherwise referred to as the Seaboard Report. www.sec.gov/litigation/investreport/34–44969.htm

[55] United States Attorneys' Manual s.9–28.000 et seq.

[56] US Department of Justice and Securities and Exchange Commission, *Resource Guide to the U.S. Foreign Corrupt Practices Act* (2012). www.justice.gov/criminal/fraud/fcpa/guidance

[57] UK Bribery Act 2010, Sec. 12(1) .

[58] Ibid. Sec. 12(2).

[59] Ibid. Sec. 7.

when the bribery is committed by a person associated with the corporation regardless of whether or not the activity took place in or outside the UK.[60] An associated person may be an employee, agent, or subsidiary.[61] This means that any foreign company that carries out a part of its business in the UK falls within the scope of the act for any of the bribery offences established under the Bribery Act. If a corporation with a subsidiary in the UK is engaged via an associated person in the commission of bribery in a third country (for example paying bribes to Nigerian government officials) and this activity took place wholly outside the UK, the fact that the foreign parent company has a close connection to the UK via its UK subsidiary brings it within the reach of the Bribery Act.[62]

The Serious Fraud Office (SFO), which is charged with implementing the UK Bribery Act, has provisions that are designed to encourage the self-reporting mechanisms that characterise FCPA enforcement.[63] The guidelines published under section 9 of the UK Bribery Act provide a framework for determining what will constitute 'adequate procedures' as a defence to the section 7 offence of failing to prevent bribery.

UK prosecutors must therefore balance public interest factors for and against prosecution. A prosecution usually takes place unless there are public interest factors against prosecution which clearly outweigh those tending in favour of prosecution.[64] Among the public factors listed that favour prosecution are the failure to report wrongdoing within

---

[60] Ibid. Sec. 12(5).

[61] Ibid. Sec. 8(3).

[62] There is a defence to this crime of failing to prevent persons associated with a company from committing bribery under Sec. 7(1) of the Bribery Act 2010. A company can escape liability if it can show that it had in place adequate procedures designed to prevent associated persons from bribing another person on behalf of the company. This defence encourages corporations to play an active role in the prevention, investigation, and reporting of corrupt activity. In 2010 the UK Ministry of Justice published the Bribery Act 2010 Guidance on the procedures that a corporation can put in place to prevent persons associated with them from bribing. These include proportionate procedures to prevent bribery risks; top-level commitment of management; periodic risk assessment; proportionate and risk-based due diligence; communication and training of bribery prevention policies; and monitoring and review of measures to prevent bribery. See www.gov.uk/government/publications/bribery-act-2010-guidance.

[63] In July 2009 the Serious Fraud Office (SFO) in the United Kingdom released Guidelines for Prosecutors on the Bribery Act 2010. See Joint Prosecution Guidance of the Director of the Serious Fraud Office and the Director of Public Prosecution as well as the Guidance on Corporate Prosecutions on the Bribery Act) (as revised in 2012, hereinafter Joint Prosecution Guidance). See generally www.sfo.gov.uk/bribery–corruption/corporate-self-reporting.aspx.

[64] Joint Prosecution Guidance, para. 31.

reasonable time of the offending coming to light[65] as well as the failure to report properly and fully the true extent of the wrongdoing.[66] Among the factors considered against prosecution is a genuinely proactive approach adopted by the corporate management team when the offending was brought to its notice, involving steps such as self-reporting and remedial actions, including the compensation of victims[67] as well as the existence of a genuinely proactive and effective corporate compliance programme.[68]

The idea of negotiated settlements has, so far, been met with mixed sentiments. In 2005 the US began an investigation into Innospec Ltd, a UK subsidiary of Innospec Inc., a company listed on a US stock exchange. Innospec Ltd pleaded guilty to charges of engaging in systematic and large-scale bribery totalling approximately $8 million paid to senior government officials in Indonesia to secure contracts for the supply of a fuel additive, tetraethyl lead. An action was brought before a UK court to approve a global settlement reached by the US and UK authorities in which the UK company Innospec Ltd agreed to pay a $12.7 million settlement. This global agreement needed to be approved by both US and UK courts. The US court approved the arrangement[69] but the UK court expressed reservations. The UK court held that, as a matter of constitutional principle, the SFO could not enter into an agreement under English law with an offender in relation to the penalty in respect of an offence. The court stressed that, for crimes of corruption, it is in the public interest for the court to rigorously scrutinise the basis of the plea bargain agreement in open courts, in the interest of transparency and good governance.[70]

Cooperation with the authorities can also lead to a settlement by way of a civil recovery order. For example, in 2012, Oxford Publishing Limited agreed to pay £1,895,435 by way of a civil recovery order of revenue that had been derived from bribery and corruption related to subsidiaries incorporated in Tanzania and Kenya, in settlement of charges brought by the SFO. Factors leading to this settlement included the fact that the OUP

---

[65]  Joint Prosecution Guidance, para. 32(e).
[66]  Joint Prosecution Guidance, para. 32(f).
[67]  Joint Prosecution Guidance, para. 32(a).
[68]  Joint Prosecution Guidance, para. 32(c).
[69]  See *United States* v. *Innospec Inc.* Court Docket Number: 10-CR-061-ESH. www.justice .gov/criminal/fraud/fcpa/cases/innospec-inc.html. See also DOJ press release, 'Innospec Inc. Pleads Guilty to FCPA Charges and Defrauding the United Nations'. www.justice .gov/opa/pr/2010/March/10-crm-278.html
[70]  See *R* v. *Innospec Limited* Crim. L.R. 665.

voluntarily reported the irregular practices and fully met with the criteria set out in SFO guidance on self-reporting matters of overseas corruption.[71]

In 2013, the SFO withdrew the guidance on corporate self-reporting because it 'contained an implied presumption that self-reported misconduct would be dealt with by civil settlement', but reiterated that there are very powerful arguments in favour of self-reporting stating that a 'self-report at the very least mitigates the chances of a corporate being prosecuted. It opens up the possibility of civil recovery or a DPA (deferred prosecution agreement).'[72] This practice of self-reporting is encouraged by Schedule 17 of the 2013 Crime and Courts Act that allows for deferred prosecution agreements. The accompanying Deferred Prosecution Agreements Code of Practice provides insight into the circumstances in which prosecutors will consider a DPA.

The next decade will no doubt show the extent to which the US model of negotiated settlements shapes good practices across the globe.[73]

### Incorporating Anti-Corruption Measures into Contract Law

A third development that promotes a climate conducive to compliance is the increasing focus on the consequences of corruption in the form of contracts or other obligations that result from successful acts of bribery. A global framework to challenge contracts that are tainted by corruption has been provided by the United Nations Convention against

---

[71] See Serious Fraud Office Press Release 'Oxford Publishing Ltd to Pay Almost £1.9 Million as Settlement after Admitting Unlawful Conduct in Its East African Operations' (3 July 2012). http://www.sfo.gov.uk/press-room/latest-press-releases/press-releases-2012/oxford-publishing-ltd-to-pay-almost-19-million-as-settlement-after-admitting-unlawful-conduct-in-its-east-african-operations.aspx

[72] See speech given by SFO Director David Green at the Pinsent Masons and Legal Week Regulatory Reform and Enforcement Conference, 24 October 2013. www.sfo.gov.uk/2013/10/24/pinsent-masons-legal-week-regulatory-reform-enforcement-conference-2

[73] An IBA study on structured criminal settlements, 'Towards Global Standards in Structured Criminal Settlements for Corruption Offences', has examined the evolving role of settlements. As the practice of structured settlements spreads, it addresses the question of whether there is a need for global standards. If so, what shape might such global standards take? Completed questionnaires have been submitted by practitioner country researchers from 63 countries. Their compiled responses provide an up-to-date and comparative overview of salient issues relating to structured settlements for corruption offences. See A. Makinwa and T. Søreide, Structured Criminal Settlements: Towards Global Standards in Structured Criminal Settlements for Corruption Offences (International Bar Association, Anti-Corruption Committee, Structured Criminal Settlements Sub-Committee, forthcoming).

Corruption. The UNCAC encourages states to view corruption as an independent vitiating factor in determining the validity of contracts. Art. 34 of the UNCAC requires states to consider corruption as a relevant factor in legal proceedings relating to the validity of contracts, the grant or withdrawal of a concession or similar instrument, or other remedial action. In addition, the prospect of private civil proceedings by victims is gaining ground. Art. 35 of the UNCAC encourages states to empower private individuals to bring actions for damage suffered as a result of corruption.

An environment that renders corruption-tainted contracts open to challenge and that encourages private litigants and self-reporting by offenders is fundamentally more open-ended and less predictable than traditional and more predictable state-centred punishment. Promoting a smart policy environment by increasing the unpredictability and risk associated with acts of corruption can positively influence the choices that corporations make. There is a tacit acknowledgement that neither the public nor the private sector acting alone is in a position to adequately tackle the problem of international corruption. There is a more diffuse pattern of enforcement with several actors, not just the state, playing a significant role. This is the approach that is emerging with respect to the enforcement of the international rules and the FCPA. The solution to impunity that results from a lack of effective sanctioning mechanisms in the fight against corruption is finding expression in a multi-actor and multilayered process of cooperation and partnership between corporations, private actors, and governments.

## The FCPA 'Box'

The above developments show that anti-corruption law and policy are developing their own dialogue and method as they streamline a global response to corruption in international business. This is influenced by the US enforcement of the FCPA as well as, albeit to a lesser extent, provisions of the UNCAC regarding contracts tainted by corruption and the right of private individuals to sue for acts of corruption. These themes are shaping the anti-corruption discourse and the quest for more effective methods of fighting corruption.

The above-mentioned examples reveal what Koskenniemi has referred to as the structural bias that is found in the institutional practices that emerge from specialised factions of international law.[74] Koskenniemi writes about a 'politics of definition, that is to say, the strategic practice of defining international situations and problems in new expert languages so as to gain control over them'.[75] He noted in a paper delivered in Australia in 2006 that: 'This approach suggests that international law comes to us in separate boxes such as "trade law" and "environmental law" that may have different principles and objectives that do not apply across the boundaries between such boxes.'[76] Current developments in the fight against corruption show how the FCPA has triggered its own 'box' with its own language.[77] This 'box' has a profound impact on the behaviour of multi-national corporations, with its own particular language, rules, and processes. Drawing on this reasoning, this 'box' is best viewed as a 'patterned exception'.[78] In discussing effective schemes of restraint for other types of corruption, such as judicial or political corruption, or in exploring sanctioning for transnational crime in general, care must be taken with anti-corruption FCPA discourse so as not to 'raise the status of that idiom to a kind of Esperanto',[79] that 'hides or obscure[s] the contingent nature of the choices made'.[80]

[74] Koskenniemi, 'Politics of International Law' (2009), 9–11.
[75] Ibid. 9. Koskenniemi noted that through specialisation – that is to say, through the creation of special regimes of knowledge and expertise in areas such as trade law, human rights law, environmental law, security law, international criminal law, European law, and so on – the world of legal practice is being sliced up into institutional projects that cater to special audiences with special interests and special ethos. The point of creating such specialised institutions is precisely to affect the outcomes that are being produced in the international world.
[76] M. Koskenniemi, 'International Law: Between Fragmentation and Constitutionalism' (2006), para 6. www.helsinki.fi/eci/Publications/Koskenniemi/MCanberra-06c.pdf
[77] Ibid. para 8. Koskenniemi noted that '[t]o be doing "trade law" or "human rights law", or "environmental law" or "European law" – as the representatives of those projects repeatedly tell us – is not just to operate some technical rules but to participate in a culture, to share preferences and inclinations shared with colleagues and institutions who identify themselves with that "box"'.
[78] Koskenniemi referred to the 'patterned exception' that 'suggests that the center may have completely collapsed'. He stated that the 'argument is that owing to "recent developments" in the technical, economic, political, or whatever field (typically linked with some sociological language about "globalization"), new needs or interests have emerged that require a new treatment. The new regime – say, a regime of environmental protection or security – seeks to respond to new "challenges" not by replacing the old rule but merely by creating an "exception" to it.' M. Koskenniemi, 'Politics of International Law' (2009), 10.
[79] Ibid. 11.
[80] Ibid. 12. Koskenniemi noted that '[t]o this extent the vocabularies act as "ideologies" in the technical sense of reifying, making seem necessary or neutral something that is partial and contested. Awareness of bias suggests two conclusions. One is to examine more closely the strategic choices that are opened by particular vocabularies of global

Koskenniemi further observed that '[a] managerial approach is emerging that envisages international law as an instrument for particular values, interests, preferences'.[81] The result of managerialism is that 'much about the search for political direction today takes the form of jurisdictional conflict, struggle between competing expert vocabularies, each equipped with a specific bias'.[82] The danger of boxes, Koskenniemi points out, is that one may present a particular solution as 'natural' and by this very act render it more than it is, in turn rendering it 'ideological'.[83] As Koskenniemi also noted:

> managerialism has its concealed normativity that privileges values and actors occupying dominant positions in international institutions and who therefore have no reason to take a critical attitude to those institutions. It solidifies the sense that questions of distribution and preference have already been decided elsewhere, so all that remain are technical questions, questions about how to smooth the prince's path.[84]

Boxes should urge users to caution. There is no natural extension of their contents to other boxes. In short, recognising the limits of the particular box of corruption in international business transactions can help to avoid circularity and encourage a more critical appraisal when extending its application or assessing the further development of its sector-specific solutions.

### Conclusion: From Plurality to Unison – A Lesson in Bias

The absence of global government in relation to corruption leaves no vacuum. However, instead of one large box of cohesion, multiple boxes are emerging. As a result there is no single approach or box that is 'truer'

---

governance. The other concerns the proper attitude to take with regard to the managerialism underlying today's international legal debates.'

[81] M. Koskenniemi, 'International Law', para 5.

[82] Koskenniemi wrote that '[i]f such regimes are bold in ambition, and able to rely on the support of some powerful sector of the political world, then they may succeed in changing the general bias in the law. For example, the rise of the bilateral investment treaty has certainly transformed the relationship between the private investor and host state from what it was 20 years ago.' Koskenniemi, 'Politics of International Law' (2009), 9.

[83] Ibid. 11. Koskenniemi pointed out that political intervention is today often a politics of redefinition, that is to say, the strategic definition of a situation or a problem by reference to a technical idiom so as to open the door for applying the expertise related to that idiom, together with the attendant structural bias. He further pointed out that 'each such vocabulary is likely to highlight some solutions, some actors, some interests. None of which is any truer than the others.'

[84] Ibid. 16.

than others. On a broader scale, the international normative framework of the rules repudiating corruption in international business frames its own particular box and sets its own standards for compliance.

Such fragmentation makes the likelihood of a broader normative framework, against which sector-specific responses can be measured, unlikely. A more overarching standard may be found in the extent to which the solution presented by any particular box contributes to the global ideals of fighting global poverty, crime, inequality, and environmental degradation. Nonetheless, some general lessons can be drawn from developments in the fight against corruption, using the cautionary words of Koskenniemi as a guide.

First, the illegality of corruption in international business has become established as a rule of law of global application. This worldwide standard repudiating corruption has emerged from a bottom-up process in which a domestic policy has become the world standard. US politics framed the regulatory framework of rules repudiating corruption in international business, and US policy continues to drive the enforcement process. The FCPA has set the baseline in the fight against corruption. It remains the primary motivator, catalyst, and driving force of the international anti-corruption movement. The politics behind these developments are at least partly reflected in the creeping internationalisation of FCPA-style processes of enforcement characterised by public–private negotiations and private-actor-led actions to supplement traditional criminal processes.

Second, the international framework of common rules repudiating corruption in business transactions is a good illustration of the arbitrariness that occurs in the international trading order. The international framework of rules and the emerging sanctioning process for international corruption offences do not represent a realisation of an ideal of global justice, but are rather the outcome of US politics and economic power. International law principles of sovereignty and non-intervention have not stood in the way of the establishment of a modality for external intervention in bribery occurring in other countries.

Third, the history of the emergence of the anti-corruption rules shows whose understanding of corruption has assumed global prominence. The American-style model is gradually spreading across the integrated market and may fundamentally change approaches to fighting white collar crime. Whatever questions may arise about the politics of the international anti-bribery rules, a new normative space in which the development of global positions on anti-corruption policy can take place now exists. Corporations have become more responsive participants in the fight against corruption, and compliance with anti-corruption rules is increasingly becoming a corporate management issue.

Fragmentation and complexity are the natural end result of sector-specific responses. Thinking in terms of boxes may be a more realistic basis for formulating theories of governance in today's international society. The language of law and the language of politics vary from box to box. The same applies to the specialist institutions associated with each particular box. In such an arrangement, the notion of the rule of law becomes layered, and the notion of universality must be re-thought. What holds true for the anti-corruption box may have no relevance to other boxes. Each box is a representative of particular interests. This makes the coexistence of the diverse boxes intensely political. By highlighting the structural biases underlying this arrangement of boxes, Koskenniemi's work on the politics of international law helps to develop a strategic awareness that assists with better navigation of the complex and fragmented space of international law.

# 7

# A Fatal Attraction? The UN Security Council and the Relationship between R2P and the International Criminal Court

MARK KERSTEN*

## Introduction: R2P and the ICC: An Under-Investigated Relationship

For twenty-five years, Martti Koskenniemi's seminal work on the politics of international law has provided scholars and practitioners alike with an invaluable framework through which to examine the nexus between global ethics, political power, and international law.[1] Koskenniemi has given us tools to imagine and interrogate developments and arguments in international law, delineating whether they are vulnerable to the critique of being too 'utopian' – when international law is a moral estate too divorced from political practice, or too 'apologetic' – when international law is merely the selective expression of the interests of powerful states.[2]

Although Koskenniemi's original observations date back to the end of the Cold War, they remain pertinent in assessing more recent developments in international law, including the doctrine of the Responsibility to Protect (R2P) and the International Criminal Court (ICC). The R2P doctrine was established in order to provide a legal framework to determine when states can and should intervene to protect civilians from mass human rights violations. The ICC was established to make international criminal justice a permanent reality of international politics. It aims to hold to account those individuals most responsible for war crimes, crimes against humanity, and genocide.

* Kersten thanks Kirsten Ainley, Toni Erskine, Naomi Head, Joe Hoover, Paul Kirby, James P. Rudolph, and Elke Schwarz for their helpful comments on earlier drafts of this chapter.
[1] See Martti Koskenniemi, 'The Politics of International Law', *European Journal of International Law*, 1 (1990), 4–32 at 9; Martti Koskenniemi, *From Apology to Utopia: The Structure of International Legal Argument* (Cambridge University Press, 2005).
[2] Ibid.

The creation of both the doctrine and the Court represents a novel means that has potential to establish a global rule of law founded on the universal promotion and protection of human rights. As such, the relationship between R2P and the ICC goes to the very heart of the politics of international law. Still, surprisingly few scholars have attempted to establish and interrogate this relationship. In light of the 2011 crisis in Libya, during which both R2P and the ICC were invoked by the UN Security Council (UNSC), there is a need to critically address how R2P and the ICC relate and operate in practice. If both are to be called upon as responses to mass atrocities, it is important to better understand the relationship between them.

In an attempt to elaborate and assess the relationship between R2P and the ICC, this chapter proceeds in four sections. First, it argues that R2P and the ICC share a common 'utopian' liberal cosmopolitan vision which seeks to displace the sovereign nation state as the primary moral referent of international politics and replace it with the rights-bearing individual. As argued in section two, the ability of either R2P or the ICC to achieve liberal cosmopolitan ends has been undermined by their relationship to the UNSC. Through an examination of the case of Libya, the third section elaborates on how both the ICC's and R2P's liberal cosmopolitan aims have been curtailed by the power politics of the UNSC. Ultimately, the thesis of Koskenniemi is reaffirmed: R2P and the ICC have not been able to escape the politics of international law. Both remain in a constant negotiation between 'utopian' liberal cosmopolitan ends and the apologia of power politics.

## A Deeper Affinity: The Liberal Cosmopolitan Intentions of R2P and the ICC

This section briefly articulates a definition of liberal cosmopolitanism and demonstrates that this common political ethos of international politics is the political and ethical tether that binds the doctrine of R2P to the institution of the ICC.

Liberalism can be broadly understood as a belief in the combined principles of individual liberty, rights, and freedom. Accordingly, liberalism advocates 'political freedom, democracy and constitutionally guaranteed rights, and [privileges] the liberty of the individual and equality before the law'.[3]

---

[3] Scott Burchill, 'Liberalism', in Burchill et al., *Theories of International Relations* (3rd edn, Palgrave Macmillan, 2005), 55.

Unlike liberalism, there is no consensus definition of cosmopolitanism.[4] Cosmopolitanism is taken here to be an ideology grounded in a 'consciousness of being a citizen of the world, whatever other affiliations we may have'.[5] It is a universalist ethic espousing the existence of a 'worldwide community of human beings' which shares universal values.[6] Cosmopolitanism has been advanced by a narrative 'which seeks to reframe human activity and entrench it in law, rights, and responsibilities' and thus seeks to affirm the 'irreducible moral status of each and every person'.[7]

Both liberalism and cosmopolitanism view the individual, and not the community or state, as the key international moral actor, placing value on individual autonomy and attributing 'to the individual a capacity to choose one's life, unencumbered by social attachments'.[8] In international relations, liberal cosmopolitanism has posed a challenge to the realist mantra, wherein states are deemed 'the crucial ethical actors in the international context' and 'the principles of international ethics [are based] on the principle of state sovereignty'.[9]

The impact of liberal cosmopolitanism on the architecture of contemporary international society has been impressive.[10] Perhaps its most obvious manifestation is the human rights regime. As Chris Brown has noted, '[t]he Universal Declaration and subsequent elaborations thereof can serve as a practical summary of what is entailed by cosmopolitan liberalism', with the human rights regime existing as 'a rough approximation of the package of norms and practices that ought to be universally observed'.[11] With the end of the Cold War, liberal cosmopolitan–inspired projects found space to flourish, challenging, if

---

[4] Samuel Scheffler, *Boundaries and Allegiances: Problems of Justice and Responsibility in Liberal Thought* (Oxford Scholarship Online Monographs, 2003), 111; Robert Fine, 'Cosmopolitanism: A Social Science Research Agenda, in Gerard Delanty, *Handbook of Contemporary European Social Theory* (Routledge, 2006), 242.

[5] Fine, 'Cosmopolitanism', 242.

[6] Martha Nussbaum, *For Love of Country?* (Beacon Press, 1996), 4.

[7] David Held, 'Violence, Law, and Justice in a Global Age', *Constellations*, 9 (2002), 75, 80.

[8] Molly Cochran, *Normative Theory in International Relations: A Pragmatic Approach* (Cambridge: Cambridge University Press, 1999), 11.

[9] See Kimberly Hutchings, *International Political Theory: Rethinking Ethics in a Global Era* (Sage, 1999), 31.

[10] Ibid.; Kirsten Ainley, 'Individual Agency and Responsibility for Atrocity', in Renee Jeffery, ed., *Confronting Evil in International Relations* (Palgrave Macmillan, 2008), 37–60.

[11] Chris Brown, *Practical Judgement in International Political Theory: Selected Essays* (Routledge, 2010), 174.

not displacing, the ethical and political primacy of state sovereignty. The result was a flurry of institutional and intellectual activity, which reflected both liberal and cosmopolitan convictions and helped spur the creation of the ICC and R2P. Central to developments in international criminal law is the notion that individuals, and not states, are responsible for violations of human rights. According to Glasius, 'holding only states responsible ... stood in the way of human rights enforcement'.[12] The ICC seeks to hold accountable individual perpetrators, those bearing the greatest responsibility for war crimes, crimes against humanity, and genocide. This reflects a shift of focus to individual agency and individual perpetrators of atrocities, wherein '[g]uilt, evil, is defined strictly in individual terms'.[13] Kirsten Ainley has described this shift as the 'result of the rise of cosmopolitan liberalism'.[14] The creation of the ICC can thus be seen as a triumph for liberal cosmopolitans. As Seyla Benhabib has noted, the Court is an acknowledgement that 'cosmopolitan norms of justice accrue to individuals as moral and legal persons in a worldwide civil society'.[15] Moreover, some argue that state support for and 'expectations of the ICC are shaped by different forms of the cosmopolitan political imagination'.[16] However, to say that the ICC constitutes a complete victory for 'utopian' liberal cosmopolitans would be misleading. As originally conceived, the ICC is the product of a 'perpetual accommodation of the hopes for cosmopolitan justice and the requirements of sovereignty and particularity'.[17] Nevertheless, the ICC stands today as a remarkable achievement for international actors inclined towards a liberal cosmopolitan vision of international politics. The Court embodies a 'cosmopolitan intent: namely, its desire to ensure

[12] Marlies Glasius, *The International Criminal Court: A Global Civil Society Achievement* (Routledge, 2006), 29.

[13] Mahmood Mamdani, 'From Justice to Reconciliation: Making Sense of the African Experience', in Colin Leys and Mahmood Mamdani, eds, *Crisis and Reconstruction: African Perspective* (Nordisk Afrikainstitutet, 1997), 22–23.

[14] Ainley (2008), 2.

[15] Seyla Benhabib, 'Reclaiming Universalism: Negotiating Republican Self-Determination and Cosmopolitan Norms', *Tanner Lectures on Human Values* (March 2004), 116.

[16] Antonio Franceschet, 'Four Cosmopolitan Projects: The International Criminal Court in Context', in Steven C. Roach, ed., *Governance, Order and the International Criminal Court: Between Realpolitik and a Cosmopolitan Court* (Oxford University Press, 2009), 181.

[17] Gerry Simpson, *Law, War and Crime: War Crimes Trials and the Reinvention of International Law* (Polity, 2007), 44. This is most evident in the failure to establish universal jurisdiction for the court. See Glasius (2006), 61–76.

state parties' primary attachment or primary loyalties to the whole of humanity'.[18]

R2P also seeks to challenge the state-centric status quo of international politics by prioritising the individual human and her experience. To resolve the inherent contradiction of espousing the universality of human rights while maintaining the inviolability of state sovereignty, an independent panel, the International Commission on Intervention and State Sovereignty (ICISS), was established by the Canadian government in 2001. Its report, *The Responsibility to Protect*, was delivered in 2001 and sought to 'square the circle ... [by reconciling] respect for human life with state sovereignty'.[19] The key to R2P, according to the ICISS, was 'that human beings sometimes trump sovereignty'.[20] R2P thus accommodated human rights with sovereignty by reaffirming the sovereign rights of states but also claiming that sovereignty itself is conditional on the state's ability and willingness to protect its own citizens from war crimes, crimes against humanity, genocide, and ethnic cleansing. When states fail or are unable to protect their people, the duty to protect those people is transferred to the international community of states.

For Lindberg, R2P 'de-centers the state as the actor par excellence in international relations in favor of people, actual human beings, who are not after all subject beyond question to the whims of their rulers'.[21] Similarly, David Chandler has written that advocates of R2P and humanitarian intervention more broadly uphold claims 'that new international norms prioritizing individual rights to protection promise a framework of liberal peace and that the Realist framework of the Cold War period when state security was viewed as paramount has been superseded'.[22] Critically, it is the liberal cosmopolitan political ethos which both determines and justifies intervention in order to 'protect' civilians. States which violate and undermine liberal cosmopolitan norms become

---

[18] Stephen C. Roach, 'Value Pluralism Liberalism, and the Cosmopolitan Intent of the International Criminal Court', *Journal of Human Rights*, 4 (2005), 475–90.

[19] Thomas G. Weiss, *Humanitarian Intervention: Ideas in Action* (Polity, 2007), 98; see International Commission on Intervention and State Sovereignty (ICISS), 'The Responsibility to Protect', December 2001.

[20] Thomas G. Weiss, 'R2P after 9/11 and the World Summit', *Wisconsin International Law Journal*, 24 (2006), 741–60 at 743.

[21] Todd Lindberg, 'Protect the People', *Washington Times* (September 27, 2005); see also Alex J. Bellamy, 'Wither the Responsibility to Protect? Humanitarian Intervention and the 2005 World Summit', *Ethics & International Affairs*, 20 (2006), 143–69.

[22] David Chandler, 'The Responsibility to Protect? Imposing the Liberal Peace', *International Peacekeeping*, 11 (2004), 59–81 at 59.

candidates for international intervention.[23] Intervention, then, is made possible and justified on the basis that it is waged in the name of a liberal cosmopolitan conception of humanity.

Neither the ICC nor R2P are diametrically opposed to sovereignty.[24] Rather, those involved in the creation of both intended to renegotiate the very meaning of sovereignty along liberal cosmopolitan lines. As Mégret has argued: 'R2P and the ICC, in their own ways, are part of projects to tame or civilize the power incarnated by sovereignty on the basis of a vigorous cosmopolitan outlook that emphasizes the transcendent and universal character of obligations owed to human beings.'[25] It is often suggested that the crimes covered by R2P and the ICC are so grave that they are in the interest of the international community of states. But responding to the perpetration of war crimes, crimes against humanity, genocide and, in the case of R2P, ethnic cleansing, is intended to be in the interests of humanity as a whole. Accordingly, international politics are to be displaced from a state-centric position and away from the prioritisation of power politics where 'right is might' to an individual-centric model based on the universal protection of human rights via international law. Both the ICC and R2P should thus be viewed as attempts to legalise and juridify international relations under the mantra of liberal cosmopolitanism. As such, they both fit within Koskenniemi's observation that the construction of a global rule of law is driven, at least in part, by 'the liberal impulse to escape politics' and to distil global politics into 'non-political rules'.[26]

## The UN Security Council, R2P and the ICC: A Fatal Attraction?

Both R2P and the ICC have drifted towards the power politics of the UN Security Council. As Mégret has poignantly argued, R2P and the ICC 'share a tendency to gravitate towards the very power that they are supposed to constrain ... a tendency to reinforce that which they claim to transcend, sovereign states on the one hand, and the UNSC on the

[23] See Karina Sangha, 'The Responsibility to Protect: A Cosmopolitan Argument for the Duty of Humanitarian Intervention', *Expressions* (Winter 2012), 1–14 at 13.

[24] See also Frederic Mégret, 'ICC, R2P, and the International Community's Evolving Interventionist Toolkit', paper presented at Helsinki Castren Institute for International Law and Human Rights (2010), 19. http://papers.ssrn.com/sol3/papers.cfm?abstract_id=1933111

[25] Ibid. 17.

[26] Koskenniemi (2005), 5–6.

other'.[27] R2P and the ICC have affirmed the Council's power, authority, and legitimacy in international law and politics.

## R2P and the UN Security Council

For the ICISS participants, it was clear that R2P was about making the Council 'work better' rather than establishing an alternative framework for intervention outside of the Council.[28] The ICISS thus endorsed a vision of R2P which fits within the mandate of the Council: 'There is no better or more appropriate body than the United Nations Security Council to authorise military intervention for human protection purposes. The task is not to find alternatives to the Security Council as a source of authority, but to make the Security Council work better than it has.'[29] However, the ICISS report also 'expressed some misgivings about relying on the Council to act as the "proper authority" for military action related to [R2P]'.[30] As a result, the report suggested that, in cases where the Council was deadlocked and unable to intervene, alternatives were available, including the possibility of the UN General Assembly considering the matter of intervention or having regional or subregional organisations intervene under Chapter VIII of the UN Charter and 'seeking subsequent authorisation from the Security Council'.[31] The ICISS firmly warned that a Security Council unable or unwilling to intervene in the face of atrocities was no justification for inaction: 'The Security Council should take into account ... that, if it fails to discharge its responsibility to protect in conscience-shocking situations crying out for action, concerned states may not rule out other means to meet the gravity and urgency of that situation.'[32] When it came to negotiating a legal consensus on R2P at the UN World Summit in 2005, the contours laid out by the ICISS inspired little agreement.[33] Looming over the negotiations was the controversial American and British invasion of Iraq, which had not received approval from the UNSC and which had been justified by the US

---

[27] Mégret (2010), 15.
[28] See Alex Bellamy, *Responsibility to Protect: The Global Effort to End Mass Atrocities* (Polity, 2009), 47–48.
[29] See ICISS (2001), XII.
[30] J. Welsh, 'Civilian Protection in Libya: Putting Coercion and Controversy Back into RtoP', *Ethics & International Affairs*, 25/3 (2011), 255–62 at 257.
[31] ICISS (2001), XIII.
[32] Ibid.
[33] Bellamy (2009), 151–2.

and the UK on (very questionable) humanitarian grounds.[34] The result was a severely diminished interest in establishing a doctrine of intervention that could be put into action or authorised from outside the UNSC.[35]

Compromise was ultimately reached with a watered-down version of the doctrine, one which was 'wedded to Security Council authorization ... [placing] the authorization of intervention squarely under the rubric of the Security Council'.[36] The final product was 'a rather curious mixture of political and legal considerations'[37] and constituted a distilled version of the ICISS's vision of the responsibility to protect, one diluted into the body of two paragraphs, the second of which clearly proclaimed that the authority of the doctrine resided solely within the UNSC.[38]

In its World Summit Outcome Document form, R2P is a product not of 'the power of humanitarian argument but [of] bargaining away key tenets of the ICISS's recommendations'.[39] Even for its greatest and most thoughtful advocates, 'the summit's language could be seen as a step backward'.[40] As Simon Chesterman observed: 'by the time [R2P] was endorsed by the World Summit in 2005, its normative content had been emasculated to the point where it essentially provided that the Security Council could authorize, on a case-by-case basis, things that it had been authorizing for more than a decade'.[41] R2P was thus virtually guaranteed to be invoked not when humanity needed it, but selectively, when the Security Council powers saw fit to do so.

### The ICC and the UN Security Council

The relationship between the UNSC and the ICC played a dominant role in the Rome Statute negotiations.[42] Proponents were concerned that

---

[34] Ibid. 153.
[35] Ibid. 168. Bellamy, however, also accepts that while R2P as outlined in the World Summit Document 'does not advance the question of how to deal with unauthorized intervention ... it does not preclude the possibility of action outside of the council'.
[36] Ibid. 155.
[37] Carsten Stahn, 'Responsibility to Protect: Political Rhetoric or Emerging Legal Norm?', *American Journal of International Law*, 101/1 (2007), 99–120 at 108.
[38] See UN General Assembly, '2005 World Summit Document', UN doc. A/RES/60/1 (24 October 2005).
[39] Bellamy (2009), 167.
[40] Weiss (2007), 117.
[41] Simon Chesterman, '"Leading from Behind": The Responsibility to Protect, the Obama Doctrine, and Humanitarian Intervention in Libya', *Ethics & International Affairs*, 25/3 (2011), 279–85 at 280.
[42] Glasius (2006), 47–60.

giving the UNSC too much influence over the functioning of the ICC would deeply politicise the Court and place international criminal justice at the whim of the Council's five permanent members. These proponents sought a Court that would be independent of the Council. Security Council members, especially the United States, Russia, and China, opposed an independent prosecutor who could handcuff the Council in its role of maintaining and restoring international peace and security.[43] The result of these debates was a compromise position which appeared to assuage the concerns of all sides, reflected in Article 16 of the Rome Statute, which proclaims that the Security Council can defer any ICC investigation or prosecution deemed to be a threat to international peace and security for a period of 12 months (renewable yearly).[44] In addition, the Council is able to refer non-member states to the Court under Chapter VII of the UN Charter.[45] To date, it has done so on two occasions: Darfur, Sudan (2005), and Libya (2011).

The practice and eager acceptance by the ICC of UNSC referrals blurs the distinction between pursuing peace and justice and inevitably might have politicised the ICC's work. As Louise Arbour, former chief prose-cutor at the International Criminal Tribunal for the former Yugoslavia and International Criminal Tribunal for Rwanda, has argued: '[I]nterna-tional criminal justice cannot be sheltered from political considerations when they are administered by the quintessential political body: the Security Council. I have long advocated a separation of the justice and political agendas, and would prefer to see an ICC that had no connection to the Security Council. But this is neither the case nor the trend.'[46] Christian Wenaweser, a former president of the ICC's Assembly of States Parties, also expressed concern about the UNSC's role in the work of the ICC, stating that '[t]here is little diplomatic political support from the Security Council on referrals and it is not likely to come . . . . In the future we have to think about the benefits for the Court'.[47] William Schabas

---

[43] Ibid. 56.

[44] Ibid. 51; Rome Statute (1998), Art. 16.

[45] Rome Statute (1998), Art. 13b.

[46] Louise Arbour, 'The Rise and Fall of International Human Rights', International Crisis Group Sir Joseph Hotung International Human Rights Lecture (17 April 2011). https://www.crisisgroup.org/global/rise-and-fall-international-human-rights accessed 27 February 2018.

[47] See remarks by Christian Wenaweser in William Schabas, 'The International Criminal Court at Ten', PhD Studies in Human Rights (15 February 2012). http://humanrightsdoc torate.blogspot.co.uk/2012/02/international-criminal-court-at-tenw.html accessed 27 February 2018.

interpreted Wenaweser's comments as suggesting that 'we don't need any more Security Council referrals'.[48]

Still, the ICC is 'stuck between a rock and a hard place' in its relationship with the Security Council.[49] Apart from UNSC referrals, the ICC can only open cases in those states which ratified the Rome Statute or which refer themselves to the Court. Many of the worst violators remain outside of the Court's judicial remit. Where this is the case, the ICC requires the UNSC to refer a situation to the Court, as has been the case with Darfur (Sudan) and Libya.[50] Yet, in accepting the UNSC as its patron, the Court may also have bound itself to the Council's power politics, thus politicising its own work. A paradox thus emerges. On the one hand, a closer relationship between the power politics of the UNSC and the ICC diminishes the independence, impartiality, and legitimacy of international criminal justice. On the other hand, without cooperation between the UNSC and the ICC some of the worst atrocities would never be investigated, a fact which itself may hinder the Court's standing and legitimacy. It is notable, however, that this dilemma appears to be rarely considered by the Court or its advocates, many of whom openly celebrate the increasingly close relationship between the ICC and the Security Council.[51]

## The Fight for Legitimacy: Who Wins?

There appears to be a trend that accepts that R2P and the ICC should work hand-in-hand with the UNSC. One justification for this position is that if the Security Council did not endorse these projects they would be largely hollow, naive, and idealistic. They would lean too far towards being 'utopian' to be relevant. By receiving the recognition of, and being

---

[48] Ibid.

[49] See also Mark Kersten, 'The UN Security Council and the ICC: Between a Rock and a Hard Place', *Justice in Conflict* (6 May 2011). http://justiceinconflict.org/2011/05/06/the-un-security-council-and-the-icc-between-a-rock-and-a-hard-place accessed 27 February 2018.

[50] On the latter see e.g. Karin Wester, 'Promise and Pitfalls of the Responsibility to Protect and Lessons to Be Learned from the Case of Libya', dissertation, University of Amsterdam, 2016.

[51] See also Mark Kersten, 'Between Justice and Politics: The International Criminal Court's Intervention in Libya', in Christian De Vos et al., eds, *International Criminal Justice and 'Local Ownership': Assessing the Impact of Justice Interventions* (Cambridge University Press, 2015), 456–78.

used by, the UNSC, both the R2P and the ICC are legitimised. They become 'concrete' in their actual usage by states.[52]

For the ICC, it has been argued that UNSC referrals create 'a mutual legitimacy push [constituting] the evolving normative benefits of mutual assistance or collaboration between institutional players sharing those values that shape the rules considered to become legitimate as well'.[53] As for R2P, it seems implausible for the doctrine to achieve legitimacy by being applied outside of the Security Council. Cases in which the doctrine has been invoked outside of the Council have been viewed as illegitimate.[54] But the biggest winner in the legitimacy sweepstakes, it would seem, is the UNSC itself.[55]

By invoking the justice of the ICC or the humanitarianism of R2P, the Security Council frames intervention within the powerful and persuasive rhetoric associated with these liberal cosmopolitan projects. Some argue that this is precisely what should occur. If done impartially and effectively, as Contarino and Lucent maintained, an enhanced relationship between R2P and the ICC 'could strengthen the credibility of the United Nations Security Council, and could be politically appealing to its five permanent members'.[56] The ICC's former Chief Prosecutor, Luis Moreno-Ocampo, has also appeared eager to combine forces, declaring that 'the International Criminal Court could add legitimacy to the Security Council's decision to apply the Responsibility to Protect'.[57]

However, there is a real risk that Security Council interventions are framed as being intended to save, protect, and bring justice to victims, while obfuscating their less altruistic motives. Humanitarian language

---

[52] Koskenniemi (1990), 7.

[53] Steven C. Roach, *Politicizing the International Criminal Court: The Convergence of Politics, Ethics, and Law* (Rowman and Littlefield, 2006), 161.

[54] See e.g. Gareth Evans, 'Russia, Georgia and the Responsibility to Protect', *Amsterdam Law Forum*, 1/2 (2009), 25–8.

[55] For another take on how the Security Council's legitimacy is bolstered by its use of R2P and the ICC, see Mégret (2010), 26–31.

[56] Michael Contarino and Selena Lucent, 'Stopping the Killing: The International Criminal Court and Juridical Determination of the Responsibility to Protect', *Global Responsibility to Protect* 1 (2009), 560–83. Contarino and Lucent also argued that 'The record to date suggests that if determination of R2P remains the sole prerogative of the UN Security Council, R2P may be little more than an ideal respected primarily in the breach' (66).

[57] As expressed during a conference presentation by Luis Moreno-Ocampo delivered on 16 November 2006. For a report of the conference see Juliette Voinov Kohler, 'The Responsibility to Protect: A Strategy for Engaging America: Conference Report', *Chicago Council on Global Affairs*, 2007. www.thechicagocouncil.org/sites/default/files/R2P%20Conference%20report.pdf accessed 27 February 2018. See also Mégret (2010), 31.

can be used to justify interventions, both judicial and military, which are not humanitarian. International protection and justice emerge as potential monopolies of the most powerful UNSC member states. For both R2P and the ICC, this signals a rather remarkable transformation from a time when the Security Council was 'seen as corrupting both the sanctity of international justice and the neutrality of humanitarian intervention'[58] to a point at which the Council is seen as the primary, perhaps only, guarantor of both.

## The UN Security Council, the ICC, and R2P: The Case of Libya

In the span of just a few weeks in February and March 2011, two unprecedented Security Council resolutions were passed in response to the clear threat to Libyan civilians posed by the regime of Muammar Gaddafi. On 26 February 2011, the UNSC passed Resolution 1970 and subsequently, on March 17, Resolution 1973. The former referred the situation in Libya to the ICC, and both invoked the R2P doctrine. As argued in this section, Resolutions 1970 and 1973 illustrated the extent to which the Court and R2P were shaped by the political machinations of UNSC states.

Prior to its invocation in the case of Libya, many questioned whether R2P would ever amount to anything more than political rhetoric.[59] While the doctrine had achieved what David Scheffer has called 'rhetorical presence'[60] in international relations and law, few substantive advances had been made in practice since its acceptance in the 2005 World Summit document, and the UNSC remained largely silent on the subject.[61] In 2008, Gareth Evans asked whether R2P was 'an idea whose time has come ... and gone', noting that states seemed to exhibit 'buyers remorse' towards the doctrine.[62] The use of R2P in Libya, however, in the words of former ICISS panellist Ramesh Thakur, was a 'game-changer', at least potentially.[63]

---

[58] Mégret (2010), 22.
[59] See Stahn (2007), 99–120.
[60] David Scheffer, 'Atrocity Crimes Framing the Responsibility to Protect', *Case Western Reserve Journal of International Law*, 40 (2008), 111–35.
[61] See Alex J. Bellamy, 'The Responsibility to Protect : Five Years On', *Ethics & International Affairs*, 24 (2010), 143–69 at 145–8.
[62] Gareth Evans, 'The Responsibility to Protect: An Idea Whose Time Has Come ... and Gone?', *International Relations*, 22 (2008), 283–98.
[63] Ramesh Thakur, 'UN Breathes Life into "Responsibility to Protect"', *The Star* (21 March 2011). www.thestar.com/opinion/editorialopinion/article/957664-un-breathes-life-into-responsibility-to-protect accessed 27 February 2018. See also Wester (2016).

Resolution 1970 recalled 'the Libyan authorities' responsibility to protect its population'.[64] Resolution 1973 invoked R2P more substantively by reiterating 'the responsibility of the Libyan authorities to protect the Libyan population and reaffirming that parties to armed conflicts bear the primary responsibility to take all feasible steps to ensure the protection of civilians', and authorising UN member states 'to take all necessary measures . . . to protect civilians and civilian populated areas under threat of attack in the Libyan Arab Jamahiriya'.[65]

For many, the invocation of R2P in Resolutions 1970 and 1973 demonstrated that the doctrine was more than rhetoric. UN Secretary-General Ban Ki-moon declared that 'Resolution 1973 affirms, clearly and unequivocally, the international community's determination to fulfil its responsibility to protect civilians from violence perpetrated upon them by their own government'.[66] Thakur claimed that Libya had 'breathed life' into the R2P doctrine.[67] Weiss similarly stated that Libya demonstrated R2P was 'alive and well'.[68] Yet the invocation of R2P as a response to the crisis in Libya also reaffirmed the absolute authority of the UNSC in shaping how R2P would, and would not, be applied.

In both Resolutions 1970 and 1973, the UNSC invoked only half of the R2P equation. The resolutions made clear that UNSC member states agreed that Libya had a responsibility to protect its citizens and that, in the absence of doing so, international intervention was appropriate. Missing from the resolutions, however, was any justification of military intervention on the basis of the international community itself bearing a responsibility to protect Libyan citizens.

It appeared that a decision was taken to avoid confirming that the international community assumed a concrete legal responsibility to protect citizens when a host state manifestly failed to do so. This was no

---

[64] UN doc. S/RES/1970 (26 February 2011). See also: Security Council, 'In Swift, Decisive Action, Security Council Imposes Tough Measures on Libyan Regime, Adopting Resolution 1970 in Wake of Crackdown on Protesters', UN Doc. SC/10187/Rev.1, 26 February 2011. www.un.org/News/Press/docs/2011/sc10187.doc.htm accessed 27 February 2018.

[65] See UN doc. S/RES/1973 (17 March 2011) and 'Security Council Approves "No-Fly Zone" Over Libya, Authorizing "All Necessary Measures" to Protect Civilians, by Vote of 10 in Favour with 5 Abstentions', UN Department of Public Information, 17 March 2011. www.un.org/News/Press/docs/2011/sc10200.doc.htm

[66] See International Coalition for the Responsibility to Protect, 'The Crisis in Libya'. www.responsibilitytoprotect.org/index.php/crises/crisis-in-libya accessed 20 July 2018.

[67] Thakur (2011).

[68] Thomas G. Weiss, 'RtoP Alive and Well after Libya' (2011) 25 Ethics & International Affairs, pp. 287–92.

accident. Security Council member states are resistant to tying themselves to the possibility of being legally obliged to act similarly in future
cases. As Pattison has put it: 'states are seemingly reluctant to accept this
responsibility for fear of being obliged to act robustly in response to
similar cases'.[69] States want to maintain the ability to select the contexts
in which they will intervene and not be dogged by legal commitments
which could further expose the hypocrisy of only protecting some people,
some of the time.

### Cosmopolitan Justice and Security Council Politics: The UN Referral of Libya to the ICC

UNSC Resolution 1970, passed on 26 February 2011, consisted of a
package of sanctions aimed at the Gaddafi regime.[70] Amongst its measures was the Security Council's second-ever referral of a situation to the
ICC. This referral was met with widespread international praise.
Observers noted that the resolution had been passed with unprecedented
speed and was authorised unanimously by all members of the UNSC.
Amnesty International described the referral as 'a historic moment in
accountability for crimes under international law'.[71] Others said it was a
'great milestone in international criminal justice'[72] and a demonstration
of 'concerted international resolve to pressure Gaddafi and his henchmen
to end their murderous attacks on the Libyan population'.[73] These
celebratory statements obfuscated the deeply politicised contours of the
ICC referral.

Three elements of the resolution in particular highlight the politicisa-
tion of the ICC's mandate through the referral. First, Resolution 1970
precluded the ICC from investigating citizens of states which were not
parties to the ICC statute, with the exception of Libya and 'unless such
exclusive jurisdiction has been expressly waived by the State'.[74] This

---

[69] James Pattison, 'Introduction', *Ethics & International Affairs*, 25 (2011), 251–54 at 253.

[70] UNSC Res. 1970.

[71] Amnesty International, 'Unanimous Security Council Vote a Crucial Moment for International Justice', 27 February 2011. www.amnestyusa.org/unanimous-security-coun cil-vote-a-crucial-moment-for-international-justice accessed 27 February 2018.

[72] See remarks by Geoffrey Robertson in 'Milestones for International Criminal Justice', *Chatham House* (22 September 2011), 3.

[73] Human Rights Watch, 'UN: Security Council Refers Libya to ICC', 27 February 2011. www.hrw.org/news/2011/02/27/un-security-council-refers-libya-icc accessed 27 February 2018.

[74] UNSC Res. 1970, para. 6.

exclusion of non-member state parties to Resolution 1970 exposed a disturbing hypocrisy in the treatment of the ICC by powerful states. This was especially the case for the US, a non-ICC-member state, which co-sponsored the referral while insisting on the exclusion of non-member state parties as a precondition for supporting the referral.[75]

The exclusion of non-member state parties runs in direct contradiction to one of the key aims of the ICC: the achievement of universal jurisdiction, whereby the ICC is able to investigate and prosecute crimes under its jurisdiction in all states. Of the ICC state parties on the Council at the time of Resolution 1970's passage, only Brazil expressed reservations on this issue, suggesting that the exemption of nations from non-member state parties went against 'the integrity and universalisation of the Rome Statute'.[76] Others had previously voiced concern about the legitimacy and legality of such exemptions. Robert Cryer's comments on the subject of the UNSC's referral of Sudan to the ICC were equally applicable in the context of Resolution 1970:

> the legitimacy of the referral is impaired by the a-priori exclusion of non-party state nationals from the jurisdiction of the ICC ... [T]he exclusion of some states' nationals fails to respect the Prosecutor's independence and makes it difficult to reconcile the resolution with the principle of equality before the law. Some states' nationals, it would appear, are more equal than others.[77]

In short, the political tailoring of the referral to exclude non-member state parties from the ICC's jurisdiction both undermined the Court's ultimate aim to achieve universal justice and confirmed that similar crimes within the same context may not be similarly investigated and prosecuted.

[75] Max du Plessis and Antoinette Louw, 'Justice and the Libyan Crisis: The ICC's Role under Security Council Resolution 1970', *Institute for Security Studies* (2011), 2; see also Tim Dunne and Jess Gifkins, 'Libya and the State of Intervention', *Australian Journal of International Affairs*, 65 (2011), 515–29 at 525.

[76] See Security Council, 'In Swift, Decisive Action, Security Council Imposes Tough Measures on Libyan Regime, Adopting Resolution 1970 in Wake of Crackdown on Protesters', UN Doc. SC/10187/Rev.1, 26 February 2011. www.un.org/News/Press/docs/2011/sc10187.doc.htm accessed 27 February 2018. 'Brazil was a long-standing supporter of the integrity and universalization of the Rome Statute, and opposed the exemption from jurisdiction of nationals of those countries not parties to it. Brazil, therefore, expressed its strong reservation to the resolution's operative paragraph 6, and reiterated its firm conviction that initiatives aimed at establishing those exemptions were not helpful to advance the cause of justice and accountability.' See UNSC Res. 1970.

[77] Robert Cryer, 'Sudan, Resolution 1593, and International Criminal Justice', *Leiden Journal of International Law*, 10 (2006), 195–222 at 217.

A second controversial feature of the referral was the inclusion of a preambular reference that recalled Article 16 of the Rome Statute. The reference to Article 16 was almost certainly included in order to assuage states that were concerned that the intervention of the ICC would complicate attempts to negotiate a political settlement to the conflict in Libya.[78] On the face of it, the inclusion of a paragraph referring to a Rome Statute article should have been of little concern. However, many international criminal justice scholars had expected that Article 16 would never become relevant in practice.[79] The invocation of Article 16 would undoubtedly run contrary to the objective of ending impunity. It was thus problematic for those who feared the ICC's work would be instrumentalised by the UNSC.

The third problematic element regarding the referral was the restriction that was placed on the temporal jurisdiction of the ICC. Article 11 of the Rome Statute provides the ICC with jurisdiction for crimes allegedly perpetrated after 1 July 2002, the date at which the Court came into existence.[80] Operative Paragraph 4 of Resolution 1970 restricted the ICC's jurisdiction to events taking place after 15 February 2011.[81] This temporal limitation on the Court's jurisdiction was a deliberate move by UNSC members and had the effect of shielding intervening states from having their pre-revolution relations with the Gaddafi regime exposed. In the years preceding the intervention, many of the states that intervened in Libya had close economic, political, and intelligence connections with the regime.[82] These

---

[78] This is also suggested by du Plessis and Louw (2011), 2. It has also been suggested that the inclusion of the reference to Article 16 was part of a compromise necessary to have Resolution 1970 pass. See 'UNSC Refers Situation in Libya to ICC, Sanctions Gaddafi & Aides', *Sudan Tribune* (27 February 2011). www.sudantribune.com/spip.php?article38116

[79] See, for example, Jessica Gavron, 'Amnesties in the Light of Developments in International Law and the Establishment of the International Criminal Court', *International and Comparative Law Quarterly*, 51 (2002), 91–117 at 109; Carsten Stahn, 'Complementarity, Amnesties and Alternative Forms of Justice: Some Interpretative Guidelines for the International Criminal Court', *Journal of International Criminal Justice*, 3 (2005) 698–9; Mark Freeman, *Necessary Evils: Amnesties and the Search for Justice* (Cambridge University Press, 2009), 81.

[80] Rome Statute 1998, Art 11.

[81] UNSC Res. 1970.

[82] 'Libya: Gaddafi Regime's US-UK Spy Links Revealed', BBC (4 September 2011). www .bbc.com/news/world-africa-14774533 accessed 27 February 2018. While the United States brushed off the reports, the UK government ordered its Gibson Inquiry to add the allegations to its docket. See also Lindsey Hilsum, *Sandstorm: Libya in the Time of Revolution* (Faber and Faber, 2012).

connections helped legitimise and sustain the regime.[83] But curtailing the ICC's temporal jurisdiction prevented investigators from shedding light on the possibly illegal and undoubtedly embarrassing political, economic, and intelligence relations between the Gaddafi regime and the states that engineered Gaddafi's demise.

Some observers have suggested that Resolution 1970 came at a significant cost to the Court. Wenawaser stated that there was 'pretty much everything wrong' with the language in Resolution 1970.[84] Similarly, Wenawaser's predecessor, Bruno Stagno Ugarte, wrote that Resolution 1970 included language 'inimical to the integrity of the Rome Statute'.[85] A group of political and academic figures, convened by Chatham House, concluded that 'too high a price was being paid [by the ICC] for the conditions for referral which were included in relevant resolutions'.[86]

Still, the ICC and a significant portion of the community which supported it eagerly accepted the UNSC's referral of Libya to the ICC, political tailorings and all. The precedent this set may be deeply problematic for the Court. While Resolution 1970 was emphatically celebrated as a victory for the pursuit of international criminal justice and was framed as a breakthrough in the relationship between the ICC and the UNSC, it may have come at a heavy price.

### Libya, the UN Security Council, R2P, and the ICC

UNSC Resolutions 1970 and 1973 have contributed to shaping the future of the ICC as an institution and of R2P as a doctrine.[87] Yet there are good reasons to be cautious of this new age of 'protection politics',[88] and some of these reasons might explain why R2P has not been invoked more recently in relation to Syria.

---

[83] See e.g. Ronald Bruce St John, *Libya: From Colony to Revolution* (Oneworld, 2011), 225–78; John Wright, *A History of Libya* (Hurst, 2010), 221–9.

[84] Remarks by Christian Wenawaser at conference: Through the Lens of Nuremberg: The International Court at Its Tenth Anniversary, Nuremberg, Germany, 5 October 2012.

[85] Bruno Stagno Ugarte, 'Enhancing Security Council Cooperation with the International Criminal Court' (2011). http://regnet.anu.edu.au/research/publications/2801/working-paper-no-62-enhancing-security-council-cooperation-international

[86] Chatham House, 'The UN Security Council and the International Criminal Court: International Law Meeting Summary, with Parliamentarians for Global Action' (16 March 2012), 7.

[87] For more, see Alex J. Bellamy and Paul D. Williams, 'The New Politics of Protection? Côte d'Ivoire, Libya and the Responsibility to Protect', *International Affairs*, 87 (2011), 825–50 at 845–7.

[88] Ibid.

The price of tethering the ICC to the UNSC has been high. Not only did Resolution 1970 politicise the mandate of the Court but, as the intervention progressed, the Court was largely abandoned by the same powers that invoked it.[89] During May and June 2011, NATO increased its military activities in order to break the apparent stalemate between the rebels and pro-Gaddafi forces. By late August, Tripoli fell to the rebels while the NATO states that had intervened began the process of jostling for the lucrative economic windfall from an NTC-controlled Libya.[90] In this context, the political calculus of Western states shifted from backing international criminal justice to other political interests and goals in a post-Gaddafi Libya. The ICC was no longer 'useful' to intervening powers. Since that time, virtually no significant political support from the Security Council has been afforded to the ICC's mandate in Libya, similar to the almost complete lack of Council interest in supporting the prosecutor's mandate in Darfur. Thus far one case has been produced, originally against three suspects, with charges of crimes against humanity (murder and persecution). In November 2011, upon his death, the arrest warrant against Muammar Mohammed Abu Minyar Gaddafi was withdrawn. Proceedings against Abdullah Al-Senussi ended in July 2014 when the inadmissibility of the case was confirmed by the Appeals Chamber. The case against Saif Al-Islam Gaddafi will remain in the pre-trial stage until the accused has been transferred to the Court in The Hague.[91] Two other warrants have since been issued, for Al-Tuhamy Mohamed Khaled and for Mahmoud Mustafa Busayf Al-Werfalli, but neither suspect has appeared before the ICC. Seven years after the Security Council referred the situation in Libya to the ICC, not a single one of the Court's targets has appeared in The Hague.

The case of Libya also seems to have cemented the selectivity that R2P was intended to transcend. Chesterman might have been correct in arguing that R2P 'may have made it harder [for the international community] to say no' to intervention in the face of mass atrocities, but doing so may have come at the expense of the underlying aim of R2P.[92]

---

[89] See Mark Kersten, 'Justice after the War: The International Criminal Court and Post-Gaddafi Justice', in K. J. Fisher and R. Stewart, *Transitional Justice and the Arab Spring* (Routledge, 2015), 192.

[90] See Rupert Cornwell, 'World Powers Scramble for a Stake in Future of the New Libya', *The Independent* (23 August 2011). www.independent.co.uk/news/world/politics/world-powers-scramble-for-a-stake-in-future-of-the-new-libya-2342212.html accessed 27 February 2018.

[91] See ICC website. www.icc-cpi.int/libya accessed 27 February 2018.

[92] Chesterman (2011), 6.

Moreover, the apparent conflation between regime change and the protection of civilians posed new problems for the R2P doctrine insofar as it mixes the political aims of removing regimes with the humanitarian goal of protecting civilians from human rights violations. Initially, there was ambivalence towards targeting Muammar Gaddafi. However, by June 2011, NATO officials admitted that they saw Gaddafi as a legitimate military target.[93] This was a far cry from Evans' claim that the intervention 'in Libya is not about bombing for democracy or Muammar Qaddafi's head ... Legally, morally, politically, and militarily it has only one justification: protecting the country's people'.[94] R2P was supposed to be 'about protecting civilians, and emphatically not about regime change'.[95] Thus the responses to the crisis in Libya may signal a step backward for R2P, moving international politics back towards a selective right to intervention rather than an international responsibility to protect.

Lastly, it is apparent that the Security Council's legitimacy and, in the case of Libya, the legitimacy of NATO forces were bolstered by framing the interventions through the language of responsibility, protection, humanity, and justice. This humanitarian language was critical in legitimising the intervention in Libya, lending political and rhetorical clout to NATO's military operations.[96]

## Conclusion: R2P and the ICC, Compromise with or Comprised by the UNSC?

The establishment of the ICC and the elaboration of R2P have been remarkable and welcome developments in international relations and international law. They have helped to calibrate ideas about international responses to mass atrocities. Moreover, where and when they have been deployed, they have had some potential to address, and perhaps even prevent, the commission of (some) international crimes.

---

[93] See 'Libya: Removing Gaddafi not allowed, says David Cameron', BBC (21 March 2011). www.bbc.co.uk/news/uk-politics-12802749 accessed 27 February 2018.

[94] Gareth Evans, 'UN targets Libya with Pinpoint Accuracy', *Sydney Morning Herald* (24 March 2011). www.smh.com.au/opinion/politics/un-targets-libya-with-pinpoint-accuracy-20110323-1c6pc.html

[95] David Rieff, 'R2P, R.I.P.', *New York Times* (7 November 2011). www.nytimes.com/2011/11/08/opinion/r2p-rip.html?pagewanted=all accessed 27 February 2018.

[96] David Kaye, 'Wanted: Qaddafi & Co. Can the ICC Arrest the Libya Three?', *Foreign Affairs* (19 May 2011). www.foreignaffairs.com/articles/67857/david-kaye/wanted-qaddafi-co accessed 27 February 2018.

But observers and scholars alike appear to have forgotten the driving liberal cosmopolitan intentions behind the ICC and R2P. Both the Court and the doctrine are increasingly at the whim of the permanent members of the UNSC. Meanwhile, proponents of the ICC and R2P increasingly reaffirm and even celebrate the role of the Security Council in dispensing ICC and R2P interventions. As demonstrated by the Court's intervention into Libya, the permanent members of the UNSC appeared content to deploy the ICC on an ad hoc basis in those situations where it served their political interests, and only after restricting and politicising the Court's mandate. This may have put the independence and integrity of the Court at risk, especially if a conscious critique of UNSC referrals was muted in favour of celebratory statements that welcomed a closer relationship between the ICC and the UNSC.

As for R2P, it is difficult to imagine how the doctrine can extricate itself from the vagaries of the UNSC. The World Summit document, subsequent resolutions, and practice have firmly entrenched R2P as a response that will be primarily, if not exclusively, invoked by the Council. We seem destined to accept Patrick Stewart's insight that '[t]here is bound to be selectivity and inconsistency in the application of the responsibility to protect norm given the complexity of national interests at stake in U.S. calculations and in the calculations of other major powers involved in these situations'.[97] Those who doubt this reality and cling to the original intent of both the ICC and R2P, it would seem, will be placed firmly within the camps of 'dreamers' and 'utopians'.

Of course, it may be that neither the ICC nor R2P were ever capable of transcending the political machinations of the Security Council. David Chandler, for example, has challenged the notion that R2P represents a moral shift away from state-centred international relations, arguing that '[t]he close relationship between *Realpolitik* and morality is not a contradictory one'.[98] Indeed, it is possible that both the ICC and R2P have always and will always constitute a compromise between the apology of UNSC power politics and the utopia of liberal cosmopolitanism. As such, they remain in constant negotiation between being too close or too divorced from power politics. Still, to retain long-term legitimacy it is important that R2P and the ICC not consistently fall prey to the selectivity and hypocrisy of UNSC realpolitik. The liberal cosmopolitan vision of

---

[97] Stewart Patrick, quoted in Jayshree Bajoria, 'Libya and the Responsibility to Protect' (2011). www.huffingtonpost.com/jayshree-bajoria/libya-and-the-responsibil_b_840586 .html accessed 27 February 2018.

[98] Chandler (2004), 59–81 at 76.

R2P and the ICC may never be fully realised, but it should be striven for. R2P and the ICC may never extricate themselves entirely from the power politics of the Council, but they need not be beholden to it. Their relationship with political power must be constantly calibrated and recalibrated for their integrity to be sustained. If not, the very liberal cosmopolitan purpose for which they were created may be irrevocably lost.

# 8

# A Return to Stability? Hegemonic and Counter-Hegemonic Positions in the Debate on Universal Jurisdiction *in absentia*

## AISLING O'SULLIVAN

## Introduction

The debate that envelops the principle of universal jurisdiction draws out a 'dark side' of the international criminal law project.[1] This remark refers to the fact that the commitment by the international community to individual criminal accountability as universal has not produced its corollary, the 'court of humanity' that will never adjourn.[2] Rather, the debate on universal jurisdiction illustrates a swing between the projects of preventing impunity and avoiding abuse.[3] As Koskenniemi and Leino

---

[1] This chapter draws from and develops a broader research project that explores the debate among international lawyers over the principle of universal jurisdiction in international criminal law. See A O'Sullivan, *Universal Jurisdiction in International Criminal Law* (London: Routledge 2017). The notion of 'dark sides' is drawn from David Kennedy, *The Dark Sides of Virtue: Reassessing International Humanitarianism* (Princeton: Princeton University Press, 2005). See also Martti Koskenniemi, *From Apology to Utopia: The Structure of the International Legal Argument* (Cambridge: Cambridge University Press, 2005), 570: 'the law constructs its own field of application as it goes along through a normative language that highlights some aspects of the world while leaving other aspects in the dark'.

[2] See *The Einsatzgruppen Trial: Trial of Otto Ohlendorf and Others* (1948) IV Trials of War Criminals before the Nuremberg Military Tribunals Green Series (1946–1949) 499: 'inconceivable that the law of humanity should ever lack for a tribunal; where the law exists a court will rise ... the court of humanity, if it may be so termed, will never adjourn ... It would be an admission of incapacity, in contradiction of every self-evident reality, that mankind ... should be unable to maintain a tribunal holding inviolable the law of humanity and by doing so preserve the human race itself.' See also G. Simpson, *Law, War and Crime: War Crimes, Trials and the Reinvention of International Law* (Cambridge: Polity Press 2007), 37, citing Finkielkraut (1992).

[3] According to the Report of the UN Secretary General Ban Ki-moon, 'The Scope and Application of the Principle of Universal Jurisdiction' (29 July 2010) UN Doc A/65/181, para. 5: 'the goal of ending impunity did not in itself generate abuse'.

have argued: 'When criminal law and diplomacy meet, the result is likely to be either undermining diplomatic freedom of action – or turning criminal justice into show trials. Any middle ground is both narrow and slippery.'[4] Theoretically, universal jurisdiction endeavours to fill a jurisdictional lacuna and therefore is considered an essential complementary mechanism for accountability. At the same time, there is a significant emphasis on avoiding the principle's 'manipulation for political ends' and the need for compliance with recognised rules of international law.[5] In this way, the debate is bound within the inevitable tension that Luban has identified between the 'momentous and radical project' and 'the religion of sovereignty'.[6] Luban has described international criminal law's dilemma as one where the 'gulf between the transcendent claims of sovereignty and its deflation in international criminal law' presents a challenge in justifying prosecutions of nationals of states who object to their trials.[7]

Endeavouring to both define and examine the practice of universal jurisdiction reveals competing approaches in academic scholarship or jurisprudential guidance. In one approach universal accountability (or fighting impunity) is emphasised, whereas in the other, state voluntary will (or avoiding abuse). Out of these competing approaches a third approach has emerged, attempting to reconcile and move these contrasting approaches to a middle ground. These contrasts are also found within the historical debates that can be traced from the end of the nineteenth century onwards. On the surface, these competing approaches in both the historical and contemporary debates have appeared to be underpinned by a recurring naturalism-positivism dichotomy that hinges upon the irreconcilable debate over whether origin of law traces to a prior legal order or to state liberty.

---

[4] Martti Koskenniemi and Päivi Leino, 'Fragmentation of International Law? Postmodern Anxieties', *Leiden Journal of International Law*, 15 (2002), 553, 579.

[5] According to the 2010 Report of the UN Secretary-General, 'Scope and Application', para. 9, universal jurisdiction is 'an essential jurisdictional instrument in the fight against impunity', and should reflect 'judicial independence and impartiality ... [in order that principle] was not manipulated for political ends'.

[6] David Luban, 'Fairness to Rightness: Jurisdiction, Legality and the Legitimacy of International Criminal Law' in Samantha Besson and John Tasioulas, eds, *The Philosophy of International Law* (Oxford: Oxford University Press, 2010), 575, 578. See also Martti Koskenniemi, 'Between Impunity and Show Trials', *Max Planck Yearbook for United Nations Law*, 6 (2002), 1–35 (characterising the irreconcilable tension as 'between impunity and show trial').

[7] Luban, 'Fairness to Rightness'.

Disrupting the notion of international law as located within a fixed political culture underpins the approach this chapter will take when examining the contentious debate on the concept of universal jurisdiction *in absentia*. This debate concerns a controversy over whether the alleged offender must be voluntarily present within the territory of the prosecuting state in order to justify exercising jurisdiction over the accused.[8] In view of its linguistic indeterminacy and its institutional bias, this approach to international law will serve as a framework through which this contentious debate will be interrogated.[9] Therein, international law is conceived of as a language that is the domain of lawyers, who engage in a practice underpinned by liberal ideas as the chosen political sensibility.[10]

This chapter draws on the themes of indeterminacy and hegemonic technique as developed in Martti Koskenniemi's work. Indeterminacy explains why the recurring naturalism/positivism (or *a priori* order (justice)/liberty (consent)) debates occur. In addition, it demonstrates how law as a language is structured by oppositions. This fundamental incoherence explains why no legal argument may be preferred over another, which compels a political choice based on either context or normative principles, such as reasonableness. Hegemonic technique explains how international law 'offers a defence for hegemonic and non-hegemonic practices equally'[11] and how international law debates suggest two projects that characterise international law: as a project of unity or of identity.[12] As we observe in competing moralist/formalist

---

[8] This issue surfaced out of the political controversies over certain proceedings before Belgian and Spanish courts against former and serving foreign state officials. In these controversial cases, international arrest warrants have been issued against foreign nationals who were not, at the time of the issuing of the warrant, on the territory of the prosecuting states. See *Re Pinochet* Tribunal de Premier Instance de Bruxelles (6 November 1998), para. 3.2.1; *Re Yerodia Ndombasi* Tribunal de Premier Instance de Bruxelles (11 April 2000), para. 3.4; *Re Sharon et al.* (2002) 126 ILR 110; *Guatemalan Generals Case*, Audiencia Nacional (13th December 2000), www.derechos.org/nizkor/guatemala/doc/autoan.html; *Cavallo* (2003) 42 ILM 888; *Scilingo* Audiencia Nacional (4th November 1998); and *Peruvian Genocide Case* (2003) 42 ILM 1200.

[9] Koskenniemi, *Apology to Utopia*, 570; Martti Koskenniemi, 'The Politics of International Law: 20 Years Later', *European Journal of International Law*, 20 (2009), 7–19 at 9.

[10] Koskenniemi, '20 Years Later' (2009), 9. International law is 'what lawyers do and how they think'. See 'Between Commitment and Cynicism: Outline for a Theory of International Law as Practice' in Martti Koskenniemi, *The Politics of International Law* (Oxford: Hart, 2011), 271.

[11] Martti Koskenniemi, *The Politics of International Law* (Oxford: Hart, 2011), 241.

[12] Martti Koskenniemi, 'International Law and Hegemony: A Reconfiguration', *Cambridge Review of International Affairs*, 17 (2004), 197–218 at 200, 201. One project claims to

approaches, these projects of unity or identity are situated in the debate that envelops the principle of universal jurisdiction and are represented by the tension between preventing impunity and avoiding abuse.

This chapter addresses the debate as bounded by a tension between competing political preferences labelled moralist (fight impunity) and formalist (avoiding abuse). This illustrates the competing logics as overarching themes at surface level. The moralist approach challenges what its proponents perceive as the injustice of impunity, privileging the moral value of criminal accountability, while champions of the formalist approach challenge what they believe is the injustice of politically motivated or show trials, privileging the moral value of maintaining order. Indeterminacy illustrates how both moralist/formalist logics are in each approach and, in this sense, merge into one another. A moralist approach that privileges the moral naturalism of the crimes (normativity) is considered simultaneously to be concrete (consent to extraterritorial jurisdiction) while a formalist approach that privileges consent to extraterritorial jurisdiction (concreteness) is considered normative (avoid arbitrary and unfettered state interference).

In this chapter, I primarily investigate the separate and dissenting opinions in the *Arrest Warrant* case on the question of universal jurisdiction *in absentia* in order to draw out the descending (more normative, less concrete) and ascending (more concrete, less normative) patterns of argument within each opinion and to identify the hegemonic and counter-hegemonic positions in the pre- and post-*Arrest Warrant* debate.[13] I observe how van den Wyngaert, Guillaume, and the Joint Separate Opinion are archetypal of the competing moralist and formalist approaches and the move to the middle ground with recourse to reasonableness. It is evident that this debate on *in absentia* trials is caught within the tension between the moralist (fighting impunity) and formalist (avoiding abuse) approaches that underpin a broader debate on the principle's justification and content. This struggle for hegemonic control illustrates how each legal outcome within the debate is not 'natural' and 'inevitable'. Rather it is a series of strategic moves that are historically contingent and accord with structural bias.

---

transform the world from 'sovereign egoism to world unity' (descending) while the other from 'oppressive homogeneity to self-determination' (ascending).

[13] Emmanuelle Jouannet, 'Koskenniemi: A Critical Introduction', in Koskenniemi, *Politics of International Law* (2011), 7, and Koskenniemi, *Apology to Utopia*, 61–4.

## The Grammar of International Law: Political Open-Endedness and Rigorous Formalism

In contrast to previous studies on universal jurisdiction, this chapter adopts an approach to international law that posits a politics of law. Thus it rejects the assumption that the rule of law is internally coherent and capable of determining legal outcomes. This approach has a 'dual insight' that describes international law as both a language 'characterized by a precise grammatical structure' and a 'site of politics'.[14] The grammatical structure of the language is constructed on a paradox in liberal theory.[15] This is exposed by a critique of liberalism that identifies the irreconcilable tension between individual freedom (as a justification for the legal order) and collective constraint (in order to protect freedom of all).[16]

In this regard, modern international law must try to 'balance' the opposing 'demands' of individual autonomy and maintaining social order, by contending that to 'preserve freedom, order must be created to restrict it'.[17] Therefore, each legal argument is both 'concrete (linked to state voluntary will as reflected in behaviour) and normative (capable of impartial ascertainment and application)'.[18] Accordingly, each argument is both to reflect (consent) and be critical (justice) of state policy regardless of which position is being argued.[19] Thus, no legal argument can be superior to its counterargument, as both argument and counterargument are structurally identical; each argument must use the same grammatical rules to adhere to 'rigorous formalism'.[20] In this sense, both patterns of argument operate simultaneously and, therefore, merge into another.

To be both critical and reflective of state policy is obviously irreconcilable. Hence, each unified argument oscillates in a constant movement between normativity and concreteness, incapable of remaining fixed or stable.[21] We observed that such a movement suggests 'two opposite

---

[14] Ibid. 24.
[15] According to Koskenniemi, *Apology to Utopia*, xiii, 'international law reproduces the paradoxes and ambivalences of a liberal theory of politics'.
[16] Roberto Unger, *Knowledge and Politics* (New York: Free Press, 1975), 66–103; Alasdair MacIntyre, *After Virtue: A Study in Moral Theory* (3rd ed., Indiana: University of Notre Dame Press, 2007).
[17] Koskenniemi, *Apology to Utopia*, 71.
[18] Ibid.
[19] Ibid. 19–20. See also David Kennedy, *International Legal Structures* (Baden-Baden: Nomos, 1987), 31, on 'hard' and 'soft' doctrines.
[20] Koskenniemi, *Apology to Utopia*, 563.
[21] Ibid. 182–223; Martti Koskenniemi, 'The Politics of International Law', *European Journal of International Law*, 1 (1990), 4–32 at 12.

projects that characterise international law'.[22] One project moves from 'oppressive uniformity of global domination into self-determination and identity', an ascending pattern, drawn from will and behaviour. The other project moves from 'sovereign egoism into world unity', a descending pattern, drawn from higher normative code or natural morality.[23] An ascending pattern privileges state power over objective binding norms. It emphasises a non-normative position and assumes that state liberty is superior to law. This presupposes that the objective (apolitical) rule of law can originate in state power. That said, to constrain state behaviour, the ascending pattern must turn to normativity in order to bind the state regardless of its consent. A descending pattern meanwhile privileges objective binding norms over state power. It emphasises a normative position and assumes that the legal order is superior to state power. This presupposes that an objective (apolitical) rule of law can originate in a higher normative code, preceding the state.[24] Yet, the descending pattern must turn to concreteness in order to bind the state by its consent.

It follows, then, that both patterns can be accused of being subjective by the opposite pattern. An ascending pattern can be read as subjective as it is too reflective of state power and, in being so, diminishes law's normative character and makes the law seem mere apology for power.[25] Equally, a descending pattern can be seen as subjective as it is too critical of state power, and thus arbitrarily constrains individual freedom and makes the law seem utopian, divorced from the realities of international affairs. Hence, projects of unity and identity 'appear as surfaces on which political actors can reciprocally make and oppose hegemonic claims' and the perception of superiority stems from each protagonist's accusation of 'subjectivity' against their opponent.[26] As competing projects are forced to recognise the validity of their counter-points, on which they depend, there is in general tendency towards a middle ground that continues to prefer a political project over another (hegemonic choice) and remains open to challenge from its counterposition.

With these observations in mind, Koskenniemi's critique of Lotus is informative. The Lotus case encapsulates the disagreement among

---

[22] Koskenniemi, 'Hegemony: A Reconfiguration', 200.
[23] Ibid.; Koskenniemi, Apology to Utopia, 65–8.
[24] Koskenniemi, Apology to Utopia, 60.
[25] Ibid. 69; Kennedy, International Legal Structures, used the themes of 'apology' and 'utopia' as a way of describing the opposing patterns within the structure of argument.
[26] Koskenniemi, Politics of International Law (2011), 201.

international lawyers on the preferred method to establish the parameters of state autonomy and collective restraint.[27] *Lotus* highlights the liberal paradox at the core of the doctrine of jurisdiction. Although the state determines the extent of its jurisdiction, it is international law that verifies the legal validity of the state's determination.[28] In mapping this paradox, Koskenniemi has contended that the doctrine of jurisdiction is torn between competing approaches to the law's origin, whether pure fact (state liberty) or legal approaches (prior legal order). In *Lotus*, the majority of the judges adopted the pure fact approach.[29] They assumed that the state's liberty pre-existed the legal order and, as such, had normative content (or value).[30] However, this assumption meant that the validity of the state's behaviour was determined according to a state's subjective preferences[31] and this cannot avoid the accusation of apology for power.[32] Consequently, the majority of the judges in *Lotus* were forced to make a descending move, namely to argue that the anterior state liberty may be subject to limitations imposed by international law.[33] This descending move is also paradoxical and its proponents may be accused of utopia because the position beyond liberty undermines the original assumption that the state's liberty is anterior and normative.[34]

In opposition, the dissenting minority in *Lotus* adopted the legal approach.[35] They assumed that an *a priori* legal order existed, imposing

---

[27] *Case of the SS Lotus (France v. Turkey)* (1927) PCIJ Ser A No 10.

[28] 'Jurisdiction, which in principle belongs solely to the State, is limited by rules of international law'; see *Nationality Decrees in Tunis and Morocco Advisory Opinion* (1923) PCIJ Rep Series B no 4, 24.

[29] In *Lotus*, the PCIJ considered that international law consisted of a general liberty of States, where 'rules of law binding upon States . . . emanate from their own free will as expressed in conventions or by usages'. As rules of law emanate from voluntary will, 'restrictions on the independence of States cannot be presumed'. As a rebuttable presumption, the PCIJ considered that international law imposes certain limitations, which require a state to remain within those limitations when exercising its inherent independence. It concluded from its analysis of the behaviour of states that the 'great variety of rules which [states] have been able to adopt without objections or complaints' demonstrated the 'wide measure of discretion' left to states by international law 'which is only limited in certain cases by prohibitive rules'. Outside of those limitations, 'every State remains free to adopt the principles, which it regards as best and most suitable'. See *Case of the SS Lotus*, 18, 19.

[30] Koskenniemi, *Apology to Utopia*, 256.

[31] Ibid. 257.

[32] Ibid. 225.

[33] *Case of the SS Lotus*, 19.

[34] Koskenniemi, *Apology to Utopia*, 225.

[35] *Case of the SS Lotus*, 34 (Judge Loder) and 52 (Lord Finlay) on the position that the Court was asked simply to determine whether Turkey was authorised under international law to

legal rights and duties on its legal subjects.[36] However, this assumption meant that the validity of state jurisdiction was determined according to theories of justice (beyond liberty) and this descending position cannot avoid the accusation of utopia either. It compels the move to an ascending pattern and the attempt to demonstrate that the jurisdictional claim is concrete based on empirical evidence in state behaviour.[37] Any empirical analysis is frustrated by competing state behaviour and in any case, it cannot escape the criticism of apology that is levelled at the pure fact approach.

This endless movement of patterns attempts to 'preserve the descending and ascending idea within itself'.[38] It follows then that the doctrine of jurisdiction fails to establish whether the law's origin is sourced to state liberty or to an international legal order pre-existing the state and that neither approach (state liberty or pre-existing legal order) can avoid accusations of being subjective and political. Both approaches conflict with the premise of a liberal rule of law because, when they are brought to their logical conclusion, the 'wide measure of discretion' negates law's normativity while the pre-existing legal order conflicts with the liberal idea of justifying the order on individual freedom. It will be apparent in the analysis of competing approaches to universal jurisdiction *in absentia* how the *Lotus* paradox is within each legal argument, that is, both positions are contained in every position.

Faced with a dispute over a state's exercise of jurisdiction, international lawyers have turned to ideas of reasonableness[39] or interest balancing[40] rather than conceiving jurisdiction as 'black letter law'.[41] Here,

---

exercise jurisdiction and not that France must demonstrate a prohibitive rule. See for support, James Brierly, 'The Lotus Case', *Law Quarterly Review*, 44 (1928), 154, 155.

[36] Koskenniemi, *Apology to Utopia*, 229. See J. G. Merrills, *The Anatomy of International Law: A Study of the Role of International Law in the Contemporary World* (2nd edn, London: Sweet and Maxwell, 1981), 45.

[37] Koskenniemi, *Apology to Utopia*, 229.

[38] Ibid. 226.

[39] Ian Brownlie, *Principles of Public International Law* (7th edn, Oxford: Oxford University Press, 2008), 308, 311 (on a 'substantial and *bona fide* connection between subject matter and source of the jurisdiction'). See also Cedric Ryngaert, *Jurisdiction in International Law* (Oxford: Oxford University Press, 2008), 145–50.

[40] Luc Reydams, *Universal Jurisdiction: International and Municipal Perspectives* (Oxford: Oxford University Press, 2003), 24.

[41] Merrills, *Anatomy of International Law*, 51. See also Louis Henkin, *International Law: Politics and Values* (Dordrecht: Martinus Nijhoff, 1995), 232 (discussing the principles as not 'black letter law' and that 'realities have refined the traditional categories, made them less rigid, less conclusive').

jurisdictional principles are conceived of as fluid categories, without stark boundary lines. However, if a final assessment is based on reasonableness and weighing interests, it is not based on a determinant rule of law and ultimately appears to be mere political choice.[42] As has been noted, if indeterminacy of rules accommodates competing positions within legal discourse, the legal rules fail to resolve the conflict on their own. Rather, the legal outcome is a political choice between competing legal arguments, namely what is termed the politics of international law.[43] Based on this observation, Koskenniemi has contended that, conscious of where the hegemony lies, lawyers operate hegemonic and counter-hegemonic techniques, and then plead in accordance with the institutional culture.[44] These hegemonic and counter-hegemonic positions[45] appeal to what Kennedy has described as moments of 'stability' or 'reforming vision'[46] or to what Koskenniemi has classified as movements towards self-determination or world unity.[47] Neither picture of the social world avoids the apology and utopia charge, as both positions are either less normative and more concrete or less concrete and more normative.[48] This means that 'the rule of law thinly hides from sight the fact that social conflict must still be solved by political means'.[49]

## The *Arrest Warrant* Case and the Debate over Universal Jurisdiction *in absentia*

The *Arrest Warrant* judgment marked a major turning point within the broader debate on the principle of universal jurisdiction because the

---

[42] The court cannot prefer any argument because each argument must draw on logics of both realism and formalism, which are themselves contradictory and incoherent. See Koskenniemi, *Apology to Utopia*, 258–303, 333–45, 461–74. See also Martti Koskenniemi, 'Occupied Zone: A Zone of Reasonableness?', *Israeli Law Review*, 41 (2008), 13. See also Jason Beckett, 'Rebel without a Cause? Martti Koskenniemi and the Critical Legal Project', *German Law Journal* 7/12 (2006), 1045–88, at 1052, 1054.
[43] Koskenniemi, *Politics of International Law* (2011) and '20 Years Later'; Nigel Purvis, 'Critical Legal Studies in Public International Law', *Harvard International Law Journal*, 32 (1991), 81.
[44] Koskenniemi, 'Hegemony: A Reconfiguration', 202.
[45] Martti Koskenniemi, *Gentle Civilizer of Nations: International Law since 1870* (Cambridge: Cambridge University Press, 2002). See also Samuel Moyn, *The Last Utopia: Human Rights in History* (Massachusetts: Harvard University Press, 2010).
[46] David Kennedy, 'When Renewal Repeats: Thinking against the Box', *New York University Journal of International and Policy* (1999–2000), 335–500 at 343.
[47] Koskenniemi, 'Hegemony: A Reconfiguration', 199.
[48] Jouannet, 'Critical Introduction', 7–8.
[49] Koskenniemi, '20 Years Later', 7.

International Court of Justice determined that personal immunity bars foreign criminal jurisdiction irrespective of whether or not the proceedings relate to crimes against international law.[50] The dispute between Belgium and the Democratic Republic of Congo (DRC) arose from a Belgian court's decision to exercise jurisdiction over (and issue an arrest warrant *in absentia* against) Yerodia Ndombasi, who, at the time, was the DRC's Minister for Foreign Affairs.[51] In issuing the arrest warrant, Judge Vandermeersch considered Belgian courts to be competent irrespective of whether or not the accused was present in Belgium at the initiation of the investigation.[52] In response, Yerodia's counsel made a series of unsuccessful interventions in the Belgian courts.[53] As the investigation was allowed to continue and the arrest warrant remained outstanding, the DRC filed an application to the International Court of Justice.[54] The DRC's application claimed a violation of *par in parem non habet*,[55] arising from an excessive and arbitrary exercise of jurisdiction and the violation of immunity of its Minister for Foreign Affairs from foreign criminal jurisdiction.[56] On the issue of immunity, it was evident that the

---

[50] *Case of the Arrest Warrant of 11 April 2000 (Democratic Republic of Congo v. Belgium)* (2002) ICJ Reports No. 121, para. 58. For approval of this finding on personal immunity, see Rosanne van Alebeek, *The Immunity of States and Their Officials in International Criminal Law and International Human Rights Law* (Oxford: Oxford University Press, 2008), 267, 273. For brevity, the phrase 'crimes against international law' will be used as a classification for war crimes, crimes against humanity, and genocide as crimes under customary international law.

[51] 'Counter-Memorial of Belgium', Part 1, para. 1.3–1.5. The civil party complaints were lodged at the Brussels Court of First Instance by twelve civil party complainants, all of whom were resident in Belgium and five of whom were of Belgian nationality.

[52] *Re Yerodia Ndombasi*, Tribunal de Premier Instance de Bruxelles (11 April 2000), para. 3.4. Here, Judge Vandermeersch interpreted the parliamentary intent for article 7 of the 1993 Belgian Law as excluding the 1993 Law from article 12(1) of the Code of Criminal Procedure (Preliminary Title), which requires the presence of the suspect in Belgium. See *Re Pinochet*, Tribunal de Premier Instance de Bruxelles (6 November 1998), para. 3.2.1.

[53] In October 2000, the Chamber du conseil rejected Yerodia's application to have access to the dossier of complaints, and his appeal to the Chamber des mises en accusation in the same month was also rejected in the interests of personal security of complainants and witnesses. See 'Counter-Memorial of Belgium', para. 1.14.

[54] See Application to Institute Proceedings Arrest Warrant of 11th April 2000 *(Democratic Republic of Congo v. Belgium)*. Subsequent to the application, there was a cabinet reshuffle and Yerodia was given the National Education portfolio, which Belgium described as a 'metamorphosis'. See 'Counter-Memorial of Belgium', para. 2.26–2.38.

[55] *Par in parem* translates as 'has no equal'. The state is 'supreme internally' but obliged not to intervene in the internal affairs of other states. See Malcolm N. Shaw, *International Law* (6th edn, Cambridge: Cambridge University Press, 2008), 647.

[56] Application to Institute Proceedings, 2.

Court addressed the aspect of the appropriateness of a tribunal in accordance with the ethos of the traditional 'centre'. As Koskenniemi has observed, the *Arrest Warrant* case was a struggle over human rights themes in which the authority of human rights bodies was challenged by alternative preferences: 'rights were trumped by traditional rules of diplomatic law'.[57]

Nevertheless, this legal outcome on the question of immunity was reached based on a corresponding hypothetical argument on the question of jurisdiction. The Court sidestepped the question of whether the Belgian legislation prescribing for universal jurisdiction *in absentia* was legally valid.[58] As Judge van den Wyngaert has observed, controversy exists because there is 'no generally accepted definition' of the principle of universal jurisdiction either in customary international law or in multilateral treaties.[59] In fact, generic descriptions of the principle are evidently open-ended.[60] It follows then that international lawyers can debate over the *veritable* content of universal jurisdiction over crimes against international law.

This use of a hypothetical argument meant that theoretically the Court's discussion of immunity in terms of the contradistinction with universal jurisdiction was premised upon the *Lotus* majority's presumption against limitations.[61] In other words, Belgium was presumed to be acting lawfully in determining the extent of its jurisdiction (ascending pattern). Yet the Court determined whether international law restricted Belgium's jurisdictional claim by imposing a prohibitive rule of immunity (descending pattern), and consequently the enforcement measures

---

[57] Koskenniemi, 'Hegemony: A Reconfiguration', 209. See also A O'Sullivan, *Universal Jurisdiction*, 165–75; van Alebeek, *Immunity of States*, 191–2.

[58] *Case of the Arrest Warrant (Judgment)*, para. 48.

[59] Ibid. (Dissent of van den Wyngaert), para. 44. On *aut dedere aut judicare* provision in multilateral treaties, see M. Cherif Bassiouni and Edward M. Wise, *Aut Dedere Aut Judicare: The Duty to Extradite or Prosecute in International Law* (Dordrecht: M Nijhoff, 1995), 49; International Law Commission 'The Obligation to Extradite or Prosecute (*aut dedere aut judicare*): Final Report of the International Law Commission' (2014) Vol II Yearbook of International Law Commission (Part Two).

[60] In general, the generic description of universal jurisdiction is the right of the state under customary international law to exercise jurisdiction without a jurisdictional link or legal nexus to the location of the offence, nationalities of the perpetrator or victim, or the State's security, vital interests or 'any other ground of jurisdiction'. For discussion, see Roger O'Keefe, 'Universal Jurisdiction: Clarifying the Basic Concept', *Journal of International Criminal Justice*, 2 (2004), 735, 746.

[61] *Case of the Arrest Warrant (Joint Separate Opinion)*, para. 71. As the Joint Separate Opinion noted, immunity reflects 'an interest which in certain circumstances prevails over an otherwise predominant interest'. '[Immunity] is an exception to jurisdiction which normally can be exercised and it can only be invoked when the latter exists. (AOS)'.

performed within its own territory were excessive. In their competing analyses on the validity of the Belgian jurisdiction, Judges van den Wyngaert and Guillaume appeared diametrically opposed to one another. The former adopted a moralist approach, whereas the latter adopted a formalist approach. Nevertheless, the structural indeterminacy means that both arguments mirror one another as they move in descending-ascending and ascending-descending patterns, respectively. Ultimately, each opinion opposes the other in determining whether the jurisdiction is reasonable in light of the chosen normative project, either preventing impunity or avoiding abuse. The incoherence in these opinions is not remedied by the Joint Separate Opinion's attempt to navigate a middle ground, as its middle ground ends up turning expressly to a notion of reasonableness in order to determine whether the jurisdiction is valid.

Van den Wyngaert's moralist approach is best situated at the margins of the *Eichmann* judgments' narrative because she drew the outermost normative position from the moral naturalism that pervaded in *Eichmann*. In this way, her approach was in keeping with the approach adopted in the earlier Spanish and Belgian *Pinochet* judgments.[62] Of course, these judgments had been made prior to the *Arrest Warrant* judgment at a time when arguments underpinned by the moralist approach had hegemonic control, leading to the 'Pinochet effect' and the persuasiveness of the preventing impunity campaign. In her Dissenting Opinion, Judge van den Wyngaert assumed that universal jurisdiction derives from the 'international reprobation for certain very serious crimes'[63] and that the principle's normative purpose is 'to avoid impunity'.[64] These interwoven arguments justify the principle of universal jurisdiction on the basis of the nature of the crimes. This combines those arguments that make an analogy between piracy committed on the high seas (conceived as an offence against the law of nations) and other offences deemed criminal under customary international law[65] with

---

[62] *Chilean Investigations (5 November 1998)* Audiencia Nacional and *Re Pinochet*, Tribunal de Premier Instance de Bruxelles (6 November 1998). For the endorsement of van den Wyngaert's approach in the literature, see Alexander Poels, 'Universal Jurisdiction *in Absentia*', *Netherlands Quarterly of Human Rights*, 23/1 (2005), 64, 76–8; Mohamed El Zeidy, 'Universal Jurisdiction *in Absentia*: Is It a Legal Valid Option?', *International Lawyer*, 37 (2003), 835, 852.

[63] *Case of the Arrest Warrant* (Dissent of van den Wyngaert), para. 46.

[64] Ibid. para. 46.

[65] See M Cherif Bassiouni, 'Universal Jurisdiction for International Crimes: Historical Perspectives and Contemporary Practice', *Virginia Journal of International Law*, 42

those that consider the principle a legal consequence of the *jus cogens* status of the crimes.[66] In *Eichmann*, the Israeli courts did not draw out the full potential from the moral naturalism that underpinned the courts' reasoning. Rather, the Israeli courts moved to be more concrete. They drew on certain historical antecedents that considered universal jurisdiction to be a subsidiary basis of jurisdiction, which prioritised the territorial jurisdiction.[67] However, both courts ultimately determined the issue on the reasonableness of Israeli courts exercising jurisdiction. Like the aforementioned *Pinochet* judgments, Judge van den Wyngaert departed here from the *Eichmann* judgments' portrayal and argued that the notion of universal jurisdiction *in absentia* was legally justifiable. In effect, her view emphasised how the purpose was to conduct the trial and prevent an injustice through impunity.[68] Thus, the voluntary presence of the accused was not the overriding factor, regardless of what format historical precedents may indicate.[69] At this outermost point, the fight against impunity campaign has become fully operational. The court of humanity could never adjourn and the political present has been transformed from sovereign egoism to world unity.

Nevertheless, by drawing out the full potential of *Eichmann*'s moral naturalism (and the 'horizon' of the moralist approach), van den Wyngaert's opinion would appear to the opposing formalist approach to be pure morality, oppressive homogeneity, and no longer the rule of law. Thus, she moved in a descending-ascending-descending pattern in her attempt to avoid the accusation of being subjective and political and

---

(2001), 81, 108; Kenneth Randall, 'Universal Jurisdiction in International Law', *Texas Law Review*, 66 (1988), 785, 798.

[66] Alexander Orakhelashvili, *Peremptory Norms in International Law* (Oxford: Oxford University Press, 2006), 288; *Prosecutor v. Furundzija*, IT-95-17/1-T (10 December 1998), para. 156; *R v. Bow Street Magistrate, ex parte Pinochet Ugarte (No.3)* (1999) 2 WLR 827; (1999) 2 All ER 97 (Lord Millet).

[67] *AG v. Eichmann* (1968) 36 ILR 5, 26–8 (citing Hyde, Glueck, and Cowles in support), 299–300.

[68] Her approach (and that of the Spanish and Belgian *Pinochet* judgments) can be traced to the *Demjanjuk* proceedings. Here, the US Court of Appeal upheld the lower courts' decision that Demjanjuk could be extradited from the US to Israel. This was notwithstanding the fact that he would, in effect, be involuntarily surrendered as opposed to being voluntarily present in Israel at the time of the proceedings. See *In re Demjanjuk*, 612 F Supp. 544 (ND Ohio) and *Demjanjuk v. Petrovsky*, 776 F 2d 571 (6th Cir. 1985), cert. denied 475 US 1016 (1986).

[69] Here, O'Keefe presented a different method by making an analogy to other principles of jurisdiction. He has argued that if there is a permission to exercise universal jurisdiction, then the 'exercise of in absentia is logically permissible also'. See O'Keefe, 'Clarifying the Basic Concept', 748.

to bind the DRC despite its clear lack of consent, that is, its objection that Belgian jurisdiction was excessive and a violation of the DRC's sovereignty. Though she justified the principle of universal jurisdiction based on her chosen moral naturalism (descending), she searched for any prohibitive rule imposed by international law constraining the anterior liberty (ascending).[70] This tried to reconcile the contradiction that there is a higher normative code (moral naturalism) that constrains liberty in order to secure communal interests, which, in van den Wyngaert's view, is greater criminal accountability. Yet at the same time, there is an anterior liberty or wide discretion for states in determining the scope of extraterritorial jurisdiction. In this sense, she analysed state behaviour and the discretion in determining jurisdiction through the lens of her chosen moral naturalism. Thus, she dismissed the higher proportion of national legislation that required custody and the limited examples of trials *in absentia* as being determinative. In her view, a prohibition could only arise if there had been a 'conscious decision' of states to prohibit jurisdiction unless the suspect was voluntarily present on the state's territory.[71] On the contrary, she tendered the Belgian and Spanish legislation as evidence of the lack of a prohibition.[72] In her view of treaty practice, the 1949 Geneva Conventions[73] and other multilateral treaty obligations did not explicitly indicate that presence of the suspect was required and may be interpreted as not prohibiting (that is permitting) a broader jurisdiction than provided for in the treaty.[74] This analysis of state behaviour will only compel those who agree that the horizon is to maximise accountability irrespective of individual state consent to jurisdiction.

In contrast, Guillaume's opinion was diametrically opposed to the *Eichmann* judgments' narrative and, in turn, drew upon (but did not go as far as) the defence counsel's arguments in *Eichmann*.[75] In this way,

---

[70] *Case of the Arrest Warrant* (Dissent of van den Wyngaert), para. 51.

[71] Ibid. para. 56.

[72] An earlier example of a similar argument, positing the lack of a prohibition against extraterritorial jurisdiction, was the reasoning used by Israeli courts in the Eichmann Trial in regard to the Israeli Nazi and Nazi Collaborators Act 1950 ('as yet no international accord exists on the question of the jurisdiction of a State to punish persons who are not its nationals for acts committed beyond its borders'). See *AG v. Eichmann*, 283–5.

[73] *Case of the Arrest Warrant* (Dissent of van den Wyngaert), para. 54.

[74] Ibid. para. 61.

[75] Eichmann's defence counsel represented the margins of this formalist approach by arguing that the charge of personal liability for acts on government order was unjustified based on official capacity and a violation of the personal immunity of state officials. Similarly, the jurisdiction was criticised as excessive based on the lack of state consent and

his approach was in keeping with what had been the counter-hegemonic position at the time of the *Arrest Warrant*, which was best represented in jurisprudence by the French courts in *Javor* and by the dissents in *Pinochet I* and *III*.[76] It was representative of the caution within scholarship against abuse of jurisdiction.[77] In Judge Guillaume's Separate Opinion, the point of departure was clearly the prohibition against non-intervention and the need for demonstrable state behaviour. In effect, there was a need for the rule of law to reflect the voluntary will of states.[78] Thus, Judge Guillaume assumed that the principle of universal jurisdiction derived from state behaviour and not from the nature of the crimes. This in turn reflected the concept of the jurisdictional principles as 'manifestations of statehood' or 'generalizations' from 'a mass of national provisions'.[79] Deriving the principle from state behaviour, he turned to the historical antecedents, the significance of which was dismissed by van den Wyngaert. He considered that jurisdiction could only be based on the absence of sovereignty over the location of the offence,[80] similar to what was presented by Eichmann's defence counsel ('absence

---

a violation of principle against non-retroactivity. See *Written Pleadings submitted by Counsel for the Appellant Adolf Eichmann*, para. 2 (a) and (b).

[76] See *Javor and Others* (2002) 127 International Law Reports 126; *R v. Bow Street Metropolitan Stipendiary Magistrate, ex parte Pinochet Ugarte* (1998) 4 All ER 897; and *R v. Bow St. Metropolitan Stipendiary Magistrate, ex parte Pinochet Ugarte (No.3)* (1999) 2 All ER 97.

[77] Even the International Law Association's generally supportive report cautioned against 'jurisdictional imperialism' and has pointed to the potential for unwarranted interference through excessive exercises of jurisdiction. International Law Association, 'Final Report on the Exercise of Universal Jurisdiction of Gross Human Rights Offences' (London, 2000), 19.

[78] Here, he emphasised the territorial character of the criminal law as fundamental and the recognition of sovereign equality in the UN Charter that strengthened the territorial principle. While he acknowledged the corpus of international criminal law and treaty obligations regarding extraterritorial jurisdiction, he argued that 'at no time' has universal jurisdiction in absentia been envisaged. '[T]to do this would, moreover, risk creating judicial chaos'. *Case of the Arrest Warrant* (Separate Opinion of Guillaume), para. 15. Reydams and Henzelin's careful inductive studies are also indicative of this point of departure. Marc Henzelin, *Le Principe de l'universalité en droit penal international* (Bruylant: Helbing & Lichtenhahn 2000), 235; Reydams, *Universal Jurisdiction*. See also see Ryan Rabinovitch, 'Universal Jurisdiction in Absentia', *Fordham International Law Journal*, 18 (2004–2005),500, 506–10.

[79] Brownlie, *Principles*, 308.

[80] On piracy, see Harvard Research on International Law, 'Draft Convention on Piracy', *American Journal of International Law Supplement*, 26 (1932), 739, 750–1, 769–85. Contrast Alfred Rubin, *The Law of Piracy* (Honolulu: University of South Pacific, 2006). On the nineteenth-century legislation, see the Austrian Penal Code of 1803, which is regarded as the earliest modern example. See Harvard Research on

of a competent court').[81] It followed, then, that the only true instance of universal jurisdiction under customary international law was the crime of piracy committed on the high seas.[82] This also accorded with the arguments of Eichmann's defence counsel, who rejected the claim that universal jurisdiction could be exercised over crimes against humanity. In effect, the purpose was to protect the anterior state liberty. Therefore, the issue of both jurisdiction over certain crimes and the precondition of voluntary presence could only be determined by the existence of historical precedents. In this way, the avoiding abuse theme has become fully realised. The court of humanity is read as a cloak for politically motivated show trials and the political present has been transformed from oppressive homogeneity to self-determination.

Nevertheless, by emphasising social description and behaviour (and reaching for the horizon of the formalist approach), Guillaume's Separate Opinion would appear to the opposing moralist approach as mere politics and sovereign egoism and to negate law's normativity. Therefore, Guillaume moved in an ascending-descending-ascending pattern to avoid the accusation of being subjective and political and to bind Belgium despite its lack of consent, that is, its contention that its exercise of universal jurisdiction was a valid exercise of its sovereignty. Though Guillaume derived the principle from state behaviour (ascending), he searched for a permissive rule, which assumed a prior legal order (descending).[83] Like van den Wyngaert, this argument tried to reconcile the contradiction that there was a wide discretion of state (or anterior freedom) in determining the scope of extraterritorial jurisdiction, and at the same time there was a higher normative code that constrained liberty in order to secure communal interests. For Guillaume, this was the protection of territorial independence and dignity of the state. In this way, he analysed state behaviour through the lens of his chosen moral naturalism. He considered the need of voluntary presence of the accused in most national legislation as significant and concluded that only Israel's Nazi and Nazi Collaborators Act 1950 would qualify as similar to the Belgian

International Law, 'Draft Convention on Jurisdiction with Respect to Crime', *American Journal of International Law Supplement*, 29 (1935), 435–652 at 574.
[81] *Written Pleadings* (31 January 1962), Part II,(b)(2)(b).
[82] *Case of the Arrest Warrant* (Separate Opinion of Guillaume), para. 5.
[83] Ibid. para. 14. He also claimed that Lotus's implication must be rejected in light of the reference to sovereign equality in the UN Charter and the application of the *uti possenditis* rule during the period of decolonisation (para. 15).

legislation.[84] In treaty practice, he considered the Hague Convention's jurisdictional clause as an incorporation of Grotius's doctrine of *aut dedere aut punire*.[85] Accordingly, Guillaume concluded that there was a near complete lack of state behaviour to justify the Belgian claim. This analysis of state behaviour would only compel those who agree that the horizon is to avoid the risk of 'creating judicial chaos'[86] and undermining state liberty, irrespective of the so-called 'universal' interests in securing greater accountability.

Relative to van den Wyngaert and Guillaume, the Joint Separate Opinion (JSO) is a middle ground between the diametrically opposed positions.[87] It clearly does not move as far as van den Wyngaert's approach at the margins, yet at the same time it does not accord entirely with Guillaume's approach. Instead, the JSO's ascending-descending pattern followed Guillaume's approach in the first instance because its point of departure was an analysis of state behaviour, appearing to emphasise state voluntary will. Yet in the second instance, it followed van den Wyngaert's approach to the analysis of state behaviour in that the inconclusiveness in state behaviour did not rule out universal jurisdiction *in absentia*.[88] This position was underpinned by the ethos of the moralist approach. Thus, the JSO dismissed the relevance of international penal conventions, as those conventions proscribed obligations to establish and exercise jurisdiction over a suspect present on state party territory.[89] Rather, these were considered as 'sensible realities' in light of the extradition component.[90] The JSO similarly discounted national legislation, as national legislation only divulged what states had decided to establish.[91] Unlike Guillaume, the JSO discounted the usefulness of the

---

[84]  Ibid. para. 12. However, he did not refer to the Spanish provision (Article 23(4) of the Organic Law of Judicial Power), which was interpreted in a manner similar to the 1993/ 1999 Belgian Law.

[85]  Ibid. para. 9. This required presence of the prosecuting state. However, Grotius's notion required a prior conviction, which is not the situation of the Hague Convention's provisions.

[86]  Ibid. para. 15.

[87]  For support in scholarship, see Institute of International Law, 'Resolution on Universal Criminal Jurisdiction with Regard to the Crime of Genocide, Crimes against Humanity and War Crimes' (Krakow, 2005).

[88]  *Case of the Arrest Warrant* (Joint Separate Opinion), para. 58 refers to the 'underlying purpose of designating certain acts as international crimes [which] is to authorize a wide jurisdiction to be asserted over persons committing them'.

[89]  Ibid. para. 32.

[90]  Ibid. para. 57.

[91]  Ibid. para. 21, 45.

punishment of piracy, given its distinction in terms of the location of the offence.[92] Rather, the JSO concluded that state behaviour was inconclusive or 'neutral'. In so doing, the JSO argued that state liberty could not determine the exact scope of the state's legal rights.[93] As states were not required to legislate as far as permitted in international law, it was evident that international law may have permitted a wider scope than that adopted by states.[94] The JSO implicitly represented state behaviour as providing evidence of a possible permission under international law (because states are not required to legislate as far as permitted). Yet at the same time, the JSO explicitly considered that treaty or national practice cannot evidence a prohibition against extradition to secure custody.

This pull on diametrically opposing positions was representative of the cautious optimism of certain earlier studies, in which universal jurisdiction was welcomed. Yet caution was also expressed against the arbitrary exercise of jurisdiction.[95] In effect, the purpose of the JSO was to move towards the bias of the international criminal law regime yet to some extent also to reflect the bias of the traditional 'centre' of public international law. This approach tried to reconcile the competing idioms through a weighing of interests and the use of reasonableness. This balancing of interests between preventing impunity and avoiding abuse could be ensured through various safeguards, including the prior offer 'to the national State of the prospective accused person the opportunity itself to act upon the charges concerned'.[96] Therefore, *in absentia* may be theoretically valid but it must be exercised in accordance with reasonableness. Here, the judges moved towards a moralist middle ground that privileged fighting impunity over its counterpoint of avoiding abuse. Thus, the JSO could appear to both van den Wyngaert and Guillaume as subjective and political, as it drew expressly on the notion of reasonableness and offered policy guidance to states. To van den Wyngaert's approach, the JSO would appear to facilitate a potential failure to secure the fundamental interests of fighting against impunity in deference to the interests of powerful states. To Guillaume's approach, it would appear to

---

[92] Ibid. para. 54.
[93] Ibid. para. 45.
[94] Ibid.
[95] Princeton Project on Universal Jurisdiction, 'Princeton Principles on Universal Jurisdiction' (Princeton: Princeton University, 2000); International Law Association, 'Final Report on Universal Jurisdiction'.
[96] *Case of the Arrest Warrant* (Joint Separate Opinion), para. 45.

have advocated the arbitrary imposition or constraint on state liberty under the guise of a so-called 'universal' interest. It is evident that the hegemony within scholarship and jurisprudence has shifted to a formalist approach in the post–*Arrest Warrant* debate. Thus, *in absentia* is deemed unlawful and does not reflect the legal concept of universal jurisdiction.[97] In fact, the aftermath of the *Arrest Warrant* has been depicted as the death knell of universal jurisdiction *in absentia*, a natural and inevitable outcome given the interstate disputes over exercises of universal jurisdiction *in absentia*.[98] Therefore, international lawyers followed Guillaume's approach, analysed state behaviour since the *Arrest Warrant*, and concluded that it has failed to indicate a permissive rule. In particular, scholars could refer to the Rome Statute incorporation acts, which generally require presence of the alleged offender,[99] and the 2009 amendment of Spain's universal jurisdiction law, inserting the requirement of voluntary presence of the accused.[100] Hence, the push and pull of mainstream sensibilities has shifted from what appeared to be a reforming vision of the moralist approach pre–*Arrest Warrant* to what appeared to be a critique of stability by the formalist approach post–*Arrest Warrant*.[101] Nevertheless, the move towards a moralist middle ground in the JSO has had some influence. Its proposal of a first offer to territorial jurisdiction has found its way into resolutions and reports that are underpinned by a moralist approach.[102] Therefore,

---

[97] Luc Reydams, 'The Rise and Fall of Universal Jurisdiction' in William Schabas and Nadia Bernaz, eds, *Routledge Handbook of International Criminal Law* (New York: Routledge, 2011); Rabinovitch, 'Universal Jurisdiction in Absentia', 500; Antonio Cassese, 'Is the Bell Tolling for Universality? A Plea for a Sensible Notion of Universal Jurisdiction', *Journal of International Criminal Justice*, 1 (2003), 589; Henzelin, *Le Principe de l'universalité*.

[98] Cassese, 'Bell Tolling', 594.

[99] See assessment in Alexander Zahar and Goran Sluiter, *International Criminal Law* (Oxford: Oxford University Press, 2008), 501.

[100] Ley Orgánica 1/2009 de 3 de noviembre complementaria de la Ley de reforma de la legislación procesal para la implantación de la nueva Oficina judicial, por la que se la Ley Orgánica 6/1985, de 1 de Julio, del Poder Judicial. http://noticias.juridicas.com/base_datos/Admin/lo1-2009.html.

[101] Kennedy, *International Legal Structures*, 335.

[102] See respectively *Report of AU-EU Technical Ad-hoc Expert Group on the Principle of Universal Jurisdiction* (15 April 2009), which promptly institutes criminal proceedings where the 'persons suspected of serious crimes of international concern are within their custody or territory'; UN Secretary-General, 'Scope and Application', referring to the fact that the general commentary in UNGA debates considered presence of the alleged offender as required; and 'Report of the International Commission of Inquiry on Darfur', 25 January 2005, www.un.org/news/dh/sudan/com_inq_darfur.pdf, highlighting the precondition of the presence of the accused.

within a broader formalist approach's hegemony, there emerged a reframed idea of universal jurisdiction *in absentia* by the moralist approach, namely investigation *in absentia*.[103] Although this approach remains counter-hegemonic, the decision in Germany and Sweden to investigate alleged crimes committed in Syria under universal jurisdiction laws gives some momentum to a moralist middle.[104]

## Conclusion

As I have observed, the debate on the principle of universal jurisdiction in absentia has been caught in the same binary tension as the wider debate on the parameters of the principle, namely between preventing impunity and avoiding abuse.[105] While there have been hegemonic and counter-hegemonic positions, the theme of indeterminacy has demonstrated how neither position can be prioritised over the other in light of each argument's fundamental incoherence. Instead, there is a struggle for hegemony between competing approaches, each of which reflects a particular project, and in turn a bias towards a certain ethos (universal accountability or maintaining order). I noted how Judge van den Wyngaert's approach was hegemonic pre–*Arrest Warrant*. Yet her approach failed to persuade others in the post–*Arrest Warrant* debate because it was set

---

[103] The Institute of International Law, in 'Resolution', Principle 3(b), has stated that 'apart from acts of investigation and requests for extradition, the exercise of universal jurisdiction requires the presence of the alleged offender in the territory of the prosecuting State . . .'. As a theoretical support for this avenue, see O'Keefe, 'Clarifying the Basic Concept', 735; Claus Kress, 'Universal Jurisdiction over International Crimes and the Institut de Droit International', *Journal of International Criminal Justice*, 4 (2006), 561. See also Article 3(5) of the Act to Introduce the Code of Crimes against International Law of 26 June 2002 and *Guatemalan Generals Case*, Judgment No. 237/2005, Constitutional Court (26 September 2005), para. 3. These only express limitation on universal jurisdiction in relation to *non bis in idem*.

[104] See Chapter 2, Section 3 of Law (2014:406) on the Punishment of Genocide, Crimes against Humanity and War Crimes, https://www.riksdagen.se/sv/dokument-lagar/doku ment/svensk-forfattningssamling/lag-2014406-om-straff-for-folkmord-brott-mot_sfs-2014-406; Section 1 of Act to Introduce the Code of Crimes against International Law of 26 June 2002 (Germany) (2003) 42 ILM 998. See also German Parliament 'Replies in German Parliament' Doc 18/12487. http://dip21.bundestag.de/dip21/btd/18/124/1812487.pdf See also ECCR and 7 Syrian natonals' criminal complaint against six high level officials in the Assad regime https://www.ecchr.eu/en/case/torture-under-the-assad-regime/

[105] The UN Secretary-General, in 'Scope and Application', para. 9, referred to universal jurisdiction being 'an essential jurisdictional instrument in the fight against impunity' yet required constraints to avoid any 'manipulation for political ends'.

against a particular context in which an imagined reformatting vision of a court of humanity appeared to precipitate a diplomatic debacle between otherwise 'friendly' states. In opposition, Judge Guillaume's approach was pitched at the moment when the shift in hegemony to the formalist approach was taking place and his privileging of an imagined return to stability had an attractive appeal in light of various diplomatic incidents. This immediate appeal is reflected in the subsequent legislative developments in numerous states which in turn are invoked to confirm his authentic description of universal jurisdiction. While the JSO's move to a moralist middle ground would appear political to both opposing positions, it was influential in various reports commissioned by regional and global actors because it tempered the 'extreme' position of Guillaume. I noted that this moralist middle ground has remained counter-hegemonic, and invariably any middle ground is 'narrow and slippery'.[106] Inevitably, this debate over universal jurisdiction in absentia is an endless series of hegemonic and counter-hegemonic positions in which a hegemonic position today may become a counter-hegemonic position tomorrow.

---

[106] Koskenniemi and Leino, 'Fragmentation', 579.

# 9

# The Domestic Politics of International Children's Rights: A Dutch Perspective

JASPER KROMMENDIJK*

## Introduction

This chapter addresses the question of whether the UN human rights treaty bodies – and especially the UN Committee on the Rights of the Child (CRC Committee) – act as engines for incorporating universal norms at the domestic level. Elements of such incorporation manifest, among other ways, in the extent to which a state changes its policy and/or legislation (partly) on the basis of the recommendations of these human rights treaty bodies. This chapter will also explore the factors which determine whether treaty body recommendations are implemented, or not.

Koskenniemi has argued that politics is about different conceptions of justice, and justice is inherently political.[1] In other words, he treats politics and justice as closely interrelated. In various ways, this observation also underlies this chapter on the domestic impact of the work of UN human rights treaty bodies on state reporting procedures. First, the work of the treaty bodies is aimed at the realisation of justice by monitoring the implementation of international human rights treaties. This was noted by former Secretary-General Ban Ki-moon when he argued that: 'the treaty bodies stand at the heart of the international human rights protection system as engines translating universal norms into social justice'.[2]

---

* This chapter is based on Krommendijk's PhD research conducted from November 2009 until March 2014, which focused on state reporting under the six main UN human rights treaties in the Netherlands, New Zealand, and Finland. See Jasper Krommendijk, *The Domestic Impact and Effectiveness of the Process of State Reporting under UN Human Rights Treaties in the Netherlands, New Zealand and Finland: Paper-Pushing or Policy Prompting?* (Antwerp: Intersentia, 2014).

[1] Martti Koskenniemi, *From Apology to Utopia: The Structure of International Legal Argument* (Cambridge: Cambridge University Press, 2006).

[2] Ban Ki-moon, 'Foreword by the Secretary-General', in Navi Pillay, *Strengthening the United Nations Human Rights Treaty Body System* (2012), 7. www2.ohchr.org/english/bodies/HRTD/docs/HCReportTBStrengthening.pdf

Second, as will be illustrated in this chapter, treaty bodies are very much engaged with politics as well. For example, they interpret open-ended treaty provisions, they formulate recommendations, and they decide how to handle information submitted by NGOs. Such acts are inherently political and imply dealing with, in the view of Koskenniemi in Chapter 2 of this book, the 'two completely different conceptual worlds' of the legal and the political.[3] Third, the process of implementation of non-binding recommendations from international legal institutions is essentially political. As will be shown in this chapter, non-legal aspects frequently determine whether the recommendations are acted upon at the domestic level. (Non-)compliance is primarily affected by political interests and preferences of the government. (Non-)compliance with recommendations is thus the result or byproduct of domestic politics.[4] The argument that there is a political dimension to the implementation of international norms also coincides with Koskenniemi's claim that international law should not 'escape politics' or treat politics as opposed to international law.[5] Similarly, the fight for an international rule of law should not be seen as a fight against politics, but a fight which takes place within politics.[6] This also implies that international norms and recommendations only have effect through the filter of domestic politics.[7] Hence, this chapter concurs with Koskenniemi's argument that 'social conflict must still be solved by political means'.[8] Fourth, the examination of this domestic political implementation process requires venturing into other disciplines than law, including political science, international relations, and sociology, as Koskenniemi noted in the early 1990s.[9]

The UN human rights state reporting procedures are based on the obligations of states which have ratified, or acceded to, these treaties (the states parties) to submit periodically, usually every four or five years, a report on the implementation of this treaty.[10] These state reports are

---

[3] See Chapter 2, 25.
[4] Oona Hathaway, 'Do Human Rights Treaties Make a Difference?', *Yale Law Journal*, 111 (2002), 1935–2042.
[5] Martti Koskenniemi, 'The Politics of International Law' *European Journal of International Law*, 1 (1990), 4–32 at 6.
[6] Ibid. 5.
[7] Martha Finnemore and Kathryne Sikkink, 'International Norm Dynamics and Political Change', *International Organization*, 52 (1998), 887–917, 893.
[8] Koskenniemi, 'Politics of International Law' (1990), 7.
[9] Ibid. 32.
[10] The six main UN human rights treaties that were included in this research and chapter are the Convention on the Elimination of All Forms of Racial Discrimination 660 UNTS 195

examined by an independent committee of experts (a 'treaty body'), through a so-called constructive dialogue with representatives of the state party. Civil society and non-governmental organisations (NGOs) are allowed to submit alternative and/or additional information to the treaty body. The assessment of a state report ends with the adoption of Concluding Observations (COs) by the treaty body, which contain suggestions and recommendations for improving implementation of the treaty standards. As stated earlier, these COs are non-binding in technical legal terms. This chapter will particularly focus on the reporting process of the UN Convention on the Rights of the Child (CRC) as regards the Netherlands, in order to explain the fact that the Dutch government has introduced laws and policies to give effect to some of the COs.[11]

The structure of this chapter is as follows. The next section will examine two theoretical explanations for the impact of COs that have inspired the empirical analysis for this chapter. The third section will examine the state reporting process conducted by the six treaty bodies and will provide four examples of COs of the CRC Committee that have been acted upon. The fourth section will explain the role of the CRC Committees' COs in the Netherlands on the basis of the two theoretical hypotheses and other factors.

## Theorising the Homecoming of International Recommendations

As explained above, this chapter analyses the extent to which the Dutch government has taken any policy or legislative measures on the basis of the COs. The methodology used to conduct this analysis primarily consists of

(opened for signature 21 December 1965, entered into force 4 January 1969) (ICERD); the International Covenant on Civil and Political Rights 999 UNTS 171 (opened for signature 16 December 1966, entered into force 23 March 1976) (ICCPR); the International Covenant on Economic, Social and Cultural Rights 993 UNTS 3 (opened for signature 16 December 1966, entered into force 3 January 1976) (ICESCR); the Convention on the Elimination of All Forms of Discrimination against Women 1249 UNTS 13 (opened for signature 18 December 1979, entered into force 3 September 1981) (CEDAW); the Convention against Torture and Other Cruel, Inhuman or Degrading Treatment or Punishment 1465 UNTS 85 (opened for signature 10 December 1984, entered into force 26 June 1987) (CAT); and the United Nations Convention on the Rights of the Child 1577 UNTS 3 (opened for signature 20 November 1989, entered into force 2 September 1990) (CRC).

[11]  To date, the CRC Committee has examined the Dutch situation four times, in 1999, 2004, 2009, and 2015. As the research project that was the basis for this chapter ended in 2014, and at the moment of writing it was rather early to assess the follow-up to the June 2015 COs, the latest set of COs has not been analysed here.

an examination of documents in which show that the government provided a reaction to the COs. These documents include in particular the periodic state reports and letters to Parliament. This analysis was complemented by sixty-three interviews with Dutch government officials and NGO and UNICEF representatives.[12] These interviews included twelve (former) Dutch government officials from five different ministries who had been involved in the process of CRC state reporting by way of drafting the state report and attending the dialogue with the CRC Committee in Geneva in 1999, 2004, and/or 2009.[13] In total, eight representatives from four different NGOs[14] involved in the CRC reporting process and from the Dutch National UNICEF Committee were interviewed as well. First of all, the interviewees were asked to give examples of implemented COs themselves (see the two columns on the right of Table 1). Second, the interviewees were asked whether particular COs have played a role in policy and legislative measures and in what way(s).

In addition to an analysis of the level of implementation of COs, this chapter explores why policy or legislative measures have (or have not) been taken on the basis of COs. The latter question has also been addressed in international relations literature on international norm compliance and implementation. In this chapter, two theoretical explanations will be provided: the compliance pull, and domestic and transnational mobilisation.[15]

## Legitimacy and Compliance Pull

Legally speaking, COs are non-binding, and the treaty bodies lack instruments to enforce and coerce compliance with their recommendations.

[12] In order to protect the anonymity of the interviewees, their names and identities are not disclosed. Instead, a randomly generated series of numbers (government officials) and letters (NGO representatives) will be used for reference. The summary reports of the interviews are on file with the author and can be accessed upon request.

[13] Officials of the following ministries were interviewed: the Ministry of Health, Welfare and Sport; the Ministry of Foreign Affairs; the Ministry of Justice; the Ministry of Social Affairs and Employment; the Ministry of Youth and Families (in existence during the period 2007–2010).

[14] Representatives of the following NGOs were interviewed: the Dutch section of Defence for Children International; Justitia et Pax; the Dutch section of the International Commission of Jurists (NJCM); and the Johannes Wier Foundation.

[15] For a more elaborate account, see also Jasper Krommendijk, 'The Domestic Effectiveness of International Human Rights Monitoring in Established Democracies: The Case of the UN Human Rights Treaty Bodies', *Review of International Organizations*, 10 (2015), 489–512.

A first theoretical implication of this feature of COs is that their implementation is contingent upon the extent to which the treaty bodies and their output exert a normative compliance pull. It has been pointed out that legitimacy is especially crucial when courts or other institutions lack coercive means.[16] Alvarez, for example, has argued that 'legitimacy is the missing link in solving the mystery of how the international system obliges without a coercive force'.[17] Similarly, Franck has observed that 'legitimacy has the power to pull toward compliance those who cannot be compelled'.[18] Legitimacy strongly relates to subjective perception and belief systems of actors.[19] For the implementation of COs it is therefore crucial that governments feel bound to comply with the COs, even though formally they are non-binding. This compliance pull depends among other things on government officials' perceptions as to the legitimacy, usefulness, persuasiveness, and legal quality of the COs, as well as the authority of the relevant treaty body. Based on this theoretical insight, this chapter will further rely on the attitudes and perceptions of Dutch government officials concerning the process of state reporting, the CRC Committee, and the COs. Information was gathered on these perceptions through semi-structured interviews with government officials. In order to determine whether a compliance pull existed, questions were raised about the views of officials concerning the quality of the constructive dialogue with the CRC Committee, the COs, and the treaty bodies.

### Domestic and Transnational Human Rights Mobilisation and Advocacy

The second compliance mechanism that features in this chapter deals with domestic and transnational human rights mobilisation and advocacy. Liberal international relations scholars have argued that international institutions are able to change the behaviour of a state through domestic institutions, such as domestic courts, and by mobilising domestic advocacy

---

[16] James Gibson and Gregory Caldeira, 'The Legitimacy of Transnational Legal Institutions: Compliance, Support, and the European Court of Justice', *American Journal of Political Science*, 39/2 (1995), 459–489 at 460, 470.

[17] Jose Alvarez, 'Book Review Essay: The Quest for Legitimacy: An Examination of the Power of Legitimacy among Nations by Thomas M. Franck', *International Law and Politics*, 24 (1991), 199–267 at 206.

[18] Thomas Franck, *The Power of Legitimacy and Institutions* (New York: Oxford University Press, 1990), at 24, 26.

[19] Ian Hurd, 'Legitimacy and Authority in International Politics', *International Organization*, 53/2 (1999), 379–408 at 381; Alvarez, 'Book Review', 206.

groups, NGOs, or political parties that pressure governments to change behaviour.[20] Several studies have even concluded that domestic change on the basis of international norms is unlikely to happen unless domestic actors take them up and demand change.[21] Moravcsik has maintained that international human rights institutions 'coopt' domestic actors who consequently pressure their governments for compliance 'from within'. He has concluded that international norms and institutions can shift the balance of power within and between domestic actors and prompt a change in coalitions and calculations underlying governmental policies, which might eventually lead to a policy change.[22] Likewise, Alter has held that international courts can act as 'tipping point actors' who support domestic compliance constituencies and provide them with 'resources'. In this way, they can tip the political balance in favour of policies in line with international norms.[23] Dai's theory on domestic compliance constituencies as 'decentralised enforcers' has noted how international norms and institutions can create a focal point for domestic actors and strengthen their leverage and legitimise their demands.[24] This also reflects Simmons' domestic politics theory on compliance with human rights treaties as 'a tool to support political mobilisation'.[25] This domestic mobilisation mechanism mirrors Keck and Sikkink's 'boomerang effect', which describes how coalitions of domestic compliance constituencies and NGOs seek international support and link up with transnational networks to bring pressure on their states from the outside. These international linkages allow such coalitions to gain leverage by introducing new issues, norms, and discourses into the debate and strengthening and amplifying their demands so that the terms of the debate

---

[20] Hathaway, 'Human Rights Treaties', 1954. Likewise, constructivist international relations theorists have pointed to the important role of domestic 'norm entrepreneurs' who use international norms to reinforce their (minority) position in domestic discussions and act as 'agents of socialisation' by demanding a policy or legislative change. Finnemore and Sikkink, 'International Norm Dynamics', 893, 902.

[21] See e.g. Tanja Börzel and Thomas Risse, 'From Europeanisation to Diffusion: Introduction', West European Politics, 35/1 (2012), 1–19 at 11.

[22] Andrew Moravcsik, 'Explaining International Human Rights Regimes: Liberal Theory and Western Europe', European Journal of International Relations, 1/2 (1995, 157–89.

[23] Karen Alter, 'Tipping the Balance: International Courts and the Construction of International and Domestic Politics', Cambridge Yearbook of European Legal Studies, 13 (2012), 1–21, at 1, 5.

[24] Xinyuan Dai, 'Why Comply? The Domestic Constituency Mechanism', International Organization, 59 (2005), 363–98.

[25] Beth Simmons, Mobilizing for Human Rights: International Law in Domestic Politics (Cambridge: Cambridge University Press, 2009), 135.

can shift.[26] In that way, they pressure states simultaneously from above and from below.[27]

In light of this theoretical premise, the extent to which domestic actors in the Netherlands have picked up, discussed, and utilised COs to lobby and pressure the Dutch government will be examined in the next section. This is supported by an analysis of parliamentary papers, court judgments, newspaper articles, and NGO websites for the period from 1 September 1995 until 31 August 2011.[28] In addition, government officials and NGO representatives were asked about their ideas concerning the impact of COs during the interviews.

## The Implementation of the COs of the CRC Committee: A Positive Exception in the Netherlands

Generally speaking, the Dutch government has hardly taken measures as a direct result of COs from the six UN human rights treaty bodies.[29] To the contrary, the government has rejected some of the concerns and recommendations of the treaty bodies.[30] In this context, it has produced

---

[26] Margaret Keck and Kathryn Sikkink, 'Transnational Advocacy Networks in International and Regional Politics', *International Social Science Journal*, 51/1 (1999), 89–101 at 90, 93; Thomas Risse and Kathryn Sikkink, 'The Socialization of International Human Rights Norms into Domestic Practices: Introduction', in Thomas Risse, Stephen Ropp, and Kathryn Sikkink, eds, *The Power of Human Rights: International Norms and Domestic Change* (Cambridge: Cambridge University Press, 1999), 1–38 at 18.

[27] Risse and Sikkink, 'Socialization', 5.

[28] These documents were traced by using, respectively, Parlando, zoek.officielebekendmakingen.nl, rechtspraak.nl, Lexis Nexis, and Google Search. The search terms and results are on file with the author and are available upon request.

[29] See also the introduction to this book (Chapter 1), which refers to Koskenniemi's observation that 'the rhetoric of law' has lost its 'transformative effect' because of 'over-legalistic explanations' as a result of which it is 'not as powerful as it claims to be' (Chapter 1, 13); Martti Koskenniemi, *The Politics of International Law* (Oxford: Hart, 2011), 133. It likewise coincided with Oomen's studies of the disconnect between national and global justice. Barbara Oomen, *Rights for Others: The Slow Home-Coming of Human Rights in the Netherlands* (Cambridge: Cambridge University Press, 2013).

[30] For further elaboration on this and other points, for CEDAW, ICERD, and ICCPR in specific, see Jasper Krommendijk, 'The Impact and Effectiveness of State Reporting under the Women's Convention: The Case of the Netherlands', in Ingrid Westendorp, ed., *The Women's Convention Turned 30: Achievements, Setbacks, and Prospects* (Antwerpen: Intersentia, 2012), 487–512; Jasper Krommendijk, 'The (Non-) Implementation of Recommendations of the Committee on the Elimination of Racial Discrimination in the Netherlands Explained', *Perspectives on European Politics and Society*, 13 (2012), 462–79; Jasper Krommendijk, 'De Beperkte Effectiviteit van de Aanbevelingen van het VN-Mensenrechtencomité in Nederland nader bekeken en verklaard' [The Limited Effectiveness of the Recommendations of the UN Human Rights Committee in the

various potential justifications for its positions, including budgetary constraints, a deliberate policy decision of a democratically elected legislature, or a conflict with other international obligations. In other instances, the government has simply argued that it did not agree with the assessment of the treaty body and that, for example, sufficient safeguards were already in place.

A further, plausible reason for the absence of any follow-up measures on the part of the Dutch government is that many of the rather broad and unspecific COs did not outline a specific course of action. Several COs have merely recommended the government to 'continue its efforts'[31] 'strengthen measures',[32] 'continue and further strengthen its efforts',[33] and even 'further strengthen the measures already taken'.[34] Other COs have recommended the Dutch government to 'take all necessary measures'[35] or 'take all appropriate measures'[36] without including concrete suggestions. Hence, the government has usually made clear that measures have (already) been taken that are in line with or address the COs sufficiently. COs have, thus, frequently coincided with measures already in place and what the government was already doing. The absence of such follow-up measures on the part of the government corresponds to the scepticism of Koskenniemi about signing a domestic bill of rights or any of the international human rights treaties. He regards the signing of such documents as a mere re-description of the existing reality, without any tangible effects.[37]

There are, however, also a couple of COs that have led to policy or legislative changes or additional measures.[38] Eleven of the twenty-four measures that were taken on this basis in the Netherlands related to COs of the CRC Committee, while the other thirteen measures were related to

Netherlands: A Closer Examination and Explanation], *Nederlands Tijdschrift voor de Mensenrechten-NJCM/Bulletin*, 38/2 (2013), 212–28.

[31] See e.g. UN Doc. CRC/C/15/Add.227 (2004), para. 22.

[32] Ibid. para. 23.

[33] See e.g. UN Doc. CRC/C/NLD/CO/3 (2009), para. 23.

[34] Ibid. para. 68.

[35] See e.g. UN Doc. CRC/C/15/Add.227 (2004), paras. 34 (b), 46, 48, 50.

[36] See e.g. UN Doc. CRC/C/NLD/CO/3 (2009), paras. 29, 52, 74 (e), 81, 83.

[37] See Chapter 2 of this book.

[38] Examples of implemented COs of other treaty bodies include the SGP court case (involving gender discrimination by a government-funded political party) and the evaluation of the gender dimension of the asylum policy (both relating to CEDAW); the increased domestic attention and debate about central storage of fingerprints (ICCPR); the integration of medical reports in the asylum procedure (CAT); and the increased domestic attention to school segregation (ICERD).

Table 1. *Overview of Implemented COs of the CRC Committee, referring to the Netherlands*

| Policy or legislative measure | COs (referred to by year of adoption) | Nr. of references in parliamentary papers by government | Nr. of references in parliamentary papers by Parliament | Nr. of gov. officials who mentioned the CO as realised | Nr. of NGO and UNICEF reps. who mentioned the CO as realised |
|---|---|---|---|---|---|
| Establishment of a Children's Ombudsman | '99, '04, and '09 | 4 | 19 | 4 | 5 |
| Abolishment of life imprisonment for minors | '99 and '04 | 3 | 2 | 1 | - |
| Separate housing of juvenile offenders | '04 | 2 | 3 | 2 | 5 |
| Prohibition of corporal punishment | '99 and '04 | 4 | 4 | 2 | 1 |
| Improvements in asylum procedure/ detention minors | '99, '04, and '09 | 3 | 12 | 1 | 3 |
| Some initiatives in the context of human rights education | '99, '04, and '09 | - | 2 | 2 | 1 |
| Increased dissemination of information on the CRC | '99, '04, and '09 | 1 | - | 1 | 3 |
| Improved interaction with NGOs | '99, '04, and '09 | - | - | - | 2 |
| Renewed consultations about foster care | '09 | - | 1 | 1 | - |
| Promotion of breastfeeding | '99 | - | 1 | - | - |
| Campaign against child abuse in 2009 | '99 | - | - | - | 1 |

*Source:* J. Krommendijk, The Domestic Impact and Effectiveness of the Process of State Reporting under UN Human Rights Treaties in the Netherlands, New Zealand and Finland (Antwerp: Intersentia, 2014), 233–4.

COs of the other five treaty bodies (Table 1).[39] The rest of this section will discuss the four implemented COs listed first in the table below as illustrations of this 'CRC exception'.

### Example 1: The Establishment of a Children's Ombudsman

On three occasions, the CRC Committee has recommended the establishment of a Children's Ombudsman to monitor the implementation of the CRC at the national level in the Netherlands.[40] The government was rather dismissive of the committee's recommendation on the first occasion in 1999.[41] These reservations notwithstanding, the first Children's Ombudsman eventually took office on 1 April 2011. The establishment of this office was the direct result of a legislative proposal by Member of Parliament (MP) Arib of the Dutch labour party (PvdA). Arib explicitly stated that her legislative proposal stemmed from the recommendations of the CRC Committee.[42] It is noteworthy that on nineteen occasions several other MPs also mentioned the COs as a reason for the establishment of the Children's Ombudsman (see Table 1).[43] This illustrates that the COs gave a necessary push and offered additional support for Arib's proposal and also reinforced the arguments of other proponents. One interviewee even argued that the

---

[39] The findings for the Netherlands do not stand alone. The implementation of the COs of the CRC Committee was also better than that of the COs of the other treaty bodies in New Zealand. Eleven out of the twenty implemented COs in the New Zealand were from the CRC Committee. This outcome was attributed to the strategic use of the reporting process and the COs by the Ministry of Youth Affairs, the advocacy by NGOs, and the Children's Commissioner. Jasper Krommendijk, 'Can Mr. Zaoui Freely Cross the Foreshore and Seabed? The Effectiveness of UN Human Rights Monitoring Mechanisms in New Zealand', *Victoria University of Wellington Law Review*, 43/4 (2012), 579–615.

[40] UN Doc. CRC/C/90 (1999), para. 12; UN Doc. CRC/C/15/Add.227 (2004), paras. 8, 20, 21; UN Doc. CRC/C/NLD/CO/3, paras. 8, 16, 17.

[41] The government did not see a need for the establishment of an ombudsman, because several of the ombudsman's potential activities were already being undertaken by other institutions. In addition, the government pointed to budgetary constraints. The government also held that the CRC does not require this either. See UN Doc. CRC/C/117/Add.1 (2002), para. 31; *TK* 2003/04, 29200 VI, nr. 21, 85; *TK* 2003/04, 29200 VI, nr. 96, 5.

[42] The initial proposal was already submitted by Arib and Van Vliet (D66) in 2001. The proposal was, however, not considered until Arib took up the issue again in 2009. See *TK* 2001/02, 28102, nr. 3; *TK* 2009/10, 31831, nr. 1–3 and 9, 20.

[43] See e.g. the statements made by Slagter-Roukema (SP), De Vries-Leggedoor (CDA) and Hamer (PvdA). *EK* 2009/10, nr. 32, 1373–6 at 1373–5. See also the references made by Langkamp (SP) *TK* 2009/10, nr. 79, 6765–77 at 6765.

Children's Ombudsman would not have been established had the committee not recommended it in its COs of 1999.[44] One representative of the Dutch section of the NGO Defence for Children International mentioned that NGOs would not have been so wound up about establishing a Children's Ombudsman had the committee not emphasised this issue so much.[45] Both government officials and NGO representatives stressed the crucial role of the pressure and political interest of Parliament in the implementation of the COs.[46]

The role of the NGOs and UNICEF was also identified as an important factor. Arib wrote her proposal together with representatives from the Dutch National UNICEF Committee and the Dutch section of Defence for Children.[47] In addition, the specificity of the COs was highlighted as a factor contributing to their implementation.[48] It was also considered important that the then Minister for Youth and Families, Rouvoet of the Christian Union (Christen Unie or CU) party (2007–2010), eventually supported the establishment of the Children's Ombudsman and even considered it a spearhead of his youth policy.[49] The latter also reflects the positive view of Rouvoet towards (reporting under) the CRC. He recognised the CRC as the starting point for his youth policy immediately after he had taken office.[50] The CRC was explicitly regarded as the foundation for the Policy Programme of Youth and Families, All Chances for All Children.[51] He even spoke about 'his' Convention and called himself the 'joint-owner' of the CRC.[52] Rouvoet was also personally involved in the process of state reporting and approached reporting as an inspiration and a boost rather than a burden. Reporting was also used in this period to create

---

[44] Interview K.

[45] Interview C.

[46] Interviews 5, 8, 11, 54, 98, C, D, J, M, W. Note that several political parties already propagated the establishment of a Children's Ombudsman before the 1999 COs. 'Pleidooi Raadgever Kinderen' [Plea for Children's Counselor], NRC Handelsblad, 15 September 1999, 5.

[47] Respectively Carla van Os and Majorie Kaandorp. Interview M.

[48] Interview 54.

[49] Interview 8. TK 2009/10, nr. 32, 1385–92 at 1387–88.

[50] TK 2006/07, 31001, nr. 1, 1.

[51] 'Alle Kansen Voor Alle Kinderen: Programma Jeugd en Gezin 2007-2011' [All Chances for All Children Programme Youth and Families 2007–2011], attached to TK 2006/07, 31001, nr. 5, 9, 38, 47.

[52] See the speech during the children's rights summit on 20 November 2009 in The Hague. www.rijksoverheid.nl/documenten-en-publicaties/toespraken/2009/11/20/kinderrech tentop-in-leiden.html

a moment of (media) attention for children's rights and to raise awareness of the issues involved.[53]

## Example 2: The Abolishment of Life Imprisonment for Minors

The COs of both 1999 and 2004 recommended that the government of the Netherlands outlaw the possibility of imposing life imprisonment on minors.[54] Following this recommendation, a bill was proposed by the Dutch government to amend the Criminal Code, the Code of Criminal Procedure, and the Youth Care Act to exclude the possibility of imposing life imprisonment.[55] The Explanatory Memorandum to the legislative proposal referred to the COs and mentioned that the bill was proposed in order to make Dutch legislation conform to the CRC.[56] The government referred to the COs on other occasions as well (see Table 1).[57] One government official interviewed, who was closely involved in the drafting of the bill, stated that the legislative amendment was a clear result of the COs. This official argued that taking up this issue was a personal initiative.[58] The official perceived political space for this proposal and anticipated that both the responsible minister and Parliament would agree with it.[59] The interviewed official argued that agreement was relatively easy to secure because life imprisonment of minors was a relative non-issue in the Netherlands and had never been applied in practice.[60] The interviewed official saw implementation of these COs primarily as a symbolic act without actual (political) costs and consequences. Be that as it may, it seems clear that the bill would not have been adopted had the CRC Committee not recommended this, because it was not considered an issue in the Netherlands.

---

[53] Interviews 49, 54.
[54] UN Doc. CRC/C/90 (1999), para. 30; UN Doc. CRC/C/15/Add.227 (2004), para. 59.
[55] *TK* 2005/06, 30332.
[56] *TK* 2005/06, 30332, nr. 3, 19.
[57] Minister for Youth and Families, Rouvoet, stated during the dialogue with the CRC Committee in 2009 that the government had amended its legislation in accordance with the COs. UN doc. CRC/C/SR.1376 (2010), para. 42. The Minister of Justice, Hirsch Ballin of the Christian Democratic party (CDA), mentioned the CO during the discussion of the bill in the Senate. *EK* 2007/08, nr. 15, 637–51 at 638.
[58] Interview 81.
[59] Bouchibti (of the Labour party or PvdA) noted that this legislative change did justice to the rights of child in the CRC, while de Wit (SP) even stated that the CO had been followed. *TK* 2006/07, nr. 56, 3197–205 at 3198, 3199, 3203.
[60] *TK* 2005/06, 30332, nr. 3, 19.

*Example 3: Housing Juvenile Offenders Separately from Children*
*Who Are Institutionalised for Behavioural Problems*

The CRC Committee also recommended, in its 2004 Cos, that the joint detention or housing of juvenile offenders with children who are institutionalised for behavioural problems should be avoided.[61] Shortly after a dialogue between the government delegation and the CRC Committee in 2004, it was decided to house these two categories of minors separately.[62] The government argued in its CRC report that this decision was made 'partly in response' to the CO.[63] The then Minister of Justice, Donner, (of the Christian Democratic party, CDA) mentioned that this change would 'at the same time' implement the recommendation of the CRC Committee.[64] However, it would take until 1 January 2010 for the process of separate housing to be completed. During this period, various domestic actors kept pressure on the government to expedite this process. Government officials and NGO representatives that were interviewed confirmed that the CRC in general and the CO in particular were two of the many factors that played a role in accelerating the separate housing of these two categories of minors.[65]

This example illustrates how international criticism clearly coincided with national politics and the broad wish of the government, Parliament, and societal actors to halt the practice. Joint detention had already been an issue in the Netherlands, widely discussed since the end of the 1990s.[66] There was political resistance in Parliament concerning the issue.[67] In addition, the media paid considerable attention to the matter and especially to the situation of children with behavioural problems who,

---

[61] UN doc. CRC/C/15/Add.227 (2004), para. 59(d).

[62] The announcement of the decision was made only two weeks after the dialogue and only four days after the adoption of the 2004 COs by the then Minister of Justice Donner. *TK* 2003/04, 28741, nr. 6, 4–5, 7. The minister himself did not refer to the COs in this context, nor did the Explanatory Memorandum to the bill refer to the 2004 COs or to the CRC. The memorandum emphasised the changed societal views and a study of the Verwey Jonker Institute as a starting point for the bill. *TK* 2005/06, 30644, nr. 3.

[63] UN doc. CRC/C/NLD/3 (2008), paras. 271–5.

[64] *TK* 2004/05, 28741, nr. 12, 2.

[65] Interviews 8, 54, C, D, J, W.

[66] The issue of joint detention had been talked about since the end of the nineties when the Youth Custodial Institutions Act was passed. *TK* 1997/98, 26 016 B, 1, 2.

[67] Already in March 2000, a motion proposed by Duijkers (of the Dutch labour party, PvdA) was adopted by Parliament stating that it was undesirable that these two groups of children were housed together. The government was requested to set up an investigation as to the possibilities to address this situation. *TK* 1999/00, 26016, nr. 13. After this motion, the issue was discussed several times in Parliament. *TK* 2003/04, 28741, nr. 8.

according to journalists, had been unlawfully detained.[68] More and more criticism was expressed by various domestic actors, including organisations of parents and magistrates in juvenile courts. The latter, for example, presented a manifesto concerning the issue.[69] Human rights and children's rights NGOs in the Netherlands, including the Dutch Lawyers Committee for Human Rights (NJCM) and the Dutch section of Defence for Children International, also lobbied on the issue. Many of these domestic actors used the CRC and the COs as a supporting argument (see also Table 1).[70] The implementation of this CO was also facilitated by the separate Minister for Youth and Families (2007–2010), who regarded the issue as important, and the related ministry.[71]

*Example 4: The Prohibition of Corporal Punishment*

In the 1999 and 2004 COs the CRC Committee recommended that the Dutch Government take legislative measures to explicitly prohibit corporal punishment.[72] On 28 September 2005, Parliament adopted a bill banning parental violence, including corporal punishment, psychological abuse, and degrading treatment.[73] The full 2004 COs were reproduced in the Explanatory Memorandum to the legislative proposal.[74] The then Dutch Minister of Justice, Donner, made clear that the bill would implement the 2004 COs as well as similar recommendations of the European Committee of Social Rights (ECSR) and the Parliamentary Assembly of the Council of Europe.[75] In a letter of 25 June 2003, Donner had already noted that he was (still) not in favour of a legal prohibition.[76] During the dialogue with the CRC Committee on 15 January 2004, the Dutch delegation pronounced that the government

---

[68]  See e.g. the front page article by Frederiek Weeda, 'Anouk Zit Onterecht in de Cel' [Anouk Is Wrongfully Locked Up], *NRC Next* (2 September 2009), 1, 4–5.

[69]  Raad voor de Rechtspraak, 'Kinderrechters in Nederland Luiden de Noodklok' [Magistrates in Juvenile Courts in the Netherlands Sound the Alarm], 10 February 2004. www .nieuwsbank.nl/inp/2004/02/10/R243.htm

[70]  See e.g. the National Audit Office that referred to the 2004 COs in a letter about youth custodial institutions. *TK* 2009/10, 31839, nr. 48, 2. The MP Voordewind (of the Christian Union party, or CU) referred to the 'request' of the CRC Committee as well. See *TK* 2009/ 10, 31839, nr. 54, 12.

[71]  Interviews 8, J.

[72]  UN Doc. CRC/C/90 (1999), para. 17. UN doc. CRC/C/15/Add.227 (2004), para. 44(d).

[73]  UN doc. CRC/C/NLD/3 (2008), para. 144.

[74]  *TK* 2005/06, 30316, nr. 3, 1–2.

[75]  *TK* 2005/06, 30316, nr. 4, 3.

[76]  *TK* 2002/03, just 030599.

was of the opinion that the existing provisions in the Dutch Civil Code were sufficient. The delegation, however, did mention that the issue was heavily debated at the domestic level, and that the position was not definitive and could change.[77] On 13 February 2004, less than a month after the dialogue, the Minister of Justice made clear that he had changed his opinion.[78]

What is then the actual role of the COs in the legislative change? On the one hand, ministers mentioned several times that the proposed legislative change would implement the COs.[79] MPs extensively referred to the 2004 COs during the discussion of the bill prohibiting corporal punishment.[80] On the other hand, Minister of Justice Donner stated that the recommendations of the CRC Committee and other actors, such as the ECSR and the Parliamentary Assembly of the Council of Europe, were not the most important reason for the bill. Rather, Minister Donner pointed to the prevention of child abuse as the primary driver for the legislative change.[81] On a later occasion, the minister noted that the legislative change was 'partly' the result of the recommendations of 'several' international organisations.[82] Whereas one interviewee held that the ban would not have been established had the committee not recommended it, government officials argued that the legislative proposal was not directly the result of the CO.[83] They pointed to the parliamentary debate since the end of the 1990s. In the view of these interviewed government officials, the COs primarily supported the introduction and eventual adoption of the bill. One government official also pointed to the important role of an official of the Ministry of Justice who was personally dedicated to the issue and had tried to convince the

---

[77] UN doc. CRC/C/SR.929 (2004), para. 72.

[78] No reference was made to the COs in relation to this announcement. *TK* 2003/04, 28345, nr. 8, 2.

[79] The then Minister of Youth and Families, Rouvoet, made clear that the proposed legislative change implemented the COs. *TK* 2006/07, 31015, nr. 1, 2, and *TK* 2003/04, 29284, nr. 3, 1.

[80] For references by the political parties PvdA, VVD, and CDA to the COs in their written questions about the bill, see *TK* 2005/06, 30316, nr. 5, 2–3, 10. Several MPs made clear that, with the act, the Netherlands would finally comply with the CRC. See *TK* 2005/06, nr. 106, 6487–500 at 6489.

[81] *TK* 2005/06, 30316, nr. 6, 2. Likewise, the minister did not point to the COs during the discussion of the bill in Parliament. He only mentioned the 2006 General Comment of the CRC Committee as well as the recommendation of the Parliamentary Assembly of the Council of Europe. See *TK* 2005/06, nr. 106, 6487–500 at 6495–7.

[82] *EK* 2006/07, 30316, nr. B, 2.

[83] Interviews K, 47, 67, 98.

Minister of Justice to introduce a legal prohibition.[84] The fact that extensive attention had been paid to the issue of corporal punishment, both at the regional and international level, at the time the matter was being debated in the Dutch Parliament, was also considered important. The CO and other recommendations thus bolstered the arguments for the opponents of corporal punishment, thereby creating a window of opportunity for and accelerating the introduction of the bill.

## The 'CRC Exception' Explained

The CRC COs show a better record of implementation in the Netherlands than the COs of other UN human rights treaty bodies. This begs an explanation. The earlier theoretical overview presented two explanations for the domestication of COs. On the basis of these two premises, the following hypotheses can be formulated to account for the 'CRC exception'. First, government officials might see the CRC Committee as more authoritative and legitimate than the other human rights treaty bodies. Officials are consequently persuaded or pulled towards compliance by the COs of the CRC Committee to a greater extent than is the case for the other treaty bodies. Second, the level of domestic and transnational mobilisation and advocacy might be higher in relation to the COs of the CRC Committee. As a result of this the government is under more pressure to implement the CRC COs than those of other treaty bodies. This section examines whether these two hypotheses are confirmed by the views of Dutch government officials, and may indeed explain the different position of the CRC.

### Hypothesis 1: The CRC Committee Is More Authoritative

Government officials that were interviewed were almost equally critical about the functioning of the six different treaty bodies. They were rather negative about the usefulness, legitimacy, and persuasiveness of the treaty bodies.[85] Government officials, for example, pointed to the basic and limited knowledge of several treaty body members about the national context and the poor preparation of some members.[86] Officials also lamented the one-sided approach of treaty bodies and the fact that they

---

[84] Interview 47.
[85] Gras also noted similar aspects in J. Gras, *Monitoring the Convention on the Rights of the Child* (Helsinki: Helsinki University Press, 2001).
[86] Interviews 5, 8, 13, 19, 61, 66, 79, 91, 93.

easily take over information and criticism of NGOs.[87] Moreover, some of the interviewed government officials had the feeling that some of the COs were completed before the actual dialogue took place, which in their view also hampered the authority of treaty bodies.[88] Several officials argued that the treaty bodies lacked independence and that the nature of the process was political.[89] All of this corresponds with Koskenniemi's observation that those serving in international legal institutions are essentially engaged with politics.[90]

The government officials were slightly more critical about the functioning, quality, and authority of the CRC Committee. One government official even counted the CRC Committee among the 'activist' committees that did not always keep a close eye on the text of the CRC.[91] Some officials noted that the dialogue between the government and the CRC Committee was usually rather emotional and based on expert members' hobbyhorses and personal feelings instead of the facts and data presented by the government.[92] Some officials even held that the CRC Committee was undeservedly critical and tendentious and in some instances approached the state delegation without respect. They specifically singled out the attack of the Indonesian chair during the dialogue in 1999, allegedly based on personal feelings related to past colonialism.[93] One official spoke about 'sneering and conceited remarks' about the 'rotten policy' in the Netherlands.[94] In addition, it was noted that the great majority of expert members of the CRC Committee had not read the report and did not seem interested in the discussion but primarily in other issues, such as their return flight or submission of their expense account.[95]

Several government officials indicated their disappointment that the discussions in 1999 and 2004 in particular also focused on issues which were not especially related to the CRC, such as homosexuality, abortion, euthanasia, same-sex marriage, and the Netherlands' drugs policy.[96] Interviewed government officials and NGO representatives both

---

[87] Interviews 5, 8, 13, 24, 57, 79, 92.
[88] Interviews 19, 42, 59, 67.
[89] Interviews 19, 49, 67.
[90] See Chapter 2 of this book.
[91] Interview 76.
[92] Interviews 47, 57, 67.
[93] Interviews 47, 81.
[94] Interview 81.
[95] Interviews 47, 81, 92.
[96] Interviews 47, 54, 81, 89.

lamented the absence of a substantive in-depth discussion on the many issues presented to them. The COs were said to be surprisingly short and lacking argumentation.[97]

The views of Dutch government officials and other interviewees illustrate that the different position of the COs of the CRC Committee cannot be explained by the fact that the committee is seen as more authoritative than the other treaty bodies or because there is a compliance pull coming from its COs. Dutch government officials have not been compelled or persuaded to act *only* because of a recommendation of the CRC Committee. The COs have never been a sufficient cause on their own. That is to say, hardly any policy or legislative measures were taken solely as a result of the COs. The four aforementioned examples illustrate that other (domestic) factors are required in order for the government to implement a CO. The next subsection will evaluate whether or not the mobilisation of domestic actors is an important prerequisite for implementation of the COs.

### Hypothesis 2: The Mobilisation of Domestic Actors Peaks in Relation to the COs of the CRC Committee

The four examples in the previous section suggest that COs might eventually be implemented when they are taken up and lobbied by domestic actors, whether NGOs, Parliament, or the media. In these four instances, the COs were a contributory cause of the follow-up measures together with many other international and national factors, such as judgements of (international) courts, NGO advocacy, and the commitment of individual government officials or MPs. The examples also illustrate that implementation of COs often required a years-long political process. Domestic actors needed to demonstrate themselves as willing and able to be persistent, spending time and attention on the issue over a long period. The examples show that parliamentary support in particular was often an essential intervening variable for the implementation of COs. This is also illustrated by Table 1, which demonstrates that the COs that were (partly) implemented were often referred to by MPs on several occasions.

---

[97] The 2009 COs e.g. included the following concern and recommendation: 'The Committee is concerned about the access to health care for migrant children without a residence permit. The Committee recommends that the State party take appropriate measures to make sure that all children in its territory have access to basic health care.' UN Doc. CRC/C/NLD/CO/3 (2009), paras. 51–2.

Another factor, also to obtain Parliament's attention, was the sustained lobbying by NGOs. The COs of the CRC Committee were frequently used by children's rights NGOs and other domestic actors to support their arguments or legitimise their work.[98] In this way, the CRC Committee supported domestic actors in framing their advocacy for legal and policy change in terms of human rights. COs thus offered a legal basis for NGO criticism and provided them with better opportunities for lobby and advocacy.[99] The findings of this research are consistent with a study conducted by Heyns and Viljoen about the impact of UN human rights treaties in twenty countries. They concluded that NGO involvement and mobilisation coupled with media coverage constitute 'an enabling domestic environment' which enhances the impact of the treaties and the COs.[100] The findings also mirror the boomerang effect previously described. That is to say, NGOs often highlighted issues in their alternative reports to the treaty bodies that they were already lobbying for domestically. They did this deliberately, with the idea of obtaining a useful and authoritative recommendation that gave extra strength and legitimacy to their claims. In this way, they used the process of reporting strategically.

Domestic mobilisation was practically absent with respect to the process of reporting under the other five treaty bodies. Table 2 shows that the COs of the CRC Committee were mentioned in more documents sent to Parliament by the government (on 24 occasions) than all the COs of the five other treaty bodies together (on 17 occasions). The same holds true for Parliament, with 56 parliamentary papers referring to the COs of the CRC Committee, as opposed to only 41 for the five other treaty bodies.

---

[98] Woll noted that COs served as 'a guide or frame of reference'. Lisa Woll, 'Reporting to the UN Committee on the Rights of the Child: A Catalyst for Domestic Debate and Policy Change', *International Journal of Children's Rights*, 8/1 (2000), 71–81 at 72–3, 76. See also Gerison Lansdown, 'The Reporting Process under the Convention on the Rights of the Child', in Philip Alston and James Crawford, eds, *The Future of UN Human Rights Treaty Monitoring* (Cambridge: Cambridge University Press, 2000), 113–28 at 116; Walter Kälin, 'Examination of State Reports', in Helen Keller and Geir Ulfstein, eds, *UN Human Rights Treaty Bodies: Law and Legitimacy*, 16–71 at 40.

[99] Andrew Clapham, 'UN Human Rights Reporting Procedures: An NGO Perspective', in Alston and Crawford, eds, *The Future of UN Human Rights Treaty Monitoring* (Cambridge: Cambridge University Press, 2000), 175–98; Scott Leckie, 'The Committee on Economic, Social and Cultural Rights: Catalyst for Change in a System Needing Reform', also in Alston and Crawford, *Treaty Monitoring*, 129–44.

[100] Christof Heyns and Frans Viljoen, 'The Impact of the United Nations Human Rights Treaties on the Domestic Level', *Human Rights Quarterly*, 23/3 (2001), 483–535 at 522–4.

Table 2. *Domestic Mobilisation in relation to the COs from 1995 to 2011 in the Netherlands*

| | ICERD COs 1998,2000, 2004, 2010 | ICESCR COs 1998, 2006, 2010 | ICCPR COs 2001, 2009 | CEDAW COs 2001, 2007, 2010 | CAT COs 2000, 2007 | CRC COs 1999, 2004, 2009 |
|---|---|---|---|---|---|---|
| Government treaty | 71 | 123 | 354 | 221 | 139 | 463 |
| COs | (5) | (0) | (1) | (10) | (1) | (24) |
| Parliament treaty | 31 | 77 | 186 | 151 | 84 | 444 |
| COs | (7) | (4) | (7) | (21) | (2) | (56) |
| National courts treaty | 17 | 127 | 1279 | 39 | 128 | 853 |
| COs | (0) | (4) | (0) | (5) | (1) | (2) |
| NGO lobbying | Limited | Practically non-existent | Limited / practically non-existent | Active | Practically non-existent | Active |
| Media coverage (newspaper articles) | 8 | 1 | 22 | 24 | 5 | 37 |

*Source:* J. Krommendijk, The Domestic Impact and Effectiveness of the Process of State Reporting under UN Human Rights Treaties in the Netherlands, New Zealand and Finland (Antwerp: Intersentia, 2014), 258.

Media coverage of the reporting process under the CRC was also significantly higher.

It is particularly noteworthy that there has been a Dutch Children's Rights Coalition of nine NGOs, chaired by the Dutch section of Defence for Children International, that has specifically focused on the domestic implementation of the CRC. This coalition has used the process of reporting strategically and has embedded the process in its broader political lobby at the national level. This also reflects the observation in the Introduction that human rights are frequently 'instrumentalised'.[101] For instance, the coalition has sent its comments on the government's reaction to the COs to Parliament and to the responsible minister. It has

[101] Chapter 1, pp. 2, 4 and 6.

also organised conferences and seminars to discuss follow-up to COs with MPs or with individual ministers. In addition, there have been structural half-yearly meetings between the coalition and an interdepartmental governmental working group on children's rights. Such NGO activities have hardly ever happened for the process of reporting under the other treaties.

Children's rights NGOs were also relatively successful lobbying on the basis of COs. The COs that led to some changes or follow-up measures mirror the policy issues that NGOs lobbied on.[102] The NGO lobby was often a reason for MPs to allude to COs or to put forward a legislative proposal, as was the case with the Children's Ombudsman. Likewise, NGOs were crucial for generating media attention. The significant role of NGOs in relation to the CRC can be explained by the historic connection of NGOs to the CRC, including involvement in the negotiations of the text of the CRC. The CRC Committee has the closest links with NGOs of all the treaty bodies.[103] In addition, there has been a Geneva-based NGO Group for the CRC (now working under the name Child Rights Connect) which has provided information and training about the process of reporting and linked domestic NGOs with the CRC Committee.

Another important explanation for the higher level of domestic mobilisation in relation to the CRC is the salience of the issue of children's rights among politicians. Children's rights meet a clear response in wider society. Nobody wants to be seen as not in favour of children's rights. It is widely acknowledged that children are by definition in a vulnerable position and in need of protection. The salience of children's rights is well illustrated by the case of Mauro in 2011. The boy Mauro faced expulsion to his country of origin, Angola, after having lived in the Netherlands in a foster family for eight years. This case was extensively covered in the media. Parliamentary attention was considerable and some MPs, the Children's Ombudsman, and the Dutch National UNICEF Committee

---

[102] Majorie Kaandorp, a former representative of the Dutch section of Defence for Children, outlined several issues for which the Dutch Children's Rights Coalition had lobbied both at the national level and among the CRC Committee and which were included in the COs 2004. Among them were several implemented COs, including three of the four examples discussed above, omitting the issue of life imprisonment. Majorie Kaandorp, 'Het Bondgenootschap tussen Niet-Gouvernementele Organisaties en het VN-Verdrag inzake de Rechten van het Kind' [The Alliance between NGOs and the CRC], in Defence for Children, *Nederland Rapporteert over Kinderrechten* [The Netherlands Reports about Children's Rights] (2004), 33–6 at 35.

[103] A.F. Bayefsky, *The UN Human Rights Treaty System: Universality at the Crossroads* (2001), 46. www.bayefsky.com/report/finalreport.pdf

as well as NGOs such as the Dutch section of Defence for Children International all framed the issue in terms of children's rights and a violation of the CRC.[104] The Mauro case exemplified that children's rights and issues are relatively easy to mobilise around, because these issues have a built-in pressure group and constituency.[105] In addition, children's rights are often perceived as less controversial and contested than other rights, such as prisoner's rights or the rights of (ethnic) minorities and asylum seekers. There seems to be a near consensus among politicians and the public that children's rights are worth promoting and protecting. Nonetheless, when it comes down to their actual implementation and the details, there is more divergence in views.

Another important reason for the higher impact of the CRC is the lack of another treaty or supervisory mechanism in the field of children's rights. Thus, the CRC is the unrivalled frame of reference for children's rights. The consequence of this is that domestic actors, and especially NGOs, are almost exclusively focused on the UN system and couch their demands in the language of children's rights under the CRC. By contrast, for nearly all the other UN human rights treaties there are authoritative or specific equivalents at the regional governance level. The substitute of the Convention against Torture (CAT) and the CAT Committee is the European Convention for the Prevention of Torture, which has a more powerful monitoring committee.[106] Likewise, the equivalent of the International Covenant on Civil and Political Rights at the European level is the European Convention on Human Rights and the European Court of Human Rights in Strasbourg.[107] The Racial Discrimination Convention (ICERD) is eclipsed by EU legislation in the field of racial discrimination and more specific Council of Europe monitoring bodies,

---

[104] See e.g. 'Kinderombudsman over Mauro' [Children's Ombudsman about Mauro], 28 October 2011. www.dekinderombudsman.nl/86/volwassen/nieuws/kinderombudsman-over-mauro/?id=54; 'Uitzetting van Mauro in Strijd met VN-Kinderrechtenverdrag' [Mauro's Expulsion Violates the CRC], 28 October 2011. www.unicef.nl/nieuws/berich ten/2011/10/uitzetting-van-mauro-in-strijd-met-vn-kinderrechtenverdrag

[105] Simmons, *Mobilizing for Human Rights*, 357–8.

[106] Redactioneel, 'Hebben Ze het Wel Goed Gezien? Hoe Om te Gaan met Oordelen van Internationale Mensenrechtencomités' [Editorial, 'Have They Really Seen It Well? How to Deal with Judgements of International Human Rights Committees], *NTM/NJCM-Bulletin* 37/4 (2012), 387–9 at 389.

[107] Krommendijk, 'De Beperkte Effectiviteit'. See also Jan-Peter Loof, 'Het Parlement, de Mensenrechten en de Zorgvuldigheid in het Wetgevingsproces' [The Parliament, Human Rights and Accuracy in the Legislative Process], in Roel de Lange, ed., *Wetgever en Grondrechten* [The Legislator and Fundamental Rights] (Nijmegen: Wolf Legal, 2008), 85–127 at 116–7.

such as the European Commission against Racism and Intolerance.[108] Even with regard to the Women's Convention (CEDAW), EU legislation in the fields of gender equality, trafficking, and violence against women has diminished the added value of the convention in the Dutch context.[109] Similarly, the European Social Charter and conventions of the International Labour Organization may outweigh, even if they do not fully substitute for, the International Covenant on Economic Social and Cultural Rights.[110]

## Conclusion

The general question addressed in this chapter was whether UN human rights treaty bodies act as engines for incorporating universal norms at the domestic level. I have argued that such incorporation has hardly taken place with respect to the process of state reporting under the majority of the UN human rights treaties. The CRC is a positive exception to this. In several instances the CRC COs have led to a policy or legislative change, often in conjunction with many other interlinking factors. On these occasions, the content of the CRC COs primarily supported, legitimised, or strengthened the arguments of domestic actors in domestic (parliamentary) debates and political decision-making. In this way, the mobilisation of these COs pushed or accelerated the adoption of policy or legislative measures. Accordingly, the rather extensive political mobilisation of domestic actors in relation to children's rights and the CRC is an important explanation for the positive exception that the CRC COs and the CRC Committee have been. Children's rights NGOs in particular have played a key role in the domestic implementation of COs and, hence, the promotion of children's rights.

---

[108] Krommendijk, *Domestic Impact and Effectiveness*.

[109] R. Janse and Jet Tigchelaar, 'Het vrouwenrechtencomité: niet bekend en niet geacht' [The Women's Committee: Unknown and Unrespected], in Nienke Doornbos, Niek Huls, and Wibo van Rossum, eds, *Rechtspraak van Buiten* (Deventer: Kluwer, 2010), 309–17 at 314; Marjolein van den Brink, 'The CEDAW After All These Years: Firmly Rooted in Dutch Clay?', in Anne Hellum and Henriette Sinding Aasen, eds, *Women's Human Rights: CEDAW in International, Regional and National Law* (Cambridge: Cambridge University Press, 2013), 482–510 at 496, 502.

[110] Reiding noted that the Dutch government has been rather positive about the ILO-system and has referred to it as 'undoubtedly the most effective ... among the worldwide systems' and 'doing a great job in the field of realising economic and social rights'. Hilde Reiding, *The Netherlands and the Development of International Human Rights Instruments* (Antwerpen: Intersentia, 2007), 151.

Ignatieff has characterised the growing development of international human rights norms and monitoring institutions as a 'human rights revolution', while Koskenniemi has referred to a proliferation of rights.[111] Although this chapter nuances the extent to which states are affected by such a revolution and the extent to which this is instigated at the international (UN) level, the findings in this chapter hint at a children's rights revolution in the Netherlands. This revolution should not necessarily be seen in terms of the material realisation of children's rights. Rather, it refers to the extent to which domestic actors couch their political demands in the language of children's rights and use international standards and monitoring processes to back this up. This is also illustrative of the political dimension of the implementation of international norms. By revealing that domestic politics and domestic mobilisation matter, this chapter corroborates Koskenniemi's thesis that international law should not regard politics as opposed to international law. Rather, domestic politics are an important prerequisite for international law's function and effectiveness.

---

[111] Michael Ignatieff, *The Rights Revolution* (Toronto: House of Anansi, 2007); see Chapter 2 of this book.

# 10

# Human Rights Cities: The Politics of Bringing Human Rights Home to the Local Level

BARBARA OOMEN*

## Introduction

Human rights cities provide a relevant case study of the politics of international law. The experiences of invoking human rights locally can clarify the benefits and drawbacks that can arise when framing policies based on human rights and when analysing social issues within the framework of international human rights law. As Koskenniemi and others have argued, international law has ceased to be the language of international relations alone. Human rights cities explicitly base their municipal urban policies upon a particular vocabulary or strand of international law, namely international human rights law.[1] In doing so, these cities illustrate the proliferation of this strand of international law as described in the introduction to this book. Analysing human rights cities can thus contribute to the study of the contemporary interrelationship between law and politics, and particularly to ideas about how the promises of international justice can be brought home.

International human rights law is much more than an idea thought up by state actors, referred to by Koskenniemi as 'billiard balls' in places like New York and Geneva, to be implemented by these actors in the national context.[2] It is invoked in local struggles for social justice by non-

* This research has been funded by the Interuniversity Attraction Poles Programme initiated by the Belgian Science Policy Office, more specifically the Global Challenge of Human Rights Integration: Towards a Users' Perspective (see www.hrintegration.be) and the Knowledge for Powerful Cities programme in the Netherlands.
1 Barbara Oomen and Moritz Baumgärtel, 'Human Rights Cities', in Anja Mihr and Marc Gibney, eds, *The Sage Handbook of Human Rights* (London: Sage, 2014), 709–30; Barbara Oomen, Martha Davis, and Michele Grigolo, eds, *Global Urban Justice: The Rise of Human Rights Cities* (Cambridge: Cambridge University Press, 2016); PDHRE, *Human Rights Learning and Human Rights Cities: Achievements Report* (New York: PDHRE, 2007).
2 Martti Koskenniemi, 'The Politics of International Law', *European Journal of International Law*, 1 (1990), 4–30; Martti Koskenniemi, 'The Politics of International Law: 20 Years Later', *European Journal of International Law*, 20 (2009), 7–19.

governmental organisations, churches, and individuals alike, through a variety of means ranging from social media to the more classic forum of the courtroom.[3] These local struggles are part of a haphazard, patchy process of rights realisation that is as much bottom-up as top-down. This process involves strategic shopping in the ever-expanding rights catalogue by unlikely alliances of actors via a wide variety of mechanisms. Local politicians can, for instance, join forces with civil society in invoking the UN Convention on the Rights of Persons with Disabilities to work towards a more inclusive city that promotes equal opportunities, including access to public buildings for people in wheelchairs. In other cases, civil society and schools might work together with the local mayor in becoming a city explicitly mobilised against racism. These efforts could not only strengthen anti-discrimination policies locally, but could also contribute to wider understandings of how to implement international human rights law.

The degree to which the invocation and realisation of international human rights law is driven by actors other than the states that have actually entered into human rights obligations has long been noted.[4] Cities, however, are relative newcomers in the process of giving explicit meaning to international human rights law.[5] This is despite the fact that cities have historically been the political communities that have bestowed individuals with rights and duties and given them citizenship status long before nation states came about.[6] Over the past decades, however, cities all around the world have begun to base their urban policies explicitly upon international human rights law, often in deviation of national government policies. The reasons for this local turn can be found in a combination of: first, the expanding numbers of urban dwellers worldwide, coupled with urban diversity; second, the rise of

---

[3] Paul Gready, ed., *Fighting for Human Rights* (London: Routledge, 2004).
[4] Andrea Bianchi, 'Globalization of Human Rights: The Role of Non-state Actors', in Gunther Teubner, *Global Law without a State* (Aldershot: Ashgate, 1997), 179–214; Jack Donnelly, *Universal Human Rights in Theory and Practice* (Ithaca: Cornell University Press, 2003), 290; Michael Goodhart, *Human Rights: Politics and Practice* (Oxford: Oxford University Press, 2009).
[5] Michele Grigolo, 'Human Rights and Cities: The Barcelona Office for Non-Discrimination and Its Work for Migrants', *International Journal of Human Rights*, 14 (2010), 896–914; Cynthia Soohoo, Catherine Albisa, and Martha Davis, *Bringing Human Rights Home: A History of Human Rights in the United States* (Pennsylvania: University of Pennsylvania Press, 2007).
[6] Engin Isin, Peter Nyers, and Bryan Turner, *Citizenship between Past and Future* (Abingdon: Routledge, 2008).

both decentralisation and multilevel governance as policy instruments; and third, the expansion of international human rights law and its justiciability.[7] The increase of urban diversity, and the fact that cities, more than ever before, are home to individuals with different nationalities, religions, and lifestyles calls for a universal moral framework in which to address local challenges. After all, the emphasis on the justiciability of socio-economic rights such as the right of access to housing, the right to education, and the rights to water, healthcare, and other basic services also strengthens the chance that local authorities will actually respond when individuals and organisations invoke these rights at the local level.[8]

This chapter explores the phenomenon of 'human rights cities', the many different ways in which this phenomenon manifests itself, and the ways in which this relates to the politics of bringing human rights home to the local level. Explicit reference to human rights in formulating urban policies might be the common denominator here, but there is a wide variance in what cities refer to international legal instruments and for what reasons; in who are the driving forces behind the choices involved; and in the results.

The experiences of three European human rights cities will be discussed in detail.[9] These are the long-established human rights city of Graz in Austria, the relative newcomer Utrecht in the Netherlands, and the British city of York, where the initiators are still in the process of evaluating the potential of making explicit reference to international human rights. Whereas human rights cities can be found all over the world, the choice of three European cities can be justified on the basis of commonalities between them. First, all three cities are part of nations that have been long-standing champions of human rights. Second, all of the initiatives in these cities not only invoke international human rights law to work towards social justice locally, but they also distance themselves from local policies and question the fairness of these policies. As such, each of these cities' experiences shed light on the interesting dynamics between the local, the national, and the international in realising international human rights. Third, initiatives in each of these cities have

---

[7] Oomen and Baumgärtel, 'Human Rights Cities'.

[8] Fons Coomans, *Justiciability of Economic and Social Rights: Experiences from Domestic Systems* (Antwerp & Maastricht: Intersentia and Maastricht Centre for Human Rights, 2006).

[9] See also, more in detail, the chapters by Graham et al., Starl, and Van den Berg in Oomen et al., *Global Urban Justice*.

consciously weighed the potential and pitfalls of reference to human rights as compared to other discursive turns in urban policies. As such, these human rights cities are well suited for a theoretical analysis of the politics of global justice along the lines offered by Koskenniemi.[10] The theoretical lines include an emphasis on the politics of definition and an awareness of how international law constitutes a strategic frame that logically leads towards certain registers of knowledge and solutions while leaving out others.[11] These emphases are important elements in the politics of human rights cities.

The second section of this chapter will discuss the ways in which actors in an urban municipal setting, as relatively new players in the field of human rights, have consciously weighed the potential added value of talking rights, and what has motivated their decisions. Generally speaking, the motivations of these actors are based on the potential of rights talk as a political tool, rather than on the legal promise that this entails.[12] Human rights, after all, can be understood not only as 'law', but also as 'values', and images of 'good governance', that far transcend their legal force alone.[13]

In line with Koskenniemi's 1990 call for awareness of the politics of international law, a third section of this chapter offers a more general investigation of the politics of human rights cities. In this section, both the ways in which human rights are invoked in local politics, including as a means for cities to distance themselves from national policies, and the constellations of actors that invoke human rights in this context will be addressed.

As argued in the fourth section, the rise of human rights cities calls for a rethinking of the notion of rights realisation as a manifestation of globalisation. A more appropriate term would be that of 'glocalisation', in which developments at the local level are constitutive of what happens globally, and the relationship between the global and the local is dialectical rather than unidirectional.[14]

---

[10] Koskenniemi, 'Politics of International Law' (1990); Koskenniemi, '20 Years Later' (2009).

[11] Koskenniemi, '20 Years Later' (2009).

[12] The term has been taken from Mary Ann Glendon, *Rights Talk: The Impoverishment of Political Discourse* (New York: Free Press, 1991).

[13] Sally Engle Merry, Mihaela Serban Rosen, Peggy Levitt, and Diana Yoon, 'Law from Below: Women's Human Rights and Social Movements in New York City', *Law & Society Review*, 44 (2010), 101–28.

[14] S. Randeria, 'Glocalization of Law: Environmental Justice, World Bank, NGOs and the Cunning State in India', *Current Sociology*, 51 (2003), 305–28; R. Robertson,

On the basis of this analysis some conclusions are drawn on how and why the language of international law is spoken at the local level, and on the relationship of international law to local politics. An emphasis is placed on human rights as a strategic frame for local policies, the politics of international law, and the local level, and on what the invocation of human rights teaches us about the character of international law in this day and age.

## The Rise of Human Rights Cities

Ever since the late 1990s, more and more cities have explicitly decided to base their urban policies on human rights in general, or on a specific subset of human rights, and to distinguish themselves from other cities on that basis. In some cases, this decision was instigated and driven by civil society. In other cases the local authorities – mayor, council, local administrators – conceptualised and drove the process. In still other cases, a whole constellation of actors worked together. One early example of a human rights city driven by civil society is Rosario in Argentina. Helped by a New York–based non-governmental organisation (NGO) called the People's Decade on Human Rights Education (PDHRE), local organisations representing women, children, workers, people with disabilities, indigenous groups, and academic and religious communities got together with the mayor of Rosario in 1997 to declare the city as 'human rights sensitive' and to sign a proclamation stating that the city would build a 'human rights community'.[15] In Barcelona, one of the first European human rights cities, progressive mayors in alliance with civil society drove the process of identifying the city with human rights, which resulted in a quick institutionalisation of human rights within the local administration.[16] Today many cities worldwide identify with the title

'Glocalization: Time-Space and Homogeneity-Heterogeneity', in Mike Featherstone, Scott Lash, and Roland Robertson, eds, *Global Modernities* (London: Sage, 1995), 25–44; Zygmunt Bauman, *Globalization: The Human Consequences* (New York: Columbia University Press, 1998).

[15] Jordy van Aarsen et al., *Human Rights Cities: Motivations, Mechanisms, Implications. A Case Study of European Human Rights Cities* (Middelburg: University College Roosevelt, 2013). http://mensenrechten.verdus.nl/upload/documents/HRC-Book.pdf; PDHRE, *Developing Sustainable Human Rights Cities: Knowing, Claiming and Securing our Right to Be Human* (New York: People's Decade on Human Rights Education, 1998); Stephen Marks and Kathleen Modrowski, *Human Rights Cities: Civic Engagement for Societal Development* (New York: UN Habitat, 2008).

[16] Michele Grigolo, 'Incorporating Cities into the EU Anti-Discrimination Policy: Between Race Discrimination and Migrant Rights', *Ethnic and Racial Studies*, 34 (2011), 1–19.

'human rights city'. For instance, one hundred cities participated in a conference for human rights cities organised by the PDHRE in 2011. The ways in which cities actually identify themselves as human rights cities and implement their human rights policies, and the types of rights to which they refer, differ strongly.[17] Some cities, like Rosario, have opted for a local proclamation of their dedication to international human rights. Others, such as Barcelona, have signed the European Charter for the Safeguarding of Human Rights in the City (ECHRC). In many other cases, cities have opted for associating with a specific subset of rights. The European Coalition of Cities against Racism (ECCAR) network, for instance, seeks to implement the UN Convention on the Elimination of All Forms of Racial Discrimination (CERD).[18] Similarly, cities like New York and San Francisco have adopted the Convention on the Elimination of all Forms of Discrimination against Women (CEDAW) as a local ordinance, incorporating it into the basis of their local gender policies in fields like combating domestic violence and enhancing participation of women in the labour market.[19] The adoption of the UN Convention on the Rights of People with Disabilities has spurred cities worldwide to ratify the Convention symbolically and to start realising the rights it contains, sometimes even before the states concerned actually ratified this particular treaty.[20] In addition, a wide variety of cities have sought to provide refuge to people persecuted in their home country, such as the International Network of Cities of Refuge (ICORN) that creates cities of sanctuary for creative professionals, or the European Shelter City Initiative.[21]

The question as to what motivates constellations of actors in a given setting to self-identify as a human rights city also yields different answers. Within the context of cities seeking to distinguish themselves from other cities, and with the rise of city-marketing, the adoption of the label

---

[17] Antoine Meyer, 'Local Governments and Human Rights Implementation: Taking Stock and a Closer Strategic Look', *Pace Diritti Umani*, 3 (2009), 7–23; Oomen and Baumgärtel, 'Human Rights Cities'; Oomen et al., *Global Urban Justice*.

[18] www.eccar.info

[19] Joan Kamuf Ward, *Bringing Human Rights Home: How State and Local Governments Can Use Human Rights to Advance Local Policy* (New York: Columbia Human Rights Program, 2012); Stacy Lozner, 'Diffusion of Local Regulatory Innovations: The San Francisco CEDAW Ordinance and the New York City Human Rights Initiative', *Columbia Law Review*, 104 (2008), 768–800.

[20] Examples are Zwolle and Wierden in the Netherlands (http://vnverdragwaarmaken.nl).

[21] Nicolaj Sønderbye, *Mapping of Temporary Shelter Initiatives for Human Rights Defenders in Danger In and Outside the EU* (London: GHK Consulting, 2012).

'human rights city' can be part of the same list as becoming a 'cultural capital' of a region, a 'city of design', a 'fair trade city' or another designation that might make the city (more) attractive to a diverse, cosmopolitan group of people. Given the degree of international support for cities working on rights realisation, both at regional (e.g. European) and at international levels, the label 'human rights city' can also serve to draw funding towards the city concerned. As will be discussed later in this chapter, a core motivation for cities can also be the desire to steer a more progressive course than the state concerned, for instance with respect to undocumented migrants. Alternatively, or simultaneously, the label 'human rights city' can serve as a discursive umbrella under which to unite and strengthen a variety of initiatives geared towards social justice in a given setting.[22]

Given the differences between the ways in which cities adopt the identity of a human rights city, and their motivations for doing so, it is worthwhile to look a bit more in detail at three specific European human rights cities. Subsequently this chapter will analyse what each of these cases may reveal in terms of using human rights as a strategic frame and the politics of international law and its glocalisation.

*Graz*

One early example of a European human rights city is Graz in Austria. In February 2001 the Municipal Council of Graz passed a Human Rights Declaration. The background to this declaration illustrates well the haphazard character of human rights implementation that is often described in the sociological literature on human rights.[23] The Austrian foreign minister at the time had to hold a speech in the United Nations (UN) on the millennium development goals. Her speechwriter was

---

[22] Amy Finnegan, Adam Saltsman, and Shelley White, 'Negotiating Politics and Culture: The Utility of Human Rights for Activist Organizing in the United States', *Journal of Human Rights Practice*, 2 (2010), 307–33; Noha Shawki, 'Global Norms, Local Implementation: How Are Global Norms Translated into Local Practice?', *Globality Studies Journal: Global History, Society, Civilization*, 26 (2011). https://gsj.stonybrook.edu/wp-content/uploads/2011/09/0026Shawki.pdf

[23] Margaret Keck and Kathryn Sikkink, *Activists Beyond Borders: Advocacy Networks in International Politics* (Ithaca and London: Cornell University Press, 1998), 228; Simon Halliday and Patrick Schmidt, *Human Rights Brought Home: Socio-Legal Perspectives on Human Rights in the National Context* (Oxford: Hart, 2004); Damian Short, 'Sociological and Anthropological Approaches', in Short, *Human Rights: Politics and Practice* (Oxford: Oxford University Press, 2009), 93–108.

befriended by Shulamith Koenig, the driving force behind PDHRE, who had often emphasised the need for a European human rights city to complement developments in Latin America and Asia. The minister of foreign affairs and Shulamith Koenig called the mayor of Graz and suggested that his city should become the first human rights city in Europe. As involved policymakers would say later, this was 'very much a rushed diplomatic operation, top-down, in which the real planning only came later'.[24]

Nevertheless, actors in the city took the announcement in the UN speech seriously, at first by adopting a Municipal Council Declaration stating that Graz would be a human rights city.[25] In this document, the council committed itself to identifying the gaps in human rights protection, to informing citizens about their rights, and to taking into account human rights in its actions. In 2002, a steering committee spearheaded by the Graz-based European Training and Research Centre for Human Rights and Democracy (ETC), part of the local university, put forward an action plan which suggested a number of specific human rights policies, including for the protection of migrants, women, and elderly people. In 2007 the city established the Human Rights Council (HRC) and charged it with the tasks of monitoring and evaluating human rights policies. The HRC, which included members from the police, the judiciary, the press, but from all political parties as well, was also tasked to recommend further actions.[26] The HRC draws up a biannual report on human rights in the city. Its fourth report, published in 2011, focused on four key areas: civil and political rights, economic and social rights, children's rights, and women's rights. In some respects the authors of the report took a critical stance, for instance pointing out how the realisation of social and economic rights was substantively impaired by political struggles. This included the struggle regarding the specific obligations that rights such as the right to housing and education set upon municipal authorities. Nonetheless, the report also mentioned positive aspects, such as the successful promotion of civic engagement

---

[24] Interview by the author with T. Rajakovics and K. Starl, Graz, 30 April 2013.

[25] Eva Schöfer, *Graz – Erste Menschenrechtsstadt Europas* (Graz: European Training and Research Centre for Human Rights and Democracy, 2002). The description of Graz as a human rights city is based upon interviews conducted by the author on 30 April and 1 May 2013; research and interviews conducted by C. Hamaker, J. Sijl, and L. Hadstein; and policy reports and newspaper articles.

[26] ETC Graz, *Was ist der Menschenrechtsbeirat?* (Graz: European Training and Research Centre for Human Rights and Democracy, 2012). www.etc-raz.at/typo3/index.php?id=1109

in neighbourhood and community work and progress in combating homelessness. Finally, Graz has taken steps to encourage actions by private groups and individuals. For instance, it has established a human rights award that is conferred every year to honour extraordinary initiatives in local human rights promotion.[27]

The four main elements in promoting Graz as a human rights city were formalisation, institutionalisation, the creation of a human rights culture, and making use of opportunities to take the concept forward. In terms of formalisation, the 2001 declaration, for instance, was not merely a political document. It referred to binding obligations contained in the Austrian Constitution, including in relation to the European Convention of Human Rights and the Universal Declaration of Human Rights, which were regarded as part of *jus cogens* and therefore binding on all states. This formal legal approach was repeated on a number of occasions. For example, when the HRC had a concern about hate speech, Graz ensured that the Municipal Council adopted a regulation that withheld campaign funding during the local government campaign from political parties which had engaged in speech that the HRC considered to be in contravention of human rights, including discrimination against particular ethnic groups. Similarly, the HRC played an important role in ensuring that the federal prohibition on begging in the city was declared to be unconstitutional by the Constitutional Court.[28]

The second important step in establishing Graz as a human rights city was a process of institutionalisation and raising awareness. Here, the HRC has been a key actor as well. In addition, there is a Council of the Disabled, and a Council for Interreligious Dialogue. For the earlier-mentioned biannual Human Rights Report that presents the state of human rights in Graz, the HRC solicits contributions from over 200 organisations. On this basis, it formulates recommendations. In the following year these recommendations are discussed in focus groups with many different stakeholders. According to a member of the Human Rights Council: 'It is these focus group discussions that really contribute to human rights awareness'.[29]

---

[27] Marie Bailloux, *Graz, City of Human Rights in Europe, or the Right to a 'Human City' in Europe? Dialogues, Proposals, Stories for Global Citizenship* (ETC Graz, 2012). http://base .d-p-h.info/en/fiches/dph/fiche-dph-8022.html

[28] Interviews conducted by the author in ETC Graz and the Graz anti-discrimination office on 30 April and 1 May 2013.

[29] Interview of T. Rajakovics, 30 April 2013.

The third step was to start a process towards the creation of a human rights culture. The strategic choice of the HRC has been to have the mayor present the yearly human rights report to the Municipal Council, and to ensure that the municipality puts the report on its website.[30] At the same time, an organisation such as ETC has put a great deal of effort in human rights education, including the training of civil servants, teachers, the police, and other key actors. When Graz became the European Cultural Capital in 2003, the driving forces behind the human rights city concept launched a project, including a lecture series, on 'a culture of human rights'.[31] As a result, it is well known throughout Graz that it is a human rights city, and civil servants and citizens alike increasingly conceive of their city as a human rights city.

A fourth step in the establishment of Graz as a human rights city has involved the city making use of opportunities to address human rights issues. One such opportunity concerned the high degree of hate speech during the 2008 local government elections. This situation led to the prosecution and conviction of Susanne Winter for hate speech.[32] The concern about events at the local level was so high among all parties that they ended up supporting the local government measure of withholding campaign funding for those parties that engaged in hate speech too often, as determined by the HRC's election monitor which was focused on assessing rights compliance in the election campaign. According to the parties involved, this led to a much friendlier local government campaign in 2012 and illustrated how the HRC made use of particular events to further its agenda.

As a result of these four steps, key actors in Graz have come to consider the city as an example of a well-established human rights city in which the link between local policies and international human rights has been formalised and institutionalised in a variety of different ways.

## Utrecht

A much more recent human rights city is the Dutch city of Utrecht. As was the case in Graz, the idea of becoming such a city came up in a rather haphazard manner. In 2010, then Utrecht mayor Aleid Wolfsen (a social democrat and former judge) received an invitation to speak at

---

[30] *Menschenrechtsberichte der Stadt Graz.* https://www.graz.at/cms/beitrag/10152653/7771447/Menschenrechtsberichte.html
[31] Focus group discussion, ETC Graz, 1 May 2013.
[32] Jonathan Turley, 'The Free World Bars Free Speech', *Washington Post* (12 April 2009).

a conference on human rights cities. While he could not make it at the time, he was intrigued by the notion and asked the municipal department of international affairs to work out a human rights policy for the city. As the mayor put it:

> Human rights do not appear to play a role at the local level. The Dutch consider them something for foreign affairs, and for Amnesty International. In reality, as a municipality, we do a lot in the field of human rights. It only has a different name, like 'care for the homeless', 'care for the elderly', 'peace education', 'gay emancipation', 'children's participation', 'protection of privacy', 'combating trafficking', 'shelter for refugees' or 'anti-discrimination policies'.[33]

One of the first products of the municipality of Utrecht's emphasis on human rights was a policy memorandum in which ten municipal policy domains were measured against the international human rights obligations of the Netherlands.[34] The memorandum described Utrecht's gay rights policy and concluded that the right to equal treatment on the basis of sexual orientation might well be soft law internationally, but was a priority for the municipality, and an issue to emphasise more strongly. In terms of combating poverty, Utrecht flagged a municipal pass that has allowed its citizens with low incomes to partake in sports activities for free. In relation to undocumented migrants, the city has pointed at treaty obligations to justify why it has disregarded national policies that do not provide shelter for individuals whose asylum claim had been turned down. The municipal policymakers have also introduced local policies to combat domestic violence and policies geared towards the homeless in line with Dutch treaty obligations.

In relation to prostitution and trafficking, there was a concern that clamping down on the people visiting prostitutes might lead to more clandestine practices and thus more violations of the rights of the prostitutes and trafficked persons involved. Although the policy memorandum deemed Utrecht's policies concerning the use of video cameras in public spaces to be in line with human rights, they were not considered to be very effective in preventing crime. Policies in the field of fair trade and human rights education were also discussed, as were the human rights implications of care for the elderly. Points of concern in relation to the

---

[33] Aleid Wolfsen, blog, 17 January 2011, translated from Dutch (www.utrecht.nl/smartsite .dws?id=353435). This site was removed after the appointment of a new mayor but the text is on file with the author.

[34] Gemeente Utrecht, *Mensenrechten in Utrecht: Hoe Geeft Utrecht Invulling Aan Internationale Mensenrechtenverdragen? Een Stedelijke Zoektocht Naar Sociale Rechtvaardigheid* (Utrecht: Gemeente Utrecht, 2011).

elderly were social isolation, the lack of care for certain groups, and the lack of attention to cultural diversity in this domain.

In addition to the policy memorandum and benchmark research on the knowledge of human rights in Utrecht,[35] the municipality also started a blog entitled 'Local Human Rights in Utrecht'.[36] On the blog, the municipality has listed a wide variety of local organisations as local human rights organisations. These include Amnesty International, the Refugee Council, and Impunity Watch, but also churches, shelters for the homeless, research institutes, and organisations working with the handicapped. From the municipal point of view, the rationale behind this broad selection of organisations has been to make use of international human rights standards as a discursive container, under which to unite and strengthen a variety of disparate actors, for instance in meetings organised during a human rights week. As one of the key policymakers formulated it: 'These are international standards on how to live and live together, a moral compass on social responsibility, a way of looking. Our objective is not to introduce a legal magnifying glass but a language for ethical discussions, and a way in which to bond and bridge different groups that might otherwise work alone.'[37]

The introduction of this 'rights talk', for instance in meetings with local actors, has built on a long tradition of progressive politics and emphasis on human rights in Utrecht. In 2013, the city extensively celebrated the 300th anniversary of the signing of the Treaty of Utrecht. International exhibitions, concerts, debates, posters throughout town, and a variety of other events underlined the city's profile as a city of peace. On a different note, Utrecht was one of the few Dutch municipalities to continue providing shelter to undocumented migrants when the national government decided to stop doing so. The social democrat Spekman, who was an alderman in Utrecht in 2002, led a national coalition of municipalities that refused to evict asylum seekers whose claim had been turned down, but who could not return to their country of origin. In terms of knowledge of human rights, this university town of 300,000 inhabitants hosts one of the main human rights research centers in the Netherlands, the Netherlands Institute of Human Rights, which is part of Utrecht University.[38] It has also hosted the National Human Rights Institute (NHRI), which opened its doors in 2012.

---

[35] Survey bestuursinformatie, Gemeente Utrecht, October 2010, on file with the author.
[36] http://humanrightsutrecht.blogspot.nl
[37] Discussion with H. Sakkers, Head of the Department of Public, International and Subsidy Affairs, Utrecht, October 2011.
[38] This institute (SIM) faced severe budget cuts over the past years.

In addition to measuring local policies against the yardstick of human rights and seeking to unite local actors under the discursive umbrella of human rights, Utrecht has also been very active in stimulating the formation of international networks on these themes. For instance, the city has participated in the Joined-Up Governance Network of Europe's Fundamental Rights Agency (FRA) and helped develop a toolkit on the implementation of fundamental rights at the local level.[39] It also hosted a conference during European Local Democracy week in 2011, with local human rights as the central theme. Here, a representative of the FRA spoke, but also mayors and aldermen from different Dutch municipalities. The policymakers from Utrecht explicitly sought connections with other cities: 'We are very lonely in this endeavor. What is the story that we tell our municipal council?'[40] The municipality of Utrecht was also one of the main participants in a research project on human rights and the city, carried out together with Utrecht University, Amnesty International, the Dutch Association of Municipalities, and the cities of Middelburg and Amsterdam.[41]

In spite of all the policy activity related to human rights, Utrecht was very hesitant to actually boast the label of human rights city. As a key policymaker put it: 'we really want to use this as a mirror for ourselves, and not as a marketing tool'.[42] It was only after the UN High Commissioner for Human Rights, Navanethem Pillay, publicly congratulated Utrecht on being the first Dutch human rights city, upon the occasion of the opening of the NHRI, that the city started to mention this title in its website. One of the reasons behind the city's hesitance to explicitly and openly refer to human rights as the basis for municipal policies could well be the vulnerability that this might cause. For example, then mayor of Utrecht, Aleid Wolfsen, had been criticised in national newspapers not only for seeking to stop publication of a critical article in a local newspaper in 2009, but also for failing to prevent the pestering of

---

[39] See http://fra.europa.eu/en/project/2011/joined-governance-connecting-fundamental-rights.

[40] Notes, conference on local democracy week, 10 October 2011, presentation of H. Sakkers and L. Lewis.

[41] The author was the leader of this research project, funded by KKS (Knowledge for Powerful Cities), from September 2012 to September 2014. See http://mensenrechten.verdus.nl.

[42] Discussion, 22 August 2012.

a gay couple.[43] These incidents could well have become more politicised had Utrecht held a higher profile as a human rights city at the time of these allegations.

## York

Whereas Graz has long been established as a human rights city and carries this identity with confidence, and Utrecht has increasingly resorted to the language of international human rights in discussing local policy considerations, the engagement of the city of York with human rights is still hesitant by comparison.[44] As a relatively prosperous university city with approximately 200,000 inhabitants, York is perhaps not the most likely city in the UK to experience the type of challenges to which reference to rights may provide an answer. Nevertheless, the York Human Rights City Project was set up in 2011 in order to explore the possibility of adopting the identity of a human rights city. One of the main driving forces, the Centre for Applied Human Rights at York University, considered the main aim of the project to be working towards the bottom-up establishment of the UK's first human rights city.

The process of looking into the relevance of rights for the local level was based on the experiences of the PDHRE in other parts of the world. Confronted with the existence of hundreds of human rights cities around the world, but none in the UK, the director of the Centre for Applied Human Rights, Paul Gready, set up a steering committee consisting of representatives of local human rights organisations. Here, as in the other cities discussed, the local university played a key role in stimulating attention for human rights at the local level. Members of the steering committee were the International Service (a local development charity), a charitable trust named after progressive industrialist Joseph Rowntree, other local organisations, and the City of York Council.

---

[43] See e.g. www.trouw.nl/tr/nl/4324/Nieuws/article/detail/1143996/2009/04/14/rsquo-Wolfsen-hield-onwelgevallige-publicatie-tegen-rsquo.dhtml and www.nrc.nl/nieuws/2011/08/30/wolfsen-door-het-stof-over-weggepest-homostel.

[44] The following discussion on the rise of York as a human rights city is among others based upon presentations and discussions during a seminar in York on 'Cities as Sanctuary' on 9–10 July 2013; discussions with P. Gready in May 2013; and documentation presented in these contacts. See also Anneloes Hoff, Jordy Van Aarsen and Maxime Van Gerven, 'York: Telling a Different Story about Human Rights', in van Aarsen, *Human Rights Cities*, 145–66; Emily Graham, Paul Gready, Eric Hoddy, and Rachel Pennington, 'Human Rights Practice and the City: A Case Study of York' in Oomen, *Global Urban Justice*.

The reasons for York to become a human rights city were manifold. On the one hand, the initiators referred to the city's history of social justice. In 1212, York became the first town in the United Kingdom to create a council of citizens, presided over by a mayor, to manage local affairs. At the end of the nineteenth century, Joseph Rowntree, the owner of two chocolate factories, introduced revolutionary social policies such as free education and healthcare and social housing. Currently, the Rowntree Foundation still plays a key role in funding human rights initiatives in York. A second reason for the reference to rights was that, as was the case in Utrecht, the driving forces behind the project felt that the notion could serve as an umbrella term for a disparate set of social initiatives, strengthening each of these initiatives and providing a foundation for new ones. More pragmatically, the Centre for Applied Human Rights at the local university considered the network a vehicle for its outreach activities, just as the city saw this particular initiative as a means to underline and strengthen its international ambitions and unique character.

Another explicit motivation for making York a human rights city was the desire for an alternative to the national discourse on human rights. The United Kingdom, possibly more than any other country in Europe at the time, was experiencing a strong and increasing resistance to rights at the beginning of the twenty-first century.[45] The UK Human Rights Act, initially passed with the ambition to 'bring human rights home' became to be perceived as an alien intervention, destined to protect 'foreigners, terrorists and pedophiles'.[46] This perception caused the Conservative Party to promote the idea of a national homegrown bill of rights, as opposed to the Human Rights Act that was essentially meant to implement the rights contained in the European Convention on Human Rights within the UK setting. It was against this background that Paul Gready, one of the driving forces behind the York Human Rights Project, stated that the ambition was to 'tell a different story about human rights' and to provide a bottom-up counter-narrative to the 'toxic national discourse'.[47]

---

[45] Michael Pinto-Duschinsky, *Bringing Rights Back Home: Making Human Rights Compatible with Parliamentary Democracy in the UK* (London: Policy Exchange, 2011).

[46] Francesa Klug, 'A Bill of Rights: Do We Need One or Do We Already Have One?', *Public Law* (Winter 2007), 714.

[47] Interviews with P. Gready (27 March 2013) and M. Kahn (Chief Inspector and Chair Black Police Association, 26 March 2013), respectively, held by A. Hoff, J. van Aarsen, and M. van Gerven, transcripts on file.

The Human Rights City Project in York was essentially based on two different mechanisms. The first centred around events, such as a week-long annual human rights festival and an 'Open Day for Social Justice and Human Rights' for local organisations working on issues of social justice. Here, the main ambition was to bring people and organisations into contact with each other and to enhance rights awareness. A second mechanism centred upon the protection of vulnerable people. York is a City of Sanctuary, which commits itself to giving vulnerable individuals – including immigrants, refugees, the homeless, and victims of domestic violence – a warm welcome.[48] Additionally, the Center for Applied Human Rights offers a protective fellowship scheme which allows for the university to host ten international human rights defenders per year.

Accordingly, York serves as an example of a city in which a coalition of civil society actors, the local municipal council, and funding organisations entertain the idea of becoming a human rights city and have developed a number of initiatives in this direction. These initiatives are strongly driven by the university. There is an ongoing discussion about the degree to which the explicit label of human rights would actually add to the degree and effectiveness of social justice initiatives within the city.

Bringing human rights home to the local level clearly involves the discursive element of framing that plays a key role in Koskenniemi's understanding of the politics of international law. It is this element – of human rights as a frame – that will be discussed in the following section.

### International Human Rights Law as a Strategic Frame

One commonality between all human rights cities, and the actors involved, is that they consciously weigh the advantages and the disadvantages of formulating urban policies in terms of international human rights over other discursive turns. Human rights, as has often been pointed out, are essentially a frame, a way of 'packaging and presenting ideas that generate shared beliefs, motivate collective action and define appropriate strategies of action'.[49] Koskenniemi has pointed out how public international law is just one competitor among many for local authority. He has also stated that 'political intervention today is often

---

[48] www.cityofsanctuary.org/york
[49] Sally Engle Merry, *Human Rights and Gender Violence: Translating International Law into Local Justice* (Chicago: University of Chicago Press, 2006), 41.

a politics of re-definition, that is to say, the strategic definition of a situation or a problem by reference to a technical idiom so as to open the door for applying the expertise related to that idiom, together with the attendant structural bias'.[50] If this is the case at the national level, it is all the more so at the local level, where reference to international law is less logical and thus constitutes more of a conscious choice. This brings up the question of how the human rights cities concerned make these strategic choices and connect to a specific expertise and set of strategies of action.

Local authorities are increasingly stimulated to refer to human rights in their policies by a variety of NGOs and international organisations. A report of the International Council on Human Rights Policy explicitly weighed the advantages of referring to human rights against other approaches, such as good governance, sustainable human development, gender analysis, the capabilities approach, or poverty reduction. The report argued that a rights-based approach shares the same principles as all the others, and has even more to offer by, for instance, emphasising accountability.[51] Similarly, a European Union publication, titled 'The Case for Human Rights at the Local Level: A Clever Obligation?', has made the business case for reference to international human rights law at the local level by underlining how such reference leads to local policies that are geared towards people's needs, societies based on equality, and accountable authorities.[52] In 2015, the United Nations Human Rights Council even adopted a report on local government and human rights emphasising how 'states and local governments have a shared responsibility and a mutually complementary role in the domestic implementation of international human rights norms and standards'.[53] In the Netherlands, a joint publication of Amnesty International and the Dutch Association of Municipalities, titled 'Well Done: The Meaning of Human Rights for Municipalities', listed the following advantages of drawing on human rights in municipal policies: strengthening social cohesion, stimulating active citizenship, offering

---

[50] Koskenniemi, '20 Years Later', 11. See also M. Ambrus, K. Arts, Ellen Hey, and H. Raulus, eds, *The Role of Experts in International and European Decision-Making Processes: Advisors, Decision-Makers or Irrelevant?* (Cambridge: Cambridge University Press, 2014).

[51] International Council on Human Rights Policy, *Local Government and Human Rights: Doing Good Service* (Versoix: ICHRP, 2005), 18.

[52] André Accardo, Jonas Grimheden, and Klaus Starl, 'The Case for Human Rights at the Local Level: A Clever Obligation?', *European Yearbook on Human Rights* (2012), 33–47.

[53] Human Rights Council, *Report of the Advisory Committee on its 9th session*, UN. Doc. A/HRC/AC/9/6, 14 August 2012, 19.

a shared vocabulary, profiling the municipality, marking its autonomy, contributing to good governance, connecting policy fields, and helping civil servants weigh different interests.[54] Finally, the authors of the joint publication emphasised how, realising that they were actually working to protect and realise human rights, they could add meaning to the work of elected officials and civil servants.

In spite of the enthusiasm that emanates from these documents, which were partially drawn up by stakeholders from Graz and Utrecht, many urban actors hesitate to label their city as a human rights city. In the European countries described, human rights are all too often associated with civil and political rights that are violated elsewhere, and to be defended elsewhere, but this is not necessarily the case in the cities discussed here. As one mayor explained: 'I am afraid that human rights simply sound too alien to the people in my city'.[55] Another mayor stated that, 'if we would label our city a human rights city I'd be scared that people would consider it as a place where human rights are violated'.[56] This fear of engaging with human rights is partly a result of the rights backlash that countries like the United Kingdom and the Netherlands have witnessed over the past years.[57] In the United Kingdom, for instance, the attempt to 'bring human rights home' by means of the Human Rights Act has led to a great deal of resistance, in which the document was described as a 'villains charter', seeking to protect foreigners, terrorists, and paedophiles instead of ordinary citizens.[58] In the Netherlands, a heated discussion on the degree to which the European Court of Human Rights was a threat to national sovereignty took place in the newspapers in 2011. This discussion was related to a more critical governmental stance towards the Strasbourg court.[59]

These developments, which can be understood in the context of an increase in xenophobia, anti-immigration policies, Euroscepticism, and

---

[54] Dave Hardy and Renske Steenbergen, *Goed Bezig: De Betekenis van Mensenrechten voor Gemeenten* (The Hague and Amsterdam: VNG and Amnesty International, 2012).
[55] Personal notes, expert meeting on human rights and the city, Utrecht, 10 October 2011.
[56] Personal conversation with the mayor of Middelburg, December 2011.
[57] Barbara Oomen, 'A Serious Case of Strasbourg-Bashing? An Evaluation of the Debates on the Legitimacy of the European Court of Human Rights in the Netherlands', *International Journal of Human Rights*, 20/ 2 (2016), 407–25.
[58] Lieve Gies, 'A Villains' Charter? The Press and the Human Rights Act'. *Crime, Media, Culture*, 7 (2011), 167–83; Francesca Klug, 'A Bill of Rights: Do We Need One or Do We Already Have One?', *Public Law* (2010), 701–19.
[59] Thierry Baudet, 'Het Europees Hof Voor De Rechten Van De Mens Vormt een Ernstige Inbreuk op de Democratie', *NRC Handelsblad* (13 November 2010).

populism, could well be the reason for a certain hesitance to engage with human rights discourse within specific cities. In York, for instance, a body advising the City Council on issues of social justice was deliberately called the Fairness Commission instead of the Human Rights Commission. Here, an explicit reference to human rights was deemed to possibly alienate citizens, who could all relate to the more 'fuzzy' notion of fairness.[60] For similar reasons, awards seeking to honour local activists initially called Human Rights Awards were redubbed the Yorkshire Region Awards. Additionally, the York Open Day for Social Justice and Human Rights referred to above was re-labelled 'Let's Get Involved' when the York Steering Committee maintained that words like justice and human rights scared people off.[61] While the city of Utrecht choose to work with the term human rights in its policy memorandum, it very consciously sought to include both 'right-wing' and 'left-wing' concerns in the choice of policy domains to analyse. Gay rights, for instance, are considered primarily a right-wing concern in the Netherlands, as they go against (Muslim) Orthodox beliefs. The right to privacy is also considered more of a right-wing concern and has received a prominent place for this reason. At the other end of the political spectrum have been concerns about the rights of undocumented migrants and the homeless.[62] Similarly, the drivers of the process in Graz took care to reformulate these rights as being of interest to businesses: having destitute people out in the streets is, after all, also a public order issue and could, according to this reasoning, affect the attractiveness of shopping streets.[63]

Where cities do turn to human rights, it is striking how they prefer to think of international public law as a discourse instead of a set of legal obligations. Merry set out three dimensions of human rights, law, values, and good governance.[64] As a legal instrument, human rights law sets out the rights of rights-holders and the obligations of authorities, as duty bearers, to respect, protect, and fulfil human rights. Both courts and international monitoring bodies have increasingly emphasised the degree to which these obligations, for instance in the field of social and economic

---

[60] Hoff et al., 'York: Telling a Different Story', 145–66.
[61] Minutes of a meeting of the York Steering Committee, 2013.
[62] Interview with H. Sakkers in Utrecht in October 2011, and presentation by H. Sakkers and L. Lewis on 22 May 2013 in Middelburg.
[63] Focus group discussion, ETC Graz, 1 May 2013.
[64] Merry et al., 'Law from Below'.

rights, also apply to local authorities.[65] Local authorities, however, prefer to invoke human rights as a set of values, a discursive framework that seeks to unite people from different backgrounds and with different interests, and thus emphasise the moral dimension of human rights over the legal side. It seems as though local authorities who engage with human rights feel that they have the choice between referring to the abstract ideal of human rights and invoking human rights as law and prefer the first approach as human rights law concerns binding claims applicable to all, whereas a general reference to rights leaves local authorities much more discretionary space. Here, one of the core activities of civil society has been to underline the legal obligations that come with this moral reference. For example, the ETC, one of the main civil society actors in the human rights city of Graz, considers the fact that Graz has consistently emphasised the legal obligations involved in being a human rights city, enshrining them at the local level and taking the government to court when needed, one of the reasons for the city's success in this field.[66]

Apart from emphasising the discursive over the legal, cities also apply a variety of different strategies to adapt international human rights discourse to local interests and concerns. One such dynamic of localisation, often described in the literature on the localisation of human rights, is that of translating human rights into the local vernacular: speaking of equality, fairness, inclusion, and other terms that are more appealing to a local audience.[67] Another mechanism explicitly refers to (internationally recognised) human rights, but couples this discourse with local traditions and history. Accordingly, York refers to the philanthropist founder of the local chocolate factory Joseph Rowntree in its discourse of human rights. Utrecht refers to its long tradition of peacemaking that started in 1713. Graz reminds its citizens of the horrors of the Second World War, but also of how welcoming it was to refugees after the Balkan Wars. Finally, human rights cities also pick up elements from the wide variety of expert vocabularies that are used in international human rights

---

[65] For a more extensive discussion of these legal obligations, see Accardo et al., 'Case for Human Rights'; Meyer, 'Local Governments'; and Oomen and Baumgärtel, 'Human Rights Cities'.

[66] Interview ETC Graz, 30 April 2013.

[67] Julia Mertus, *Human Rights Matters: Local Politics and National Human Rights Institutions* (Stanford: Stanford University Press, 2008); Merry, *Local Justice*. On processes of localising human rights in general see e.g. Koen de Feyter, *The Local Relevance of Human Rights* (Cambridge: Cambridge University Press, 2011).

law to suit local interests, for example where these are geared towards women, children, refugees, persons with disabilities, the Roma, fair trade, or combating domestic violence.[68]

Koskenniemi also has pointed to the structural biases that underlie the institutional practices of searching for a suitable political vocabulary to address concerns in the field of social justice.[69] In this regard, it is clear that urban actors are well aware of this process, and seek to use it to their advantage.

## The Politics of Human Rights Cities

In his contribution to this book, Koskenniemi has made a distinction between talking either 'Rabbit' or 'Duckalese', respectively the language of politics or that of the law. The discussion in this chapter, however, suggests that it might not be that simple. In a context in which it is less common to refer to human rights, doing so is an inherently political choice and opens the door to another subset of political choices. Which rights should be underscored, out of an ever-expanding agenda, and in what manner? An understanding of the choice of rights talk as a form of politics also calls for an eye to the coalitions united by such rights talk and the actors against whom human rights are mobilised.

There is a virtually unlimited repertoire to choose from for cities wanting to 'talk rights'. In this sense today's world has seen a true rights proliferation: these days, virtually every social concern can be rephrased as a rights claim.[70] With the right to privacy in the ECHR expanded to include topics as divergent as shelter for the elderly and protection against environmental disasters, the international human rights catalogue has grown to include newcomers like the right to development, the right to water, and even the right to the city itself.[71] This wide repertoire of rights is only augmented by the indeterminacy of many of these rights. The fact that they are negotiated in multilateral settings often results in very general provisions, which give little policy guidance. The rise of

---

[68] Koskenniemi, '20 Years Later'.

[69] Ibid. 11.

[70] Jane Cowan, Marie-Benedicte Dembour, and Richard Wilson, eds, *Culture and Rights: Anthropological Perspectives* (Cambridge: Cambridge University Press, 2001).

[71] Hannah Miller, 'From "Rights-Based" to "Rights-Framed" Approaches: A Social Constructionist View of Human Rights Practice', *International Journal of Human Rights*, 14 (2010), 915–31; Margit Mayer, 'The "Right to the City" in the Context of Shifting Mottos of Urban Social Movements', *City*, 13 (2006), 362–74.

monitoring bodies and special rapporteurs and the increase in the judicial enforcement of human rights may have mitigated all of this somewhat, but many rights are still open to highly varied interpretations. The European Court of Human Rights and the 'margin of appreciation' for member states is a case in point: the legal doctrine allows state parties to the ECHR to interpret rights in line with local cultures and constitutional traditions.

One example of the politics involved in selecting the particular rights to refer to is that of Graz. Whereas the city, as we have seen, proudly boasts the identity of being a human rights city, there is hardly any attention for those people who are not citizens but, in the words of Hannah Arendt, are 'mere naked human beings'.[72] 'The rights of undocumented migrants', as one of the main drivers behind the human rights city put it, 'are a no-go area. Illegality is a crime in Austria. There must be undocumented migrants, but they are not the focus of the human rights city.'[73] The Utrecht civil servants who drew up their city's relevant policy documents did not only consciously pick 'left-wing' and 'right-wing' human rights topics, but struggled to read through international instruments and decide how to actually translate them to the local level. The freedom given to countries by the vague formulations in international legal instruments constitutes a political space that is far removed from the idea of 'setting-boundaries-to-power' classically associated with human rights. The vagueness of the rights concerned enables authorities to reinterpret them in line with their interests and the status quo, thus taking away part of their potentially transformative power.

In the freedom to choose the words, verbs, sentences, and messages conveyed by rights talk also lies the paradox of human rights. Once applied, human rights tend to lose their radical nature, and become embedded in politics and political possibilities, instead of functioning as an alternative.[74] This also has much to do with the constellations of actors that are the driving forces behind a human rights city. Far from fitting into the classical individuals-as-rights-holders versus states-as-duty-bearers dichotomy, these actors include combinations of active civil servants, enthusiastic politicians, mayors, civil society, universities, churches, and individuals brought together by 'pragmatic

---

[72] Hannah Arendt, *The Origins of Totalitarianism: Introduction by Samantha Power* (New York: Harcourt, 1951; repr. 2004).
[73] Interview with K. Starl, Graz, 30 April 2013.
[74] Halliday and Schmidt, *Human Rights Brought Home.*

politics' and connected closely enough to international networks to draw a variety of resources from them.[75]

Does this mean that rights talk and political power play can be conflated, and that reference to rights is a mere reflection of political possibilities? Not always. Apart from being utopian ideals and comprising an evocative language, rights do possess the legal quality to empower those who are otherwise marginalised just as they can serve as an additional endorsement for certain policy measures. This becomes visible in the way in which cities use human rights in political negotiations with central governments. Cities that are confronted, in daily practice, with the consequences of budget cuts and harsh immigration policies increasingly refer to human rights in order to draw a red line. This has happened in the United Kingdom, in which cities of sanctuary have refused to go along with harsh national immigration policies.[76] It has also happened in the Netherlands, where the city of The Hague protested against national budget cuts on care at home by claiming that the policies constituted a violation of Dutch human rights treaty obligations.[77] It is precisely because of the way in which states are classical duty bearers within international law, and the jurisprudence on the duties involved, that such an appeal often is powerful.

As another political dimension, an appeal to human rights is often made in order to protect local interests against national policy proposals. Such appeals are particularly powerful if seconded by international organisations or courts. In this context, the 'rights boomerang' resulting from the collaboration of local and international actors to pressurise national governments towards rights compliance, described by Risse, Ropp, and Sikkink, consists of local authorities siding with international organisations in order to ensure compliance with a particular obligation.[78] The role of these local authorities in actually developing international law, both in theory and in its application, is often neglected. As municipalities test the real value of human rights locally and feed their experiences back into international discussions, they contribute to the

---

[75] Benjamin Barber, *If Mayors Ruled the World: Dysfunctional Nations, Rising Cities* (Yale: Yale University Press, 2013).

[76] See e.g. www.cityofsanctuary.org/news/1937/bristol-council-stands-destitute-asylum-seekers.

[77] 'Gemeente Den Haag: Korting op Thuiszorg in Strijd met de Wet', *De Volkskrant* (6 September 2013).

[78] Thomas Risse, Stephen Ropp, and Kathryn Sikkink, *The Power of Human Rights: International Norms and Domestic Change* (Cambridge: Cambridge University Press, 1999), 22–4.

spread of human rights, which is more adequately described as glocalisation than as globalisation. The city of Graz, for instance, was proud to note that the European Coalition of Cities against Racism left its imprint on the Durban Review Conference destined to assess the state of the International Convention on the Elimination of all Forms of Racial Discrimination, held in in Geneva in 2009.[79]

## Conclusion

A focus on human rights cities, as relative newcomers in the field of human rights application and implementation, can teach us something about the added value of contemporary reference to international human rights (law). A number of lessons can be drawn. For one, human rights cities are vivid illustrations of the expansion of human rights described in the introduction to this book. Whereas international human rights were once the sole domain of nation states, today more and more cities explicitly refer to international human rights in setting their local policies. The degree to which they do this, the actors that are involved, the strategies that are followed, and the actual outcomes that emerge differ strongly, as the examples of Graz, Utrecht, and York make clear.

Nevertheless, some general remarks on the relationship between rights talk and politics can be made. Cities that adopt a human rights frame of reference very consciously weigh the potential added value of references to rights, but also recognise a number of perils involved. The potential value is discursive rather than legal: reference to universal rights holds the promise of uniting disparate groups under one linguistic umbrella. The perils, according to some actors, are that human rights can be considered leftish; they can be seen to hold the potential of polarisation or to be of relevance only to foreign countries, thus alienating the public instead of involving them. This fear can partially be explained by the rise of populism and xenophobia in various Western countries, and the rights resistance which this can lead to.

A close look at the practice of human rights cities also reveals how the rise of these cities defies easy dichotomies. Instead of being a manifestation of the classic divide of rights holders versus duty bearers, human rights cities are characterised by coalitions of state and civil society actors combining forces for the realisation of the rights

---

[79] Interview with K. Starl, Graz, 30 April 2013. See also: www.unesco.org/new/fileadmin/MULTIMEDIA/HQ/SHS/pdf/ECCAR%20Final%20declaration_eng.pdf

concerned. The choice of what rights to promote or to protect, out of the vast international catalogue, is inherently political and subject to complex negotiations. The choices made can only succeed if they are upheld by a broad local coalition. Rights talk, far from being an apolitical and technical alternative to political power play, is merely another manifestation of power relations. The larger the alliance of state and non-state actors behind it, the bigger its chances of success.

Nevertheless, human rights do possess a unique legal quality that other discourses lack. This becomes apparent in the way in which human rights cities invoke international human rights to defy unwelcome national policies, often with the aid of international institutions. The difference between the global and the local, then, is a final dichotomy that befits textbooks more than it does reality. Far from being the domain of states, in Koskenniemi's terms 'billiard balls' in the international playing field, global justice these days is glocal, and just as political at the local level as it is internationally.

# 11

## Taking Seriously the Politics of International Law: A Few Concluding Remarks

JEFF HANDMAKER AND KARIN ARTS

### From a Politics of Re-Description to Legal Mobilisation

The authors in this volume have explored various dimensions of Koskenniemi's 'politics of re-description'. By explicitly acknowledging and grappling with both legal and political aspects of mobilising legal norms in attempts to obtain justice, these authors have explicitly responded to Koskenniemi's call for lawyers to seriously engage with the politics of international law and legal practice. In addition, they have offered explanations for (and in some cases, deeper critical analyses of) the selected global justice issues that they address, whether one speaks, as Koskenniemi has put it, the law of 'Duckalese' or the politics of 'Rabbit', or both at the same time.

In an effort to explain how international law is shaped, experienced, and enforced, the following three different types of engagement have been explored in particular. First, contributors have engaged with the nature and role of international justice, against what have become highly pluralistic and frequently competing legal regimes, which other authors have sought to re-frame as 'regime interaction'.[1] For example, the international regulation of global trade can significantly clash with international law designed to preserve biological diversity or fair labour standards, which in turn asks fundamental questions of the liberal legal order. Second, contributors have engaged with the way in which specific vocabularies have been invoked in attempts to solve political problems (but which sometimes make matters worse). Examples include the adoption of numerous UN Security Council Resolutions to condemn the actions of persistently violating states, such as Israel's decades-long

---

[1] Margaret Young, ed., *Regime Interaction in International Law: Facing Fragmentation* (Cambridge: Cambridge University Press, 2012).

occupation of Palestinian territories, including Resolution 2334.[2] In the absence of accompanying measures to hold such persistently violating states accountable through acts of retortion or third-country reprisals, a situation of impunity can be created, which may in turn necessitate other, more creative forms of legal mobilisation such as the ones that Saba has addressed in her contribution. In addition, those at the receiving end of violations might develop a deepened sense of cynicism, and the legitimacy of the Security Council possibly can be undermined. The third form of engagement by contributors of this book is with efforts to 'localise' international law; from supranational efforts to enforce international criminal law, as O'Sullivan's contribution addressed, to municipal recognition of international human rights obligations as in Oomen's contribution, albeit with varied success.

Especially when grounded in hard, empirical examples, these different engagements with law and politics – some deeper than others – reveal the potential of what we can term legal mobilisation. By this we mean the way in which law is instrumentalised by a collection of different actors, usually including civic actors, either to reinforce the hegemonic positions or actions of states, or to serve as a countervailing effort to confront states, individuals, or corporations with their obligations in international law.[3] Such mobilisation, in contrast with retrogressive, discriminatory, or other oppressive forms of legal instrumentalism, represents a legitimate political claim that is vested in the capacity of civic and other relevant actors to challenge states in relation to their international legal obligations, and especially in relation to the human rights obligations of states. Legal mobilisation furthermore involves a skilful translation of global rules in locally relevant contexts that reinforces the inherent structural bias of law and legal institutions (i.e. embedded assumptions contained within them that are aimed at particular outcomes) in very deliberate, progressive, and often creative ways.[4] Iain Scobbie has characterised the

---

[2] United Nations, *Resolution Adopted by the Security Council at Its 7853rd Meeting on 23 December 2016* (New York: United Nations, 2016).

[3] Balakrishnan Rajagopal, *International Law From Below: Development, Social Movements and Third World Resistance* (Cambridge: Cambridge University Press, 2003). See also Muthucumaraswamy Sornarjah, 'On Fighting for Global Justice: The Role of a Third World International Lawyer', *Third World Quarterly*, 37 (2016), 1972–89; and Jeff Handmaker, *Advocating for Accountability: Civic-State Interactions to Protect Refugees in South Africa* (Antwerpen, Intersentia, 2009).

[4] Jeff Handmaker 'Evaluating the Potential of Law and Development through the Lens of Legal Mobilization', European Law and Development Research Conference, Oostende, 2016.

notion of structural bias, a concept originally developed by Koskenniemi in relation to a given specialisation of international law (e.g. human rights law, humanitarian law, international labour agreements, bilateral migration agreements), as 'dominant expectations about the values, actors and solutions appropriate to that specialisation, which thus affect practical outcomes'.[5] Beyond the normative questions that this raises, such an approach is consistent with one of the core principles underpinning socio-legal studies, as articulated by Cotterell: 'legal ideas are a means of structuring the social world'.[6] In this regard, the normativity of law (to accomplish a particular set of goals or to entrench general or specific interests) interacts explicitly with its functioning (through various actors, institutions, and structures). Hence, legal mobilisation, which focuses on the interactions between mainly civic actors and state or intergovernmental institutions, serves as a useful analytical lens to explain how the structural bias of international law is 'instrumentalised'.[7]

On the one hand, the structural bias of law can also be instrumentalised in very negative ways, for example reinforcing the gender-based discrimination inherent in certain (legally protected) traditional practices, or preserving the hegemonic power of powerful states such as the UN Charter's configuration of voting power within the Security Council. On the other hand, structural bias can be championed by human rights advocates to reinforce social justice claims, such as the doctrine of equality before the law (i.e. due process), to stimulate a more even playing field against powerful legal opponents, such as states or multinational corporations.

In Chapter 3 of this volume, ten Kate and Nouwen presented a critical take on legal instrumentalism, referring to the many international actors engaged in supranationalised processes of criminal justice that select which cases are worthy of pursuing and which claimants are worthy of supporting. This paternalistic approach to legal mobilisation, they argue, may be seriously questioned, since the process of 'amplifying' some voices and 'silencing' others not only raises concerns about the legitimacy of such claims but in several cases has been decidedly out of touch with the local context and then is also likely to be of questionable relevance.

---

[5] Iain Scobbie, 'On the Road to Avila? A Response to Koskenniemi', *EJIL Talk*, 2009. www .ejiltalk.org/on-the-road-to-avila-a-response-to-koskenniemi

[6] Roger Cotterrell, 'Why Must Legal Ideas Be Interpreted Sociologically?', *Journal of Law and Society*, 25 (1998), 171–92 at 192.

[7] Sanne Taekema, 'The Many Uses of Law: Interactional Law as a Bridge between Instrumentalism and Law's Values' (February 3, 2016). https://ssrn.com/abstract=2745206

To illustrate their point, the authors make compelling reference to the dominant approach to transitional justice in northern Uganda, which has tended to amplify the US-backed Ugandan government's military-oriented solutions. Such an approach has tended to silence the majority civilian population in northern Uganda that has been most directly affected by armed conflict in that region.

By contrast, examples of legal mobilisation that are much more grounded in a locally relevant context were revealed in Chapter 4, in Saba's discussion of actions in solidarity with Palestinians in Gaza, and in Oomen's illustrations in Chapter 10 of how global human rights can be translated through the establishment of human rights cities. Both ten Kate and Nouwen and Saba also gave examples of how law has been 're-described' in a manner that best reinforces the claims of those mobilising the law.

Accordingly, some authors in this volume have shown how critical it is not only to understand law in relation to a particular social, cultural, and political context, but also to appreciate how law can be mobilised in order to advance human rights and justice claims. But the ways in which law is being re-described by those mobilising the law, and the strategies through which law is mobilised, are revealed even more vividly through certain dilemmas that legal mobilisers encounter when seeking to translate international law in a way that best supports their justice claims. For example, ten Kate and Nouwen illustrate how the Ugandan government's legal referral to the International Criminal Court of their case against the Lord's Resistance Army re-described the nature of the conflict in northern Uganda as essentially adversarial and reinforced the government's military approach to the conflict. By contrast, Saba illustrates how the Free Gaza Movement re-described their operations in their media statements as strictly humanitarian, and how this served to undermine Israel's insistence that a military response was necessary to disrupt the movement's operations. In the following section we elaborate further dilemmas encountered by legal mobilisers.

### Dilemmas in Translating International Law into Justice

For each of the forms of global justice explored in the introduction to this book – social justice and criminal justice – three key dilemmas often arise in the way law is invoked to promote or realise these objectives. These are: the cultural embeddedness of justice understandings, the frequent non-enforcement of international obligations, and the existence of significant socio-economic gaps at both the global and the national level. Each of these dilemmas presents significant obstacles to the realisation of justice through legal mobilisation. They can fundamentally impede the realisation of global justice, whatever specific form legal mobilisation might take. These obstacles furthermore make it very difficult to go beyond normative gains (such as the formal domestication of international legal norms) and seek to realise global norms in a manner that is locally/culturally relevant. The latter is a principal preoccupation of many social justice and human rights activists.[8]

The first of these dilemmas is that understandings of justice are culturally embedded in the institutions or movements involved in legal mobilisation. To put it bluntly, what is considered just in one country may be considered fundamentally unjust in another (and vice versa). This was vividly illustrated in the way in which international legal systems and individual states responded in an apologist manner concerning the apartheid regime in South Africa, from the emergence of the regime in 1948 even until democratic elections in 1994. Throughout this period, internally in South Africa the apartheid government regarded Nelson Mandela as a terrorist. Many governments in the global North, notably the United States and the United Kingdom, took the same position.[9] But within these same states, a somewhat utopian global, civic-led, anti-apartheid movement that shared a culture of global solidarity and social justice also emerged, which regarded Mandela as the epitome of a just struggle. This view was shared by numerous governments in the global South. Were it not for this culturally embedded understanding of justice within the global anti-apartheid movement, it is highly unlikely that pressure through civic-led boycotts and other such actions would ever have taken hold, let alone swayed the views of the movement's own governments.[10]

---

[8]  Sally Merry, 'Transnational Human Rights and Local Activism: Mapping the Middle', *American Anthropologist*, 108 (2006), 38–51.

[9]  Elleke Boehmer 'Postcolonial Terrorist: The Example of Nelson Mandela', *Parallax*, 11 (2005), 46–55 at 46.

[10]  Richard Ballard, Adam Habib, Imraan Valodia, and Elke Zuern, 'Globalization, Marginalization and Contemporary Social Movements in South Africa', *African Affairs*, 104 (2005), 615–34. For accounts of the global anti-apartheid movement, see: Håkan Thörn, *Anti-apartheid and the Emergence of a Global Civil Society* (New York: Palgrave Macmillan, 2006); Stephen Ellis and Tsepho Sechaba, *Comrades against Apartheid: The ANC and the South African Communist Party in Exile* (Bloomington: Indiana University Press, 1992); Roger Fieldhouse, *Anti-Apartheid: A History of the Movement in Britain, A Study in Pressure Group Politics* (London: Merlin Press, 2005); Conny Braam, *Operation Vula* (Bellevue: Jacana Books, 2004); Jos van Beurden, *Vinger op de Zere Plek* (Amsterdam: de

A contemporary example from this volume that has also revealed this cultural embeddedness is ten Kate and Nouwen's emphasis, in Chapter 3, on the importance of civic participation in international criminal justice which has also shown how socio-cultural understandings of local justice are necessary in order to ensure that the views of ordinary persons, who are directly affected by the crimes committed, inform international justice interventions, including criminal justice.

The second dilemma concerns the non-enforcement of international obligations, including the failure of states to respect the obligation to prosecute international crimes, combined with difficulties in securing universal support for international criminal justice. This is particularly pressing as countries have proven reluctant to prosecute international crimes in their own jurisdictions, at the same time expressing cynicism about - and in the case of South Africa, Kenya, The Gambia, and Burundi announcing their intentions to withdraw from - the International Criminal Court.[11] This situation has been further complicated by a high degree of selectivity in prosecutions when they do take place, which in the case of the International Criminal Court has been described as 'politically pragmatic'.[12] Meanwhile, Western notions of criminal justice may be regarded as irrelevant, even counterproductive to or sidelining local notions of justice in non-Western environments. Ten Kate and Nouwen's review of criminal justice interventions in Uganda and Kersten's analysis of the ICC's impotent role in relation to the situation in Libya have addressed this dilemma in Chapter 3 and Chapter 7, respectively. These factors, and many others, form a considerable threat to the notion of global (criminal) justice and may even breed antagonism towards this notion.

Other examples in this book that reveal the dilemma of non-enforcement of international obligations include Abiola's stark overview of the very different compliance standards between states when addressing

---

Geus, 1996); and Janice Love, *The U.S. Anti-Apartheid Movement: Local Activism in Global Politics* (New York: Praeger, 1985).

[11] Sewell Chan and Marlise Simons, 'South Africa to Withdraw from International Criminal Court', *New York Times* (21 October 2016), www.nytimes.com/2016/10/22/world/africa/south-africa-international-criminal-court.html?_r=0. Kenya has not yet effectuated its withdrawal. The Gambia and South Africa, respectively in February and March 2017, rescinded their notification of withdrawal from the Rome Statute. Burundi's withdrawal from the Rome Statute took effect in October 2017. See end note 2 at https://treaties.un.org/Pages/ViewDetails.aspx?src=TREATY&mtdsg_no=XVIII-10&chapter=18&clang=_en#2.

[12] Adam Branch, 'Uganda's Civil War and the Politics of ICC Intervention', *Ethics and International Affairs*, 21 (2007), 179–98.

international corruption (in Chapter 5), as well as O'Sullivan's analysis (in Chapter 6) of how challenging it is to prosecute international crimes in a national jurisdiction.

There are some positive, contrasting examples as well. For instance, efforts to secure common standards in the enforcement of international law by states can be accomplished through technocratic efforts of inter-governmental frameworks, as explained in Groff's analysis of the Hague Conference on Private International Law in relation to harmonising child support, abduction, and protection orders (in Chapter 4). Similarly, Krommendijk's insights (in Chapter 10) into how the Netherlands has sought to harmonise its international children's rights obligations reveals how otherwise soft enforcement bodies such as the UN Committee on the Rights of the Child can trigger a 'compliance pull'.

A final dilemma concerns the massive socio-economic gaps between the global North and the global South, which echo Thomas Nagel's contention that '[w]e do not live in a just world'.[13] The current preoccupation of powerful countries and some global governance institutions, reinforced by a plethora of academic literature by mainstream economists, is to stabilise the world economic order, not to seriously revisit the reasons that led to the recent financial crises[14] or to truly step up efforts to realise the right to development for all.[15] There is certainly no effort at hand to shift the fundamentals of the world economy that remain massively skewed. Responses to the problems involved have, indeed, tended to mask these inequalities, rendering world-wide socio-economic justice a distant dream.[16] Saba's chapter has highlighted this dilemma well (Chapter 3). She showed how efforts to 're-describe' international obligations, and in particular international humanitarian law obligations towards civilian populations, can lead to increased international

---

[13] Thomas Nagel, 'The Problem of Global Justice', *Philosophy and Public Affairs*, 33 (2005), 113–47 at 113.

[14] See e.g. Ralph de Haas and Iman van Lelyveld, 'Multinational Banks and the Global Financial Crisis: Weathering the Perfect Storm?', *Journal of Money, Credit and Banking*, 46 (2014), 333–64; Augusto Lopez-Claros, 'Fiscal Challenges after the Global Financial Crisis: A Survey of Key Issues', *Journal of International Commerce, Economics and Policy*, 5 (2014), 1-34; Jon Gregory, *The Global Financial Crisis and the Clearing of OTC Derivatives* (Chichester: Wiley, 2014).

[15] Karin Arts and Atabongawung Tamo, 'The Right to Development in International Law: New Momentum Thirty Years Down the Line?', *Netherlands International Law Review*, 63 (2016), 221–49.

[16] Bob Jessop, 'Recovered Imaginaries, Imagined Recoveries: A Cultural Political Economy of Crisis Construals and Crisis Management in the North Atlantic Financial Crisis', in Mats Benner, ed., *Before and Beyond the Global Economic Crisis: Economics, Politics and Settlement* (Cheltenham: Edward Elgar, 2013).

attention (and possibly pressure), especially when they are combined with other forms of legal mobilisation. Such efforts of international activists tend to be more effective than those of others who simply seek to raise attention for the desperate humanitarian plight of Palestinians in the occupied Palestinian territory of Gaza. In other words, direct action on its own, in the absence of strong legal argumentation, often merely affirms the nature of Israel's regime, with its relatively high socio-economic standards and a well-armed military, backed by powerful European and North American states that are all far more privileged, socio-economically speaking, than the socially and economically deprived enclave of Gaza.

## Taking the Politics of International Law Seriously

The underlying, and somewhat obvious, message here is that, ultimately, international law is riddled with politics, not to mention a myriad of social, economic, and cultural factors, which lawyers especially must take far more seriously than they generally do. This challenge was taken up in the individual contributions to this volume in which their authors asked myriad questions about not simply the content of law, but also about the political, social, economic, and cultural working of the law.

In Chapter 2 of this volume Koskenniemi launched this debate, as he so often has done in the course of his prolific writings on the topic, by asking what both lawyers and political scientists should think of the relationship between politics and law. His suggestion that we regard the legal and political dimensions as a metaphor of the same Wittgenstein image of the duck and the rabbit is compelling. But he didn't stop there. Ultimately, he has argued, deciding on whether to emphasise the legal or political dimensions of a problem to be solved is a matter of choice. This could be in relation to the frame one adopts, or to the language one regards as 'more just' or as likely to produce the best possible outcome. Such a flexible approach allows one to critically assess the functionality and indeed legitimacy of international law and accompanying legal enforcement institutions. For example, as Kersten has shown, the Security Council and the International Criminal Court make competing claims for legitimacy on how to respond most appropriately to mass atrocities. The role of international criminal justice in responding to such atrocities is a particularly challenging field in this regard, although Nouwen and ten Kate insist that we interrogate the processes of justice, rather than the legal norms or institutions set up to enforce these norms.

Evaluating whether the outcome of such processes can be considered good or bad, they argue, is highly conditional 'on one's normative and political framework'.[17] The processual nature of international criminal lawmaking is also a valuable basis for O'Sullivan's discussion of whether to prosecute an international crime in a third country domestic court. Put another way, international criminal law enforcement institutions, whether at the domestic or international level, can be regarded as legitimate in relation to whether they are, as Koskenniemi has put it, 'about legal punishment or show trials?; the enforcement of law or of (Western/imperial) bias?; legal or victor's justice?'[18]

This brings us to another key challenge in international law enforcement, particularly when international law and enforcement institutions are widely regarded as having manifestly failed to address the problem at hand. In such circumstances, what is the potential of civic actors to try and shift the structural bias of international law to reinforce social justice claims? Saba has explored this question through vividly illustrating the work of the Freedom Flotilla movement, a global solidarity effort that has combined direct action with an explicit invoking of international legal humanitarian and human rights vocabularies and articulating both through strategic campaigning. The need for such alternative strategies, she has argued, is due to widespread frustration among Palestinian solidarity activists about what they regard as the ineffective manner in which reports sanctioned by core United Nations agencies have responded to humanitarian crises, (re)producing 'legally incoherent conclusions', most of which are not legally binding. So, do such alternative civic interventions 'have any impact'? Saba asked.[19] She has argued that they do, not necessarily based on strict legal readings, but on the extensive media attention and framing of the issues that the Freedom Flotilla activists have managed to generate.

The principal lesson that one can take home from all of this is, in line with the words of Koskenniemi, to 'learn to be better at the politics of re-description'; in other words, to try and re-describe problems in the language in which one has expertise, whether this be legal Duckalese or political Rabbit, and above all to challenge the mainstream within one's respective fields of expertise by other, contested visions.[20]

---

[17] Chapter 3 in this book, 48.
[18] Chapter 2 in this book, 29.
[19] Chapter 4 of this book, 83.
[20] Chapter 2 of this book, 44.

Oomen, however, has offered a slightly different vision to Koskenniemi's. On the one hand, she acknowledges that the decision to observe human rights is inherently a matter of political choice on the part of municipal bureaucrats, although arguably the same could be said for other 'actors against whom human rights are mobilised', whether these be national legislators or international policymakers.[21] On the other hand, Oomen emphasises that one cannot ignore the multilayered networks through which 'rights talk' reaches the attention of these actors who ultimately have the power to ensure that human rights, and by extension notions of justice, are – as described earlier in this chapter – culturally embedded in the institutions and movements engaged in legal mobilisation. She maintains: 'rights talk, far from being an apolitical and technical alternative to political power play, is merely another manifestation of power relations. The larger the alliance of state and non-state actors behind it, the bigger its chances of success.'[22] Accordingly, lawyers need to take both the politics of law and the cultural embeddedness of justice claims much more seriously, as well as the potential for broad-based coalitions to address complex social justice claims, as the global anti-apartheid movement so effectively did in relation to pre-1990s South Africa.[23] Some scholars of global justice have indeed begun to take this cultural embeddedness seriously, not least the authors in this book, who have taken up Koskenniemi's challenge to look beyond international law's simple normativity. But, much more research remains needed before we can fully appreciate the potential of legal mobilisation through broad-based interest coalitions.

Meanwhile, as touched upon earlier, commentators have questioned the challenges involved in enforcing international law in the face of weak systems of global governance, in the process challenging the ideological tendencies of the liberal internationalists[24] or the new realists.[25] International law and international relations theorists have posited interpretive guides that address the ethical basis of international law.[26] Accordingly, scholars have sought to integrate statist and cosmopolitan perspectives of justice, as to some extent Kersten also pursued in his

[21] Chapter 11 of this book, 228.

[22] Ibid. 232.

[23] Richard Abel, *Politics by Other Means: Law in the Struggle against Apartheid, 1980–1994* (New York: Routledge, 1995).

[24] Richard Falk, 'Legality and Legitimacy: The Quest for Principled Flexibility and Restraint', *Review of International Studies*, 31 (2005), 33–50.

[25] Jens Ohlin, *The Assault on International Law* (Oxford: Oxford University Press, 2015).

[26] Steven Ratner, *The Thin Justice of International Law: A Moral Reckoning of the Law of Nations* (Oxford: Oxford University Press, 2015).

contribution to this book.[27] Other contributors to this volume have explained the extent to which international legal rules affect state behaviour, such as Saba, Groff, O'Sullivan, and Krommendijk.[28]

Hence, this book makes a contribution to the growing body of literature on the potential of mobilising international law for global justice by evaluating two important, albeit under-explored dimensions of international law and the justice systems created to enforce it: the politics of re-description and the potential for legal mobilisation to lead to structural change. Koskenniemi's politics of re-description allows for a candid look at how law and politics interact in a variety of international and globalised contexts. The authors of this book furthermore have explored the ways in which different actors promote progressive structural change by way of legal mobilisation, instrumentalising law as part of a legitimate political project.

Through evaluating a few of the myriad ways in which international law is being understood, (re)interpreted, and even mobilised by different international organisations, domestic enforcement agencies, and civic actors, we have taken stock and revisited the politics of international law and global justice. By engaging in this discussion, we have sought to show how mobilising international law can – sometimes dramatically – expand the boundaries of legal and political possibilities. Accordingly, these conscious engagements with the politics of international law and justice are instructive of the ways in which both legal scholars and practitioners are instrumentalising the structural bias of international law in a progressive manner to serve as an instrument for social and political change.

---

[27] See also Mathias Risse, *On Global Justice* (Princeton University Press, 2012).

[28] See also Mark Klamberg, *Power and Law in International Society: International Relations as the Sociology of International Law* (London: Routledge, 2015); and Edwin Egede and Peter Sutch, *The Politics of International Law and International Justice* (Edinburgh: Edinburgh University Press, 2013).

# INDEX

For EU product safety concerns, contact us at Calle de José Abascal, 56–1°, 28003 Madrid, Spain or eugpsr@cambridge.org.

www.ingramcontent.com/pod-product-compliance
Ingram Content Group UK Ltd.
Pitfield, Milton Keynes, MK11 3LW, UK
UKHW020332140625

459647UK00018B/2120